UNDER DISCUSSION
Donald Hall, General Editor

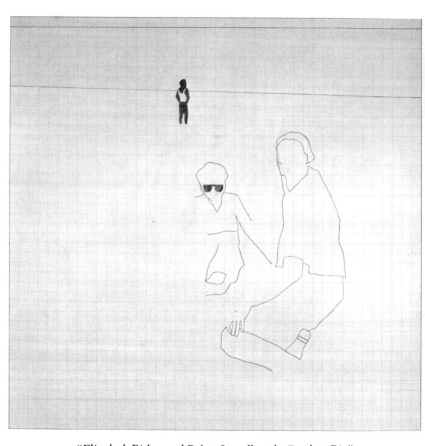

"Elizabeth Bishop and Robert Lowell on the Beach at Rio"
Ralph Hamilton

Elizabeth Bishop and Her Art

Edited by Lloyd Schwartz and Sybil P. Estess

Foreword by Harold Bloom

Ann Arbor
THE UNIVERSITY OF MICHIGAN PRESS

Copyright © by The University of Michigan 1983
All rights reserved
Published in the United States of America by
The University of Michigan Press and simultaneously
in Rexdale, Canada, by John Wiley & Sons Canada, Limited
Manufactured in the United States of America

1986   1985   1984   6   5   4   3   2

Library of Congress Cataloging in Publication Data
Main entry under title:

Elizabeth Bishop and her art.

  (Under discussion)
  Bibliography: p.
  1. Bishop, Elizabeth, 1911–   —Addresses,
essays, lectures. 2. Poets, American—20th century—
Biography—Addresses, essays, lectures. I. Schwartz,
Lloyd, 1941–   . II. Estess, Sybil P., 1942–
III. Series.
PS3503.I785Z65   1983   811'.54   82-20235
ISBN 0-472-09343-6
ISBN 0-472-06343-X (pbk.)

Frontispiece courtesy of Ralph Hamilton, "Elizabeth Bishop and
Robert Lowell on the Beach at Rio," pencil study on graph paper
(21″ × 21″), 1974.

Paperbound edition cover photograph of Elizabeth Bishop courtesy of *World
Literature Today*. © 1977, University of Oklahoma Press.

Acknowledgments

Grateful acknowledgment is made to the following publishers, journals, organizations, and individuals for permission to reprint copyrighted materials:

Book-of-the-Month Club for Elizabeth Bishop's excerpts from Book-of-the-Month Club *News*, May, 1977. Copyright © Book-of-the-Month Club, 1977. Reprinted by permission.

Ashley Brown for "Elizabeth Bishop in Brazil," *Southern Review*, Fall, 1977.

Farrar, Straus and Giroux for the following: "An Inadequate Tribute" from *Randall Jarrell 1914–1965*, edited by Robert Lowell, Peter Taylor, and Robert Penn Warren, copyright © 1967 by Farrar, Straus and Giroux, Inc.; "Statement for the English Memorial Service for Robert Lowell," October 12, 1977; lines written in a copy of *Fannie Farmer's Boston Cooking School Cookbook,* given to Frank Bidart, copyright © 1982 by Alice Methfessel, executrix of the estate of Elizabeth Bishop; introduction to *The Burglar of Babylon,* copyright © 1968 by Elizabeth Bishop; excerpt from the introduction to *The Diary of "Helena Morley,"* copyright © 1957 by Elizabeth Bishop; excerpts from two letters to Marianne Moore about "A Miracle for Breakfast" from *Elizabeth Bishop: A Bibliography 1927–1979,* by Candace MacMahon, copyright © 1980 by Alice Methfessel; excerpt from "What the Young Man Said to the Psalmist," first published in *Poetry,* copyright 1952; excerpt from "Gregorio Valdes, 1879–1939," first published in *Partisan Review,* copyright 1939; excerpt from "A Brief Reminiscence and A Brief Tribute," first published in the *Harvard Advocate,* copyright © 1975 by Elizabeth Bishop; "As We Like It," first published in the *Quarterly Review of Literature;* review of E. E. Cummings' *Xaipe: Seventy One Poems,* first published in *U.S. Quarterly Book Review;* "On *Life Studies* by Robert Lowell"; "On *Golden State* by

"On Elizabeth Bishop," by Frank Bidart, from *World Literature Today* 1 (Winter, 1977).

Oxford University Press for "Elizabeth Bishop: Questions of Memory, Questions of Travel" from *Five Temperaments: Elizabeth Bishop, Robert Lowell, James Merrill, Adrienne Rich, John Ashbery*, by David Kalstone. Copyright © 1977 by David Kalstone. Reprinted by permission of the author and Oxford University Press.

Paris Review for "From an Interview," excerpts from an interview with Frederick Seidel, *Paris Review* 7, 1961.

Parnassus for "Elizabeth Bishop's Mappings of Life," by John Hollander, *Parnassus*, Spring/Summer, 1977.

Robert Pinsky for "The Idiom of a Self," *American Poetry Review*, January–February, 1980; and "Elizabeth Bishop, 1911–1979," *New Republic*, November 10, 1979.

Ploughshares for an excerpt from a conversation with Mark Strand and Norman Klein, *Ploughshares* 2, no. 3; and for "One Art: The Poetry of Elizabeth Bishop, 1971–1976," by Lloyd Schwartz, *Ploughshares* 3, nos. 3 & 4.

Lloyd Schwartz for "Elizabeth Bishop, 1911–1979," *Boston Phoenix*, October 16, 1979.

Sewanee Review for excerpts from "Thomas, Bishop, and Williams," by Robert Lowell, *Sewanee Review*, Summer, 1947.

Willard Spiegelman, for "Elizabeth Bishop's 'National Heroism,'" *Centennial Review*, Winter, 1978.

Twayne Publishers, a division of G. K. Hall & Co., Boston, for an excerpt from "It All Depends" from *Mid-Century American Poets*, edited by John Ciardi.

Time for "On 'Confessional Poetry'" from "Poets," June 2, 1967, reprinted by permission.

Vassar College for an excerpt from "Time's Andromedas," first published in *Vassar Journal of Undergraduate Studies*, copyright 1933; and an excerpt from "Gerard Manley Hopkins: Notes on Timing in his Poetry," first published in *Vassar Review*, copyright 1934.

Viking Penguin for "Comment on 'In the Waiting Room' and Herbert's 'Love Unknown,'" by Richard Howard, from *Preferences*.

Richard Wilbur for "Elizabeth Bishop: A Memorial Tribute

Read at the American Academy of Arts & Letters, 7 December 1979," published in *Ploughshares* 6, no. 2 (1980).

The editors have made every effort to secure permission for every item included in this volume. Where no acknowledgments are given, there has been no response to our continued requests. We therefore apologize here for any omissions.

We are grateful to Candace MacMahon, Elizabeth Bishop's bibliographer, for calling to our attention four of the items by Elizabeth Bishop included here. We would also like to express our thanks to the following people for their invaluable advice, encouragement, cooperation, and continual efforts on behalf of this volume: Frank Bidart, Harold Bloom, Pat Botacchi, Ted Estess, Donald Hall, Ralph Hamilton, David Kalstone, David Lehman, Allen Mandelbaum, Alice Methfessel, Joyce Peseroff, Robert Pinsky, and Helen Vendler. Our debt to Elizabeth Bishop for all her help is greater than we can say.

Foreword

The principal poets of Elizabeth Bishop's generation included Roethke, Lowell, Berryman, Jarrell, and, in a different mode, Olson. Whether any of these articulated an individual rhetorical stance with a skill as sure as hers may be questioned. Her way of writing was closer to that of Stevens and Marianne Moore, in the generation just beyond, than to any of her exact contemporaries. Despite the differences in scale, her best poems rival the Stevens of the shorter works, rather than the perhaps stronger Stevens of the sequences.

Bishop stands, then, securely in a tradition of American poetry that began with Emerson, Very, and Dickinson, and culminated in aspects of Frost as well as of Stevens and Moore. This tradition is marked by firm rhetorical control, overt moral authority, and sometimes by a fairly strict economy of means. The closing lines in *Geography III* epitomize the tradition's self-recognition:

> He and the bird know everything is answered,
> all taken care of,
> no need to ask again.
> —Yesterday brought to today so lightly!
> (A yesterday I find almost impossible to lift.)

These poignant lines have more overt pathos than the poet ever allowed herself elsewhere. But there is a paradox always in the contrast between a poetry of deep subjectivity, like Wordsworth's or Stevens's or Bishop's, and a confessional poetry, like Coleridge's or that of Bishop's principal contemporaries. When I read, say, "The Poems of Our Climate," by Stevens, or "The End of March," by Bishop, I encounter eventually the overwhelming self-revelation of a profoundly subjective consciousness. When I read, say, "Skunk Hour" by Lowell or one of Berryman's sonnets, I confront finally an opacity, for that is all the confessional mode can yield. It is the strength of Bishop's tradition that its clarity is more than a surface phenomenon. Such strength is cognitive, even analytical, and surpasses philosophy and psychoanalysis in its power to expose human truth.

There are grander poems by Bishop than the relatively early "The Unbeliever," but I center upon it here because I love it best of all her poems. It does not compare in scope and power to "The Monument," "Roosters," "The Fish," "The Bight," "At the Fishhouses," "Brazil, January 1, 1502," "First Death in Nova Scotia," or the extraordinary late triad of "Crusoe in England," "The Moose," and "The End of March." Those ten poems have an authority and a possible wisdom that transcend "The Unbeliever." But I walk around, certain days, chanting "The Unbeliever" to myself, it being one of those rare poems you never evade again, once you know it (and it knows you). Its five stanzas essentially are variations upon its epigraph, from Bunyan: "He sleeps on the top of a mast." Bunyan's trope concerns the condition of unbelief; Bishop's does not. Think of the personae of Bishop's poem as exemplifying three rhetorical stances, and so as being three kinds of poet, or even three poets: cloud, gull, unbeliever. The cloud is Wordsworth or Stevens. The gull is Shelley or Hart Crane. The unbeliever is Dickinson or Bishop. None of them has the advantage; the spangled sea wants to destroy them all. The cloud, powerful in introspection, regards not the sea but his own subjectivity. The gull, more visionary still, beholds neither sea nor air but his own aspiration. The unbeliever observes nothing, but the sea is truly observed in his dream:

> which was, "I must not fall.
> The spangled sea below wants me to fall.
> It is hard as diamonds; it wants to destroy us all."

I think that is the reality of Bishop's famous eye. Like Dickinson's, its truest precursor, it confronts the truth, which is that what is most worth seeing is impossible to see, at least with open eyes. A poetry informed by that mode of observation will station itself at the edge where what is most worth saying is all but impossible to say. I will conclude here by contrasting Bishop's wonderful trope of the lion, in "The End of March," to Stevens's incessant use of the same figure. In Stevens, the lion tends to represent poetry as a destructive force, as the imposition of the poet's will-to-power over reality. This image culminates in "An Ordinary Evening in New Haven":

> Say of each lion of the spirit
>
> It is a cat of a sleek transparency
> That shines with a nocturnal shine alone.
> The great cat must stand potent in the sun.

Against that destructive night in which all cats are black, even the transparent ones, Stevens sets himself as a possible lion, potent in the light of the idea-of-ideas. Here, I take it, is Bishop's affectionate riposte:

> They could have been teasing the lion sun,
> except that now he was behind them
> —a sun who'd walked the beach the last low tide,
> making those big, majestic paw-prints,
> who perhaps had batted a kite out of the sky to play with.

A somewhat Stevensian lion sun, clearly, but with something better to do than standing potent in itself. The path away from poetry as a destructive force can only be through play, the play of trope. Within her tradition so securely, Bishop profoundly plays at trope. Dickinson, Moore, and Bishop resemble Emerson, Frost, and Stevens in that tradition, with a difference due not to mere nature or mere ideology but to superb art.

Harold Bloom

Contents

Introduction

On a recent television program, publisher Robert Giroux spoke of the period of neglect, the decline in reputation, that often follows the death of a well-known poet. With Elizabeth Bishop, however, the reverse seems to be the case. After years of critical misconception, effusion, or condescension (Oscar Williams, for example, setting the tone in 1946 by praising her "exquisite detail" and "charming little stained-glass bits"), she has finally come to be regarded as one of the major voices of our century.

Not that she hadn't always her more serious supporters. Early on, reviewing *North & South,* both Robert Lowell and Arthur Mizener (in seminal pieces never before reprinted) caught the complexity at the heart of Bishop's work. Anne Stevenson's 1966 book-length study, though now out of date, marked another important step. But it is only since *Geography III,* Bishop's fifth and last collection of poems, that the fundamental issues in her work have begun to be fully and more systematically explored. The emotional openness of these poems, their clarity and directness of exposition (what Robert Pinsky in *The Situation of Poetry* calls "the prose virtues") seemed to supply a clue to the elusiveness of the earlier work, and to create a need for the revaluation of Bishop's total accomplishment. Suddenly, we have essays called "The Power of Reticence" (Octavio Paz) and "The Poet of Feeling" (Alan Williamson). The most important recent criticism takes as a point of departure the inevitable and automatic commonplaces about Bishop's characteristic imagery, technique, and tone—geography and love of travel, descriptive precision, formal control, understatement and detachment, smallness of scale—and shows how complex yet coherent, how connected to the largest issues of modern literature, Bishop's work has always been.

The nine essays in the first section of this volume, from David Kalstone's extensive and probing overview to Penelope Laurans's examination of the nuances of versification, all begin with this deeply revaluating approach. Helen Vendler sees not only the poignance, but also the strangeness and mystery, the "threat of death," within Bishop's adumbration of familiar, domestic scenes. Robert Pinsky sees language itself as Bishop's real cartography, the "geographical situation of the soul," and shows how Bishop, like Wordsworth, expresses in her poems nothing less than the central effort of the individual artistic consciousness to impose order on the world. David Lehman focuses on an unexpected and largely unexplored area of Bishop's geographical image—not travel, but her frequently stated desire for confinement, her "need to make peace with the certitude of loss." Both Alan Williamson, in his discussion of Bishop's love poems, and Penelope Laurans, in her analysis of Bishop's metrics, find her "restraint" not the result of cool objectivity but of an urgent need to hold back feelings all too difficult to control. In the uncertainties expressed in Bishop's continual questioning, Bonnie Costello sees an emblem of Bishop's desire for self-location in an impersonal world: "Home seems to be in question, or rather, in questioning." By examining Bishop's "double tone" in the poems of *Geography III,* Lloyd Schwartz finds the emotional complexities of her later poems consistent with attitudes maintained throughout her work. And Willard Spiegelman sees in Bishop's understated realism a fundamental "natural heroism" that "internalizes the external." For all their diversity of interest, these essays dovetail in their common underlying conviction of Bishop's powerful moral, psychological, and emotional force.

This assumption is reinforced by the chronology of shorter articles and reviews, poems, memoirs, and memorials that make up the second part of this volume. Many of these are by those who were closest to Elizabeth Bishop—Marianne Moore, Robert Lowell, Randall Jarrell, and more recently, James Merrill and Frank Bidart. Many of these pieces are by poets (John Ashbery once called Bishop "a writer's writer's writer"). The memoirs are filled with useful and touching detail, both personal and literary, and though some of the shorter pieces have been chosen for their "historical" value, most of them make up in depth what they lack in length.

The third and final part is a chronological selection of Elizabeth Bishop's own words about writers and writing, about herself and her own writing—a miniature anthology spanning the length of her career: lively, eloquent passages from college essays, several reviews, a previously unpublished, amusingly self-aware piece of light verse, "occasional" statements, quotations from interviews, and two full-length interviews (from 1966 and 1977).* Her thoughtful, memorably imaged comments on "timing" (written in her twenties), her remarks on translation, on forms, her comments on Lowell, Jarrell, Moore, Auden, Cummings, Bidart, all have a double edge of truth, each penetrating word doubling back as self-revelation—just as in her poems.

"The two kinds of poetry are, Excellent and Other," William Meredith wrote in an affectionate and witty piece delivered at a special program of the Modern Language Association honoring Elizabeth Bishop (New York, 1976). "Elizabeth Bishop, so far as we know, writes only the one kind. Most other poets show off, in print, their greater versatility." The contents of this volume, we trust, will help demonstrate that this "one art" has been—and remains—not only singular, but both many-sided and inexhaustibly deep.

---

*All of these were gone over and, in several places, rewritten by Elizabeth Bishop.

PART ONE *Critical Essays*

DAVID KALSTONE

Elizabeth Bishop
Questions of Memory, Questions of Travel

Elizabeth Bishop, to her credit, has always been hard to "place." In the surveys of American poetry she is not linked to any particular school. She has had, from the very start, her share of prizes and praise; her work is admired by many poets who do not admire one another. Though on occasion she has had the grants and university positions which keep poets alive in America, she only rarely gives the public readings which keep poets visible. She has lived abroad for long stretches of her life, most recently in Brazil. Her books of poems, eagerly awaited, appear infrequently. *North & South* (1946), *A Cold Spring* (1955), *Questions of Travel* (1965); *The Complete Poems* (1969); *Geography III* (1976).

Bishop is probably the most honored yet most elusive of contemporary poets. Who else, with some of her best poems still to be written, would have entitled a volume *The Complete Poems?* She was, until very recently, "read unreasonably little and praised reasonably much," as Randall Jarrell said of Marianne Moore. There are many reasons for this, but the ones which interest me here have to do with the accidents of critical attention. Bishop's first book was so individual and striking that certain pieces from *North & South*—poems like "The Fish" and "The Man-Moth"—have been reprinted over and over in anthologies. She has become known as the author of single stunning poems, fewer from the later volumes than from the earlier. Wonderful as the anthologized poems may be, they give, even for anthologies, an unusually stunted version of Bishop's variety, of the way her writing has emerged, of her developing concerns.

Five Temperaments (New York: Oxford University Press, 1977), pp. 12–41.

There is a second problem: the deceptively simple surface of Bishop's work. Critics have praised her descriptive powers and treated her as something of a miniaturist. As mistakenly as with the work of Marianne Moore, they have sometimes asked if Bishop's is poetry at all. Bishop's early poems show a deep affinity with Marianne Moore's exact observant style: "An appropriately selected foundation for Miss Bishop's work," said Randall Jarrell. But he was also quick to see Bishop as "less driven into desperate straits or dens of innocence, and taking this Century of Polycarp more for granted."[1] Jarrell is one of those critics who urges us to look for the inner landscape and not to treat a poet's descriptive powers as if they were ends in themselves, or a weaker form of expression. He was able to show Moore's accuracy and understatement to be an instrument of ironic self-protectiveness. ("Her Shield" is the title of his essay.) By implication, he teaches us to ask similar questions about Bishop. Unlike the relatively armored approach of Marianne Moore, Bishop's precise explorations become a way of countering and encountering a lost world. Merely to praise her "famous eye" would be a way of avoiding larger issues. We need to know what is seen, and how the eye, with what Kenneth Burke calls its "disguised rituals," initiates us into human fears and wishes.

I

Robert Lowell, thinking back to the time before he wrote *Life Studies,* felt that Bishop's work "seemed to belong to a later century."[2] It wasn't so much a matter of experimental forms. In *North & South* (1946) there were a number of emblematic poems—"The Map," "The Monument," "The Gentleman of Shalott" among them—some in formal stanzas, some strictly rhymed. Still, from the very start, there was something about her work for which elegantly standard literary analysis was not prepared. Readers have been puzzled, as when one critic writes about "Florida": "the poet's exuberance provides a scattering of images whose relevance to the total structure is open to question. It is as though Miss Bishop stopped along the road home to examine every buttercup and asphodel she saw."[3] First of all, Bishop writes about alligators, mangrove swamps, skeletons and shells—things exotic and wild, not prettified. More important, there is some notion of neat and total structure which the critic expects and imposes, but which the poem subverts. What makes the quoted critic nervous is a quality which becomes more and more prominent in Bishop's work—her apparent lack of insistence on meanings beyond the surface of the poem, the poem's seeming randomness and disintegration. There is something personal, even quirky, about her apparently straightforward descriptive poems which, on early readings, it is hard to identify. This is an offhand way of speaking which Bishop has come to trust and master, especially in her important book of 1965, *Questions of Travel,* and in the extraordinary poems she has published since then.

I am talking about matters of tone, the kind of authority a single voice will claim over the material included in a poem. Anyone who has heard Miss Bishop read will know how flat and modest her voice is, how devoid of flourish, how briefly she holds her final chords and cadences and allows a poem to resonate. Here is the beginning of "In the Waiting Room":

> In Worcester, Massachusetts,
> I went with Aunt Consuelo
> to keep her dentist's appointment
> and sat and waited for her
> in the dentist's waiting room.

Or another opening ("Filling Station"):

> Oh, but it is dirty!
> —this little filling station,
> oil-soaked, oil-permeated
> to a disturbing, over-all
> black translucency.
> Be careful with that match!

And this is the end of "The Bight":

> Click. Click. Goes the dredge,
> and brings up a dripping jawful of marl.
> All the untidy activity continues,
> awful but cheerful.

I have chosen the plainest and most provocative examples of the apparently random in order to raise questions common to much poetry after Wallace Stevens: how is meaning developed from individual and unamplified details? How does the observer's apparent lack of insistence, devoid of rhetorical pressure, rise to significance (if, indeed, that is the word for it)? Howard Nemerov gives us one answer: "Vision begins with a fault in this world's smooth façade."[4] But Bishop finds that fault, that break from observation into the unknown, almost impossible to locate. "There is no split," she remarks in a letter:

> Dreams, works of art (some) glimpses of the always-more-successful surrealism of everyday life, unexpected moments of empathy (is it?), catch a peripheral vision of whatever it is one can never really see full-face but that seems enormously important. I can't believe we are wholly irrational—and I do admire Darwin—But reading Darwin one admires the beautiful solid case being built up out of his endless, heroic observations, almost unconscious or automatic—and then comes a sudden relaxation, a forgetful phrase, and one feels that strangeness of his undertaking, sees the lonely young man, his eye fixed on facts and minute details, sinking or sliding giddily off into the unknown. What one seems to want in art, in experiencing it, is the same thing that is necessary for its creation, a self-forgetful, perfectly useless concentration.[5]

Heroic observation; eyes fixed on facts and minute details, sinking, sliding giddily off into the unknown; a self-forgetful, perfectly useless concentration. What she sees in Darwin, we can see in her own efforts. Take "Florida" (the poem our critic found disorganized)—a poem of almost Darwinian concentration.

The opening line is so disarming, almost trivializing, that we are in danger of taking what follows for granted: the odd changes of scale that are among this poem's secrets.

> The state with the prettiest name,
> the state that floats in brackish water,
> held together by mangrove roots

that bear while living oysters in clusters,
and when dead strew white swamps with skeletons,
dotted as if bombarded, with green hummocks
like ancient cannon-balls sprouting grass.

The scale changes as rapidly as Gulliver's: first the whole state, afloat, intact with its boundaries, the mapmaker's or aerial photographer's vision; then an organism (held together by mangrove roots), the geologist's or botanist's fanciful X ray. Her Florida is a barnacled world refined to residues. Oysters dot the mangrove roots; dead mangroves strew the swamps with skeletons. Dead turtles leave their skulls and their shells, which are themselves hosts to other growths, barnacled. The coastline is looped with seashells painstakingly and exotically named. There is sediment in the water; solvents in wood-smoke; charring on stumps and dead trees. Yet the charring is "like black velvet." The residues studding this landscape are its principal ornaments as well: artistic and historical growths, like the "tide-looped strings of fading shells" turning the "monotonous . . . sagging coast-line" to something else.

At first the description occurs in a free-floating eternal present, a series of phrases which don't commit the observer to any main verb at all. They seem if anything to exclude her, reawakening memories of geological change that stretch far before and beyond her in scale, habitually repeated historical action. The strange shifts of scale—of size and space—in a seemingly timeless, self-renewing present remind us constantly, by implication, of the frailty of our merely human observer. A descriptive poem, which in other hands, say Whitman's, appropriates landscapes and objects, here makes us aware just how, just why we are excluded from such appropriations.

Only when we get to the buzzards, two-thirds of the way through the poem, is there a form of the present tense (they "are drifting down, down, down") restricted to her particular moment of watching, a definite *now*. Here also, two strange mirrors in which we do not find ourselves. First:

Thirty or more buzzards are drifting down, down, down,
over something they have spotted in the swamp,

in circles like stirred-up flakes of sediment
sinking through water.
Smoke from woods-fires filters fine blue solvents.

And then:

After dark, the fireflies map the heavens in the marsh
until the moon rises.

The four elements form a self-enclosed world. Creatures of
the air mirror the earth's discards (are they really there?) floating
through water; and fire, as if completing the cycle, exhales fine
smoke into the blue. Then again with the fireflies, air and flicker-
ing fire are reflected in the marsh, earth and water together. In
other words, alternate creations dwarf or frame the poet's own:
the long scale of eroding nature with its fossils and predators
(buzzards, mosquitoes with "ferocious obbligatos"), and then
the daily repeating creations and fadings. When the moon comes
up, the landscape pales. Its wonderful sounds and colors—the
flashy tanagers, the pelicans gold-winged at sunset, the musical
screeching—turn skeletal once more.

The world in its processes provides a delicate model for the
poet's work, for art—its shells with beautiful names, its finely
observed (and alliterative) oysters in clusters. But the poem con-
tinually stresses how such contrivance is made for fading and
how nature's contrivances survive the artist's own. Building
toward a phrase whose effect is worthy of what she admires in
Darwin ("a sudden relaxation, a forgetful phrase"), Bishop
sums up the impact of the scene, grasped for the fullness of her
own understanding:

Cold white, not bright, the moonlight is coarse-meshed,
and the careless, corrupt state is all black specks
too far apart, and ugly whites; the poorest
post-card of itself.

At the end Florida contracts to the alligator's five primitive calls
("friendliness, love, mating, war, and a warning"), and with its

whimper is restored to darkness and its mysterious identity as "the Indian Princess."

Bishop exposes us to a more ambitious version of her almost toneless observer in a poem which reaches back to her Nova Scotia childhood, "At the Fishhouses." Here is the opening:

> Although it is a cold evening,
> down by one of the fishhouses
> an old man sits netting,
> his net, in the gloaming almost invisible
> a dark purple-brown,
> and his shuttle worn and polished.
> The air smells so strong of codfish
> it makes one's nose run and one's eyes water.
> The five fishhouses have steeply peaked roofs
> and narrow, cleated gangplanks slant up
> to storerooms in the gables
> for the wheelbarrows to be pushed up and down on.
> All is silver: the heavy surface of the sea,
> swelling slowly as if considering spilling over,
> is opaque, but the silver of the benches,
> the lobster pots, and masts, scattered
> among the wild jagged rocks,
> is of an apparent translucence
> like the small old buildings with an emerald moss
> growing on their shoreward walls.
> The big fish tubs are completely lined
> with layers of beautiful herring scales
> and the wheelbarrows are similarly plastered
> with creamy iridescent coats of mail,
> with small iridescent flies crawling on them.

At first, as in "Florida," a landscape seems almost without a spectator, the speaker comically unwelcome in an air which smacks of another element and which makes her eyes water and her nose run. She slowly exposes the scene, present tense, with a tempered willingness to let it speak for itself in declarative simplicity. Things *are;* things *have*. The lone fisherman, a Wordsworthian solitary, is worn into the scene, his net "almost invisible," his shuttle "worn and polished," his "black old knife" with a blade "almost worn away." The dense opening description—deliberately slow, close to fifty lines of the poem—is in all details of sight, sense and sound intended to subject us to the landscape, to draw us deeply into it. "The five fishhouses have steeply peaked roofs/ and narrow, cleated gangplanks slant up": even the clotted consonants and doubling of adjectives force these words apart and force us to dwell on them, as if to carve out some certainty of vision. The reader is meant to become what the speaker jokingly claims herself to be later in this poem: "a believer in total immersion."

From this immersion a pattern gathers, unhurried but persistent: present, for example, in the odd half-rhyme of *codfish* and *polished,* or in the unassuming repetition of *iridescent.* The wheelbarrows are "plastered / with creamy iridescent coats of mail, / with small iridescent flies crawling on them." The crudeness and the delicacy of these details are made to appear strokes of the same master, of the landscape's age-old subjection to the sea, to the caking, the plastering, the lining, the silvering-over which turns everything to iridescence or sequins, as at the same time it rusts them and wears them away.

In its fidelity to setting—to what is both jagged and strangely jewelled—the poem accumulates the sense of an artistry beyond the human, one that stretches over time, chiselling and decorating with its strange erosions. The human enterprise depends upon and is dwarfed by the sea, just as the fishhouse ramps lead out of, but back into the water: "Down at the water's edge, at the place / where they haul up the boats, up the long ramp / descending into the water." Precisely by imagining these encircling powers, the speaker wins some authority over them. This is her largest gesture, reflected in some smaller moments of propitiation: offering a cigarette to the fisherman, and with odd simplicity singing Baptist hymns to a moderately curious seal, true creature of that "element bearable to no mortal." Behind them—or more to the point "behind us"—as if left behind in merely human history "a million Christmas trees stand / waiting for Christmas."

This "believer in total immersion," through her patient

wooing or conjuring, finally wins a certain elevation of tone, a vision, in a twice-repeated phrase, of the sea "Cold dark deep and absolutely clear."

> . . . The water seems suspended
> above the rounded gray and blue-gray stones.
> I have seen it over and over, the same sea, the same,
> slightly, indifferently swinging above the stones,
> icily free above the stones,
> above the stones and then the world.
> If you should dip your hand in,
> your wrist would ache immediately,
> your bones would begin to ache and your hand would burn
> as if the water were a transmutation of fire
> that feeds on stones and burns with a dark gray flame.
> If you tasted it, it would first taste bitter,
> then briny, then surely burn your tongue.
> It is like what we imagine knowledge to be:
> dark, salt, clear, moving, utterly free,
> drawn from the cold hard mouth
> of the world, derived from the rocky breasts
> forever, flowing and drawn, and since
> our knowledge is historical, flowing, and flown.

The poet returns knowledge to concreteness, as if breaking it down into its elements (dark, salt, clear). The speaker herself seems drawn into the elements: at first jokingly in the fishy air which makes the nose run, the eyes water; then in the burning if one dips one's hands, as if water were a "transmutation of fire that feeds on stones." The absorbing and magical transformations of earth, air, fire and water into one another (as in "Florida") make it impossible—and unnecessary—to distinguish *knowledge* from the *sea,* to determine what, grammatically, is "derived from the rocky breasts / forever." With a final fluency she leaves her declarative descriptions behind and captures a rhythm at once mysterious and acknowledging limitations ("flowing and drawn . . . flowing and flown").

"At the Fishhouses" makes explicit what is usually implicit, invisible and vital in Miss Bishop's poems, like a pulse: a sense of the encircling and eroding powers in whose presence all minute observations are valuably made. She is, in fact, rather like a sandpiper she describes in another poem: the bird pictured as subject to the water's roar, the earth's shaking—imagined in "a state of controlled panic, a student of Blake." He watches the sand, no detail too small ("Sandpiper"):

> The world is a mist. And then the world is
> minute and vast and clear. The tide
> is higher or lower. He couldn't tell you which.
> His beak is focussed; he is preoccupied,
>
> looking for something, something, something.
> Poor bird, he is obsessed!
> The millions of grains are black, white, tan, and gray,
> mixed with quartz grains, rose and amethyst.

Here again are those shifts of scale which, instead of unsettling, actually strengthen our perspective. The poem is a critique of Blake's auguries of innocence: his seeing the world in a grain of sand. "The world is a mist. And then the world is / minute and vast and clear." The adjectives appear to make a quiet claim. Yet what an odd collocation—minute and vast and clear. The scales are not really commensurable; one sees the world, one sees the grain of sand, and the clarity comes in making a primitive and definite distinction about what is and is not within our grasp. The bird, on the one hand, is battered and baffled by the waves, the misty "sheets of interrupting water"; on the other hand it attends and stares, is preoccupied, obsessed with the grains of sand, a litany of whose colors, minutely and beautifully distinguished, ends the poem. That is all it knows of the world.

These poems both describe and set themselves at the limits of description. Bishop lets us know that every detail is a boundary, not a Blakean microcosm. Because of the limits they suggest, details vibrate with a meaning beyond mere physical presence. Landscapes meant to sound detached are really inner landscapes. They show an effort at reconstituting the world as if it were in danger of being continually lost. It is only this sense of *precarious*

possession that accounts for the way Bishop looks at the city
waking up ("Love Lies Sleeping"):

> From the window I see
>
> an immense city, carefully revealed,
> made delicate by over-workmanship,
>> detail upon detail,
>> cornice upon façade,
>
> reaching so languidly up into
> a weak white sky, it seems to waver there.
>> (Where it has slowly grown
>> in skies of water-glass
>
> from fused beads of iron and copper crystals,
> the little chemical "garden" in a jar
>> trembles and stands again,
>> pale blue, blue-green, and brick.)

That human contrivance is frail and provisional is clear not only
from the "wavering" but also from the odd, habitual changes of
scale: an immense city, carefully revealed, is also a little chemical
garden in a jar. That it should be seen as workmanship at all is a
miracle of freshness, a confusion of proportions, part aerial vi-
sion, part closeup as of some miraculous insect civilization.
Bishop triumphs in the surprising coincidence of mechanics and
natural growth, fused beads of crystal, a little chemical garden—
a balancing act to portray our fragile ingenuity.

The ability to see such accomplishments as provisional ex-
plains the power of one of Bishop's apparently random poems,
"The Bight." It is subtitled "on my birthday," the only sug-
gestion of much resonance beyond the impression of a tide-
battered inlet—muddy at low tide, with dredges, pelicans, marl,
sponge boats, sharktails hung up to dry, boats beached, some
wrecked. What animates the scene this time is the observer's
deliberate activity, celebrating her birthday in an off-key way
with an unrelenting and occasionally mischievous series of com-

parisons: pilings dry as matches; water turning to gas (and which Baudelaire might hear turning to marimba music); pelicans crashing like pickaxes; man-of-war birds opening tails like scissors; sharktails hanging like plowshares. The whole rundown world is domesticated by comparisons to our mechanical contrivances, our instruments of workaday survival, enabling, in turn, an outrageous simile (stove-boats "like torn-open, unanswered letters") and an equally outrageous pun ("The bight is littered with old correspondences"). The letters wickedly enough bring Baudelaire back into the poem, merge with his "correspondences." They are unanswered letters to boot, in a poem where the author has shot off one comparison after another, like firecrackers. No wonder then that a dredge at the end perfectly accompanies this poet's activities:

> Click. Click. Goes the dredge,
> and brings up a dripping jawful of marl.
> All the untidy activity continues,
> awful but cheerful.

This is what she allows for her birthday: the pointed celebration of small-craft victories in a storm-ridden inlet.

It is no accident that much of Bishop's work is carried on at the mercy of or in the wake of the tides. There are divided and distinguished stages in her encounters: moments of civilized, provisional triumph; and then again, times when landscapes leave us behind—the northern seas of "At the Fishhouses," the abundant decay of "Florida" and later, of her adopted Brazil, magnetic poles sensed even in the title of her first volume, *North & South*. Our mortal temperate zones seem in some ways the excluded middle where we possess a language of precarious, even doomed distinctions.

2

The fact that Bishop sought worlds which dwarf us, landscapes from which we are excluded, is best glossed by a wonderful and very important story, "In the Village." The tale reaches back to a Nova Scotia childhood, a version of her own. Her mother was taken to a sanitarium when Bishop was five; she never saw her again. The story is told through the child's eyes. In one scene the young girl watches her mother, who is just back from a sanitarium and coming out of two years of mourning, being fitted for a new dress. "The dressmaker was crawling around and around on her knees eating pins as Nebuchadnezzar had crawled eating grass." The child stands in the doorway.

Clang.
Clang.
Oh, beautiful sounds, from the blacksmith's shop at the end of the garden! Its gray roof, with patches of moss, could be seen above the lilac bushes. Nate was there—Nate, wearing a long black leather apron over his trousers and bare chest, sweating hard, a black leather cap on top of dry, thick, black-and-gray curls, a black sooty face; iron filings, whiskers, and gold teeth, all together, and a smell of red-hot metal and horses' hoofs.
Clang.
The pure note: pure and angelic.
The dress was all wrong. She screamed.
The child vanishes.[6]

The child vanishes literally, and metaphorically as well, in that moment of awakening and awareness of inexplicable adult pain. From this point on the story is told in the first person and in the present tense, as if she had been jolted into reclaiming something first seen as a distant tableau and dream. Memories of the mother's scream echo through scenes which are also, as in the pungent energy of the blacksmith shop, rich strong recollections of life in a Nova Scotia village. At the end, the mother gone for good, the threats and village harmonies come together for the last time.

Every Monday afternoon I go past the blacksmith's shop with the package under my arm, hiding the address of the sanitarium with my arm and my other hand.
Going over the bridge, I stop and stare down into the river. All the little trout that have been too smart to get

caught—for how long now?—are there, rushing in flank movements, foolish assaults and retreats, against and away from the old sunken fender of Malcolm McNeil's Ford. It has lain there for ages and is supposed to be a disgrace to us all. So are the tin cans that glint there, brown and gold.

From above, the trout look as transparent as the water, but if one did catch one, it would be opaque enough, with a little slick moon-white belly with a pair of tiny, pleated, rose-pink fins on it. The leaning willows soak their narrow yellowed leaves.

Clang.

Clang.

Nate is shaping a horseshoe.

Oh, beautiful pure sound!

It turns everything else to silence.

But still, once in a while, the river gives an unexpected gurgle. *"Slp,"* it says, out of glassy-ridged brown knots sliding along the surface.

Clang.

And everything except the river holds its breath.

Now there is no scream. Once there was one and it settled slowly down to earth one hot summer afternoon; or did it float up, into that dark, too dark, blue sky? But surely it has gone away, forever.

Clang.

It sounds like a bell buoy out at sea.

It is the elements speaking: earth, air, fire, water.

All those other things—clothes, crumbling postcards, broken china; things damaged and lost, sickened or destroyed; even the frail almost-lost scream—are they too frail for us to hear their voices long, too mortal?

Nate!

Oh, beautiful sound, strike again![7]

What sounds like a bell buoy out at sea? The scream? The blacksmith's anvil? The two finally merging? "In the Village" is the vital center from which many of Bishop's poems radiate, the darker side of their serene need to reclaim "the elements speaking: earth, air, fire, water." She printed it among the poems of her 1965 volume, *Questions of Travel,* as if to make that point.

For a moment "In the Village" offers a radiant primal world, available to human energies. It is almost unique in Bishop's work for the way it resolves tensions between the remembered, inaccessible, inhuman call of the four elements and her affectionate grasp of the more precarious details of human life. In the glow of memory she is for once licensed to glide from the scream ("But surely it has gone away, forever") to the noise of the anvil, the two distantly merged like the bell buoy at sea, the elements speaking. For once, in the suffused light of childhood, she is allowed to hear those perfectly inhuman elements as if they were the voices of paradise, a fulfilled retreat from the intense inescapable world of change and loss. For once, losing hold of details is not an engulfment or a drowning, but a situation quietly accepted with a muted question:

All those other things—clothes, crumbling postcards, broken china; things damaged and lost, sickened or destroyed; even the frail almost-lost scream—are they too frail for us to hear their voices long, too mortal?

No wonder then that Bishop was drawn again and again to her Northern and tropical landscapes whose scale and temperature are so different from our own. Exile and travel are at the heart of her poems from the very start—and sometimes as if they could reconstitute the vision of "In the Village," as if they led somewhere, a true counter to loss. Bishop is spellbound by the polar world in an early poem, "The Imaginary Iceberg." "Self-made from elements least visible," the iceberg "saves itself perpetually and adorns / only itself." Of that tempting self-enclosed world, a frosty palace of art, she writes, "We'd rather have the iceberg than the ship, / although it meant the end of travel." This is, in an idiom fraught with danger, "a scene a sailor'd give his eyes for."

Again, in the wonderful "Over 2000 Illustrations and a Complete Concordance," a traveller is tantalized by the promise of vision beyond the random encounter. Childhood memories of etchings of the Holy Land in an old Bible make her yearn for something beyond the *and* and *and* of pointlessly accumulated travel. This is the end of the poem:

> Everything only connected by "and" and "and."
> Open the book. (The gilt rubs off the edges
> of the pages and pollinates the fingertips.)
> Open the heavy book. Why couldn't we have seen
> this old Nativity while we were at it?
> —the dark ajar, the rocks breaking with light,
> an undisturbed, unbreathing flame,
> colorless, sparkless, freely fed on straw,
> and, lulled within, a family with pets,
> —and looked and looked our infant sight away.

Like the "scene a sailor'd give his eyes for," that last phrase ("looked and looked our infant sight away") carries a mysterious yearning to stop observing, which it also guards against. Bishop never entirely gives in. She glimpses the terrifying folk truth behind the apparent satisfactions of a sight "we'd give our eyes for." And if we are to see the old Nativity in "Over 2000 Illustrations," if the memory of engravings in a beloved childhood book allows us once more to trust experience as sacramental, if such travel will reconstitute the blasted family of "In the Village" (the poem envisions rocks breaking with light "and, lulled within, a family with pets"), then what will it mean to "look and look our infant sight away"? Where or when is *away*? Is it a measureless absorption in the scene? Or, on the contrary, a loss of powers, as in "to waste away"? Or a welcome relinquishment, to be gathered back into the world of childhood, to return to "infant" sight—it keeps its Latin root, "speechless."

Bishop, sensing dangers, only hints at satisfaction. "Over 2000 Illustrations and a Complete Concordance" is almost a farewell to such temptations. There are in her poems no final visions. She moves away from "We'd rather have the iceberg than the ship, / although it meant the end of travel" to the "Questions of Travel" entertained in her third book. There, in tones more relaxed than ever before, she learns to trust the saving, continuous, precise pursuits of the exile's eye.

3

The volume *Questions of Travel* in effect constitutes a sequence of poems, its Brazilian landscapes not so much providing answers as initiating us into the mysteries of how questions are asked. It is important that the book also includes poems about her Nova Scotia childhood and the central story of that period, "In the Village." In the light of those memories, the Brazilian poems become a model of how, with difficulty and pleasure, pain and precision, we re-introduce ourselves into a world.

There are three important initiating poems: in order, "Arrival at Santos," "Brazil, January 1, 1502" and "Questions of Travel." The first is deliberately superficial, comic, sociable. We watch her straining from tourist into traveller, after the disappointments of Santos, which like all ports is like soap or postage stamps—necessary but, "wasting away like the former, slipping the way the latter / do when we mail the letters we wrote on the boat." The familiar and merely instrumental melt away and we know something more than geographical is meant by the last line: "We are driving to the interior."

We go there by means of one of Bishop's characteristic changes of scale. "Arrival at Santos"—it's not Bishop's usual practice—had been dated at the end, *January, 1952*. The next poem is "Brazil, January 1, 1502," and its first word is the generalizing *Januaries*. No longer in the "here" and "now" of the uninstructed tourist, the poem fans out into the repeating present of the botanist and the anthropologist. Our drive to the interior is through the looking glass of natural history. There is a comforting epigraph from Lord Clark's *Landscape into Art*, "embroidered nature . . . tapestried landscape," that seems to familiarize the scene, appropriate it for European sensibilities. Yet this is a wild burgeoning tapestry, not "filled in" with foliage but "every square inch *filling in* with foliage," tirelessly self-renewing. Its distinctions of shade and color force her into relentless unflagging specificity: "big leaves, little leaves, and giant leaves, / blue, blue-green, and olive." A parade of shades: silver-gray, rust red, greenish white, blue-white. The powers of description are deliberately and delightfully taxed; it's hard for mere humans to keep up.

Then, with a bow to our desire for a familiar tapestry, Bishop draws our attention to something in the foreground. It is first identified as "Sin: / five sooty dragons near some massy rocks." The rocks are "worked with lichens" and "threatened from underneath by moss / in lovely hell-green flames." Then, in a deliberate change of scale, the little morality play turns to something wilder, more riveting, making fun of our tame exaggerations. Those dragons are, in fact, lizards in heat.

> The lizards scarcely breathe; all eyes
> are on the smaller, female one, back-to,
> her wicked tail straight up and over,
> red as red-hot wire.

Then the most daring change of all:

> Just so the Christians, hard as nails,
> tiny as nails, and glinting,
> in creaking armor, came and found it all,
> not unfamiliar.

For a moment, until we unravel the syntax, "just so" identifies the invaders with the lizards in heat. Tiny in scale, dwarfed by the scene, the settlers, after Mass, are out hunting Indian women:

> they ripped away into the hanging fabric,
> each out to catch an Indian for himself—
> those maddening little women who kept calling,
> calling to each other (or had the birds waked up?)
> and retreating, always retreating, behind it.

The tapestry—initially it seemed like a device to domesticate the landscape—instead excludes invaders from it. At the beginning we were identified with those settlers of 1502: "Nature greets our eyes / exactly as she must have greeted theirs." At the end that proves to be a dubious privilege. Nature's tapestry endures, renews itself. After our initial glimpse of order, we shrink like Alice or Gulliver—toy intruders, marvelling.

Bishop's book, then, imagines first the mere tourist, then the invader, and finally, in the title poem, faces what is actually available to the traveller. "Questions of Travel" anticipates a new submissive understanding, taking what comes on its own terms, as she does with the magical powers of "The Riverman" or the mysterious quirks of the humble squatter-tenant, "Manuelzinho." The key to this new openness and affection is in the movement of the title poem. It proceeds through a cautious syntax of questions, with tentative answers in negative clauses. The glutted, excluded observer of the two opening poems ("There are too many waterfalls here") hallucinates mountains into capsized hulls, her own sense that travel might turn into shipwreck. Her first questions are asked with a guilty air: "Should we have stayed at home and thought of here? . . . Is it right to be watching strangers in a play . . . ?"

> What childishness is it that while there's a breath of life
> in our bodies, we are determined to rush
> to see the sun the other way around?
> The tiniest green hummingbird in the world?
> To stare at some inexplicable old stonework,
> inexplicable and impenetrable,
> at any view,
> instantly seen and always, always delightful?

You can hear Bishop's spirits rise to the bait of detail, the word "childishness" losing its air of self-accusation and turning before our eyes into something receptive, *childlike,* open to wonder. This is finally a less ambiguous approach than that of the traveller yearning to "look and look our infant sight away." "Questions of Travel" does not expect, as "Over 2000 Illustrations" did, that vision will add up, restore our ancient home. The yearning remains ("Oh, must we dream our dreams / and have them, too?"). But the observer is drawn very cautiously by accumulating detail, and questions themselves begin to satisfy the imagining mind. The following passage, all questions, proceeds by the method Bishop admired in Darwin ("a self-forgetful, perfectly useless concentration"):

> But surely it would have been a pity
> not to have seen the trees along this road,
> really exaggerated in their beauty,
> not to have seen them gesturing
> like noble pantomimists, robed in pink.
> —Not to have had to stop for gas and heard
> the sad, two-noted, wooden tune
> of disparate wooden clogs
> carelessly clacking over
> a grease-stained filling-station floor.
> (In another country the clogs would all be tested.
> Each pair there would have identical pitch.)
> —A pity not to have heard
> the other, less primitive music of the fat brown bird
> who sings above the broken gasoline pump
> in a bamboo church of Jesuit baroque:
> three towers, five silver crosses.
> —Yes, a pity not to have pondered,
> blurr'dly and inconclusively,
> on what connection can exist for centuries
> between the crudest wooden footwear
> and, careful and finicky,
> the whittled fantasies of wooden cages.
> —Never to have studied history in
> the weak calligraphy of songbirds' cages.

Bishop has the structuralist's curiosity. She probably enjoys Lévi-Strauss, who also studies "history in / the weak calligraphy of songbirds' cages" in the Brazil of *Tristes Tropiques*. Bishop rests in doubts, proceeds by a tantalizing chain of negative questions (surely it would have been a pity . . . not to have seen . . . not to have heard . . . not to have pondered . . . etc.). The closing lines revisit the world of "Over 2000 Illustrations and a Complete Concordance" but with more abandon, more trust to the apparent randomness of travel and the state of homelessness:

"Is it lack of imagination that makes us come
to imagined places, not just stay at home?
Or could Pascal have been not entirely right
about just sitting quietly in one's room? .

Continent, city, country, society:
the choice is never wide and never free.
And here, or there . . . No. Should we have stayed at home,
wherever that may be?"

I said earlier that details are also boundaries for Elizabeth
Bishop, that whatever radiant glimpses they afford, they are also
set at the vibrant limits of her descriptive powers. "In the Vil-
lage" and "Questions of Travel" show us what generates this
precarious state. "From this the poem springs," Wallace Stevens
remarks. "That we live in a place / That is not our own and,
much more, not ourselves / And hard it is in spite of blazoned
days."[8] Bishop writes under that star, aware of the smallness
and dignity of human observation and contrivance. She sees
with such a rooted, piercing vision, so realistically, because she
has never taken our presence in the world as totally real

4

"How had I come to be here?" Bishop asks in a recent poem,
"In the Waiting Room."[9] Even more than "In the Village," "In
the Waiting Room" invites us to understand Bishop's efforts in
an autobiographical light. Revisiting childhood experience, less
open to ecstasy than the earlier short story, "In the Waiting
Room" recalls the sense of personal loss so often implied behind
Bishop's observations. The poem is a melancholy visitation to a
childhood world Bishop has earlier ("In the Village") described
more joyfully. This time she is accompanying her aunt to the
dentist's office.

> while I waited I read
> the *National Geographic*
> (I could read) and carefully

studied the photographs:
the inside of a volcano,
black, and full of ashes;
then it was spilling over
in rivulets of fire.
Osa and Martin Johnson
dressed in riding breeches,
laced boots, and pith helmets.
A dead man slung on a pole
—"Long Pig," the caption said.
Babies with pointed heads
wound round and round with string;
black, naked women with necks
wound round and round with wire
like the necks of light bulbs.
Their breasts were horrifying.

The scream of "In the Village" is heard once again in a return to youthful memories of women in pain. But the scream, this time, is not banished.

Suddenly, from inside,
came an *oh!* of pain
—Aunt Consuelo's voice—
not very loud or long.
I wasn't at all surprised;
even then I knew she was
a foolish, timid woman.
I might have been embarrassed,
but wasn't. What took me
completely by surprise
was that it was *me:*
my voice, in my mouth.
Without thinking at all
I was my foolish aunt,
I—we—were falling, falling,
our eyes glued to the cover
of the *National Geographic,*
February, 1918.

The memory is astonishing, especially in the telling: the way in which "inside" allows us the little girl's own moment of confusion, as the cry seems to be her own. The child, entirely a spectator to others' pain "In the Village," finds unexpectedly that she is prey to it herself at the moment which sentences her to adulthood "In the Waiting Room."

Observation, the spectator's clear and lonely power, is a kind of life-jacket here. The poem is detailed and circumstantial: the child clings to details so as to keep from "sliding / beneath a big black wave, / another, and another."

> But I felt: you are an *I*
> you are an *Elizabeth*,
> you are one of *them*.
> *Why* should you be one, too?

The "I" that enters this poem, bearing her very name (the first time Bishop uses it in a poem) has the same staying power, no more, no less than the furniture of the waiting room, the arctics, the overcoats, the shadowy gray knees of the adults in the waiting room—all the sad imprisoning litany of human identity, like the numbers she takes pains to mention: three days until she is seven years old; the fifth of February, 1918. These read like incantations to "stop / the sensation of falling off / the round, turning world / into cold, blue-black space." The very plainness of the poem is what saves her; she is a realist *faute de mieux,* she observes because she has to.

"In the Waiting Room," like other poems Bishop has published since her *Complete Poems* appeared in 1969, rounds a remarkable corner in her career. My impression is that these pieces, collected in *Geography III* (1976), revisit her earlier poems as Bishop herself once visited tropical and polar zones, and that they refigure her work in wonderful ways. "Poem" looks to a small landscape by what must be the same great-uncle, an R.A., who painted the "Large Bad Picture" in her first book, *North & South*. "In the Waiting Room" revisits an awakening to adulthood as seen by a child, the world of "In the Village." "The Moose" recalls the pristine wonder of her Nova Scotia poems, and "Crusoe in England" looks back at a Southern hemisphere even more exotic than her tropical Brazil. In these and other poems, returning to earlier scenes, Bishop has asked more openly what energies fed, pressured, endangered and rewarded her chosen life of travel and clear vision.

Her "questions of travel" modulate now, almost imperceptibly, into questions of memory and loss. Attentive still to landscapes where one can feel the sweep and violence of encircling and eroding geological powers, poems such as "Crusoe in England" and "The Moose" pose their problems retrospectively. Crusoe lives an exile's life in civilized England, lord in imagination only of his "un-rediscovered, un-renamable island." In "The Moose" we are city-bound, on a bus trip away from Nova Scotia, and the long lean poem reads like a thread the narrator is laying through a maze—to find her way back?

"Crusoe in England" re-creates the pleasures and the pains of surviving in a universe of one. News that a new volcano has erupted trips Crusoe's memories of his own island. His way of thinking about it is that an island has been *born:*

> at first a breath of steam, ten miles away;
> and then a black fleck—basalt, probably—
> rose in the mate's binoculars
> and caught on the horizon like a fly.
> They named it. But my poor old island's still
> un-rediscovered, un-renamable.
> None of the books has ever got it right.

The shock of birth, the secret joy of naming, of knowing a place "un-renamable"—these emotions shadow the surface, as they do for the child of "In the Waiting Room." Crusoe's whole poem is pervaded by the play of curiosity. He asks questions, concentrates and then, as Bishop says elsewhere of Darwin, one sees him, "his eye fixed on facts and minute details, sinking or sliding giddily off into the unknown." The drifts of snail shells on Crusoe's island look from a distance like beds of irises. The next thing we know, they *are* iris beds:

> The books
> I'd read were full of blanks;
> the poems—well, I tried

reciting to my iris-beds,
"They flash upon that inward eye,
which is the bliss. . . ." The bliss of what?
One of the first things that I did
when I got back was look it up.

No point in finishing Wordsworth's quote: *imagination* would
fill the blank better than *solitude* in this case, but neither is neces-
sary in the presence of Crusoe's joy in the homemade and under
the pressure of having to re-invent the world: "the parasol that
took me such a time / remembering the way the ribs should go";
the baby goat dyed red with the island's one kind of berry "just
to see / something a little different"; a flute, "Home-made,
home-made! But aren't we all?" The poem is crowded with
fresh experience: hissing turtles, small volcanoes. Crusoe has his
longings—one fulfilled when Friday appears. He also has his
nightmares. When he is on the island, he dreams about being
trapped on infinite numbers of islands, each of which he must in
painful detail explore. Back in England the nightmare is just the
opposite: that such stimulation, imaginative curiosity and ener-
gy will peter out. His old knife ("it reeked of meaning, like a
crucifix") seems to have lost its numinous power. The whole
poem poses a question about imagination when it is no longer
felt to be intimately related to survival. Biship seems involved
with the figure of Crusoe because of the questions *after* travel, a
kind of "Dejection Ode" countered by the force and energy that
memory has mustered for the rest of the poem. It acts out ways
of overcoming and then re-experiencing loss.

Elizabeth Bishop has always written poetry to locate herself—
most obviously when she is challenged by the exotic landscapes
of North and South. She now performs her acts of location in
new ways—sometimes showing the pains and joys of domes-
tication, in poems like "Five Flights Up" and "12 O'Clock
News" (the imaginative transformation of the writer's desk into
a war-torn landscape). More important is the relocation in time,
no longer seeing herself and her characters in long geological—
Northern or tropical—perspectives, but in a landscape scaled
down to memory and the inner bounds of a human life. What
she finds are the pleasures and the fears of something like
Crusoe's experience: the live memories of naming, the sudden

lapse of formerly numinous figures. Early morning "Five Flights Up," listening to an exuberant dog in a yard next door, to a bird making questioning noises, she feels alive enough to imagine

> gray light streaking each bare branch,
> each single twig, along one side,
> making another tree, of glassy veins . . .

apart enough to conclude

> —Yesterday brought to today so lightly!
> (A yesterday I find almost impossible to lift.)

In another sense the past has its sustaining surprises. "Poem" is about the feelings awakened by a small painting passed down in her family, a landscape apparently by the great-uncle responsible for the "Large Bad Picture" which Bishop approached with diffidence and only submerged affection in *North & South*. In the new poem, the painter's work is welcomed as it brings alive, slowly, a scene from her childhood.

> I never knew him. We both knew this place.
> apparently, this literal small backwater,
> looked at it long enough to memorize it,
> our years apart. How strange. And it's still loved,
> or its memory is (it must have changed a lot).
> Our visions coincided—"visions" is
> too serious a word—our looks, two looks:
> art "copying from life" and life itself,
> life and the memory of it so compressed
> they've turned into each other. Which is which?
> Life and the memory of it cramped,
> dim, on a piece of Bristol board,
> dim, but how live, how touching in detail
> —the little that we get for free,
> the little of our earthly trust. Not much.
> About the size of our abidance
> along with theirs: the munching cows,

the iris, crisp and shivering, the water
still standing from spring freshets,
the yet-to-be-dismantled elms, the geese.

I hear in these guarded, modest, still radiant lines a new note in Bishop's work: a shared pleasure in imaginative intensity, almost as if this remarkable writer were being surprised (you *hear* the surprise in her voice) at the power over loss and change which memory has given her writing. What else is it that we hear in "The Moose," as the bus gets going through a lovingly remembered trip from salt Nova Scotia and New Brunswick, world of her childhood, toward Boston where she now lives? The fog closes in, "its cold, round crystals / form and slide and settle / in the white hens' feathers." They seem to enter an enchanted forest, and she is lulled to sleep by voices from the back of the bus, "talking the way they talked / in the old feather-bed, / peacefully, on and on." A long chain of human speech reassures her: " 'Yes . . .' that peculiar / affirmative. 'Yes . . .' / A sharp indrawn breath, / half groan, half acceptance." It is almost as if this discourse and its kinship to her own powers, the storyteller's powers handed down, summon up the strange vision which stops the bus: a moose "towering, antler-less . . . grand, otherworldly"—primitive, but giving everyone a "sweet / sensation of joy." It is "homely as a house / (or, safe as houses)" like the very houses the quieting talk on the bus recalls. The moose seems both to crystallize the silence, security and awe of the world being left behind and to guarantee a nourishing and haunting place for it in memory.

In "The End of March" Bishop follows a looped cord along a deserted beach to a snarl of string the size of a man, rising and falling on the waves, "sodden, giving up the ghost. . . . / A kite string?—But no kite." It might be an emblem for these recent poems which touch on lost or slender connections. Bishop seems more explicit about that than she used to be. Where loss was previously the unnamed object against which the poems ventured forth, it is now one of the named subjects. Her poems say out very naturally: "the little that we get for free, / the little of our earthly trust. Not much." Memory is her way of bringing to the surface and acknowledging as general the experience of losing which has always lain behind her work and which the work attempts to counter. "One Art" is the title Bishop gives to a late villanelle which encourages these very connections.

> The art of losing isn't hard to master;
> so many things seem filled with the intent
> to be lost that their loss is no disaster.
>
> Lose something every day. Accept the fluster
> of lost door keys, the hour badly spent.
> The art of losing isn't hard to master.

The effort to control strong feeling is everywhere in this poem. What falls away—love, homes, dreams—is hopelessly intertwined with the repeating rhymes which challenge each other at every turn: *master, disaster.*

> I lost my mother's watch. And look! my last, or
> next-to-last, of three loved houses went.
> The art of losing isn't hard to master.
>
> I lost two cities, lovely ones. And, vaster,
> some realms I owned, two rivers, a continent.
> I miss them, but it wasn't a disaster.
>
> —Even losing you (the joking voice, a gesture
> I love) I shan't have lied. It's evident
> the art of losing's not too hard to master
> though it may look like (*Write* it!) like disaster.

The last stubborn heartbreaking hesitation—"though it may look like (*Write* it!) like disaster"—carries the full burden, and finally confidence, of her work, the resolve which just barely masters emptiness and succeeds in filling out, tight-lipped, the form.

If Bishop's writing since *Complete Poems* still displays her tough idiosyncratic powers of observation, it also makes a place for those observations in very natural surroundings of the mind.

The title *Geography III* (and its epigraph from "First Lessons in Geography") is at once a bow to her real-life relocation and a deep acknowledgment of the roots of these poems in childhood memory and loss. The time and the space these poems lay claim to are more peculiarly Elizabeth Bishop's own—less geological, less historical, less vastly natural; her poems are more openly inner landscapes than ever before.

NOTES

1. Randall Jarrell, *Poetry and the Age* (1953; reprint ed., New York: Random House, Vintage, 1959), p. 213.

2. Robert Lowell, "On 'Skunk Hour,'" reprinted in *Robert Lowell: A Collection of Critical Essays,* ed. Thomas Parkinson (Englewood Cliffs, N.J.: Prentice-Hall, 1968), p. 133.

3. Stephen Stepanchev, *American Poetry Since 1945* (New York: Harper and Row, 1965), p. 74.

4. Howard Nemerov, *Reflexions on Poetry & Poetics* (New Brunswick, N.J.: Rutgers University Press, 1972), p. 6.

5. Quoted in Anne Stevenson, *Elizabeth Bishop* (New York: Twayne, 1966), p. 66.

6. "In the Village," in *Questions of Travel* (New York: Farrar, Straus and Giroux, 1965), pp. 48–49.

7. Ibid., pp. 76–77.

8. *The Collected Poems of Wallace Stevens* (New York: Alfred A. Knopf, 1954), p. 383.

9. Poems in this section are cited from *Geography III* (New York: Farrar, Straus and Giroux, 1976).

HELEN VENDLER

Domestication, Domesticity, and the Otherworldly

Elizabeth Bishop's poems in *Geography III* put into relief the continuing vibration of her work between two frequencies—the domestic and the strange. In another poet the alternation might seem a debate, but Bishop drifts rather than divides, gazes rather than chooses. Though the exotic is frequent in her poems of travel, it is not only the exotic that is strange and not only the local that is domestic. (It is more exact to speak, with regard to Bishop, of the domestic rather than the familiar, because what is familiar is always named, in her poetry, in terms of a house, a family, someone beloved, home. And it is truer to speak of the strange rather than of the exotic, because the strange can occur even in the bosom of the familiar, even, most unnervingly, at the domestic hearth.)

To show the interpenetration of the domestic and the strange at their most inseparable, it is necessary to glance back at some poems printed in *Questions of Travel*. In one, "Sestina," the components are almost entirely innocent—a house, a grandmother, a child, a Little Marvel Stove, and an almanac. The strange component, which finally renders the whole house unnatural, is tears. Although the grandmother hides her tears and says only "It's time for tea now," the child senses the tears unshed and displaces them everywhere—into the dancing waterdrops from the teakettle, into the rain on the roof, into the tea in the grandmother's cup:

> . . . the child
> is watching the teakettle's small hard tears

First printed in *World Literature Today* 1 (Winter 1977). Reprinted in *Part of Nature, Part of Us* (Cambridge, Mass.: Harvard University Press, 1980), pp. 97–110.

> dance like mad on the hot black stove
> the way the rain must dance on the house . . .

> . . . the almanac
> hovers half open above the child,
> hovers above the old grandmother
> and her teacup full of dark brown tears.

The child's sense of the world is expressed only in the rigid house she draws (I say "she," but the child, in the folk-order of the poem, is of indeterminate sex). The child must translate the tears she has felt, and so she "puts . . . a man with buttons like tears" into her drawing, while "the little moons fall down like tears / from between the pages of the almanac / into the flower bed the child / has carefully placed in the front of the house."

The tercet ending the sestina draws together all the elements of the collage:

> *Time to plant tears*, says the almanac.
> The grandmother sings to the marvellous stove
> and the child draws another inscrutable house.

The absence of the child's parents is the unspoken cause of those tears, so unconcealable though so concealed. For all the efforts of the grandmother, for all the silence of the child, for all the brave cheer of the Little Marvel Stove, the house remains frozen, and the blank center stands for the definitive presence of the unnatural in the child's domestic experience—*especially* in the child's domestic experience. Of all the things that should not be inscrutable, one's house comes first. The fact that one's house always *is* inscrutable, that nothing is more enigmatic than the heart of the domestic scene, offers Bishop one of her recurrent subjects.

The centrality of the domestic provokes as well one of Bishop's most characteristic forms of expression. When she is not actually representing herself as a child, she is, often, sounding like one. The sestina, which borrows from the eternally childlike diction of the folktale, is a case in point. Not only the diction of the folktale, but also its fixity of relation appears in the poem, especially in its processional close, which places the almanac, the grandmother, and the child in an arrangement as unmoving as those found in medieval painting, with the almanac representing the overarching Divine Necessity, the grandmother as the elder principle, and the child as the principle of youth. The voice speaking the last three lines dispassionately records the coincident presence of grief, song, necessity, and the marvelous; but in spite of the "equal" placing of the last three lines, the ultimate weight on inscrutability, even in the heart of the domestic, draws this poem into the orbit of the strange.

A poem close by in *Questions of Travel* tips the balance in the other direction, toward the domestic. The filling station which gives its name to the poem seems at first the antithesis of beauty, at least in the eye of the beholder who speaks the poem. The station is dirty, oil-soaked, oil-permeated; the father's suit is dirty; his sons are greasy; all is "quite thoroughly dirty"; there is even "a dirty dog." The speaker, though filled with "a horror so refined," is unable to look away from the proliferating detail which, though this is a filling station, becomes ever more relentlessly domestic. "Do they live in the station?" wonders the speaker, and notes incredulously a porch, "a set of crushed and grease- / impregnated wickerwork," the dog "quite comfy" on the wicker sofa, comics, a taboret covered by a doily, and "a big hirsute begonia." The domestic, we perceive, becomes a compulsion that we take with us even to the most unpromising locations, where we busy ourselves establishing domestic tranquillity as a demonstration of meaningfulness, as a proof of "love." Is our theology only a reflection of our nesting habits?

> Why the extraneous plant?
> Why the taboret?
> Why, oh why, the doily? . . .
>
> Somebody embroidered the doily.
> Somebody waters the plant,
> or oils it, maybe. Somebody
> arranges the rows of cans
> so that they softly say:
> ESSO–SO–SO–SO

to high-strung automobiles.
Somebody loves us all.

In this parody of metaphysical questioning and the theological argument from design, the "awful but cheerful" activities of the world include the acts by which man domesticates his surroundings, even if those surroundings are purely mechanical, like the filling station or the truck in Brazil painted with "throbbing rosebuds."

The existence of the domestic is most imperiled by death. By definition, the domestic is the conjoined intimate: in American literature the quintessential poem of domesticity is "Snowbound." When death intrudes on the domestic circle, the laying-out of the corpse at home, in the old fashion, forces domesticity to its ultimate powers of accommodation. Stevens' "Emperor of Ice-Cream" places the cold and dumb corpse at the home wake in grotesque conjunction with the funeral baked meats, so to speak, which are being confected in the kitchen, as the primitive impulse to feast over the dead is seen surviving, instinctive and barbaric, even in our "civilized" society. Bishop's "First Death in Nova Scotia" places the poet as a child in a familiar parlor transfixed in perception by the presence of a coffin containing "little cousin Arthur":

> In the cold, cold parlor
> my mother laid out Arthur
> beneath the chromographs:
> Edward, Prince of Wales,
> with Princess Alexandra,
> and King George with Queen Mary.
> Below them on the table
> stood a stuffed loon
> shot and stuffed by Uncle
> Arthur, Arthur's father.

All of these details are immemorially known to the child. But focused by the coffin, the familiar becomes unreal: the stuffed loon becomes alive, his taciturnity seems voluntary, his red glass eyes can see.

> Since Uncle Arthur fired
> a bullet into him,
> he hadn't said a word.
> He kept his own counsel
>
> . . .
>
> Arthur's coffin was
> a little frosted cake,
> and the red-eyed loon eyed it
> from his white, frozen lake.

The adults conspire in a fantasy of communication still possible, as the child is told, "say good-bye / to your little cousin Arthur" and given a lily of the valley to put in the hand of the corpse. The child joins in the fantasy, first by imagining that the chill in the parlor makes it the domain of Jack Frost, who has painted Arthur's red hair as he paints the Maple Leaf of Canada, and next by imagining that "the gracious royal couples" in the chromographs have "invited Arthur to be / the smallest page at court." The constrained effort by all in the parlor to encompass Arthur's death in the domestic scene culminates in the child's effort to make a gestalt of parlor, coffin, corpse, chromographs, loon, Jack Frost, the Maple Leaf Forever, and the lily. But the strain is too great for the child, who allows doubt and dismay to creep in—not as to ultimate destiny, oh no, for Arthur is sure to become "the smallest page" at court, that confusing place of grander domesticity, half-palace, half-heaven; but rather displaced onto means.

> But how could Arthur go,
> clutching his tiny lily,
> with his eyes shut up so tight
> and the roads deep in snow?

Domesticity is frail, and it is shaken by the final strangeness of death. Until death, and even after it, the work of domestication of the unfamiliar goes on, all of it a substitute for some assurance of transcendent domesticity, some belief that we are truly, in this world, in our mother's house, that "somebody loves us all." After a loss that destroys one form of domesticity, the effort to reconstitute it in another form begins. The definition of death in

certain of Bishop's poems is to have given up on domesticating
the world and reestablishing yet once more some form of inti-
macy. Conversely, the definition of life is the conversion of the
strange to the familial, of the unexplored to the knowable, of the
alien to the beloved.

No domesticity is entirely safe. As in the midst of life we are
in death, so, in Bishop's poetry, in the midst of the familiar, and
most especially there, we feel the familiar as the unknowable.
This guerilla attack of the alien, springing from the very bul-
warks of the familiar, is the subject of "In the Waiting Room."
It is 1918, and a child, almost seven, waits, reading the *National
Geographic,* while her aunt is being treated in a dentist's office.
The scene is unremarkable: "grown-up people, / arctics and
overcoats, / lamps and magazines," but two things unnerve the
child. The first is a picture in the magazine: "black, naked wom-
en with necks / wound round and round with wire / like the
necks of light bulbs. / Their breasts were horrifying"; and the
second is "an *oh!* of pain / —Aunt Consuelo's voice" from in-
side. The child is attacked by vertigo, feels the cry to be her own
uttered in "the family voice" and knows at once her separateness
and her identity as one of the human group

> But I felt: you are an *I,*
> you are an *Elizabeth,*
> you are one of *them.*
> *Why* should you be one too?
>   . . .
> What similarities—
> boots, hands, the family voice
> I felt in my throat, or even
> the *National Geographic*
> and those awful hanging breasts—
> held us all together
> or made us all just one?

In "There Was a Child Went Forth" Whitman speaks of a
comparable first moment of metaphysical doubt:

. . . the sense of what is real, the thought if after all it should prove
    unreal,

The doubts of day-time and the doubts of night-time, the curious
     whether and how,
Whether that which appears so is so, or is it all flashes and specks?
Men and women crowding fast in the streets, if they are not flashes
     and specks what are they?

It is typical of Whitman that after his momentary vertigo he
should tether himself to the natural world of sea and sky. It is
equally typical of Bishop, after the waiting room slides "beneath
a big black wave, / another, and another," to return to the sober
certainty of waking fact, though with a selection of fact dictated
by feeling.

> The War was on. Outside,
> in Worcester, Massachusetts,
> were night and slush and cold,
> and it was still the fifth
> of February, 1918.

The child's compulsion to include in her world even the most
unfamiliar data, to couple the exotica of the *National Geographic*
with the knees and trousers and skirts of her neighbors in the
waiting room, brings together the strange at its most horrifying
with the quintessence of the familiar—oneself, one's aunt, the
"family voice." In the end, will the savage be domesticated or
oneself rendered unknowable? The child cannot bear the con-
junction and faints. Language fails the six-year-old. "How—I
didn't know any / word for it—how 'unlikely.'"

That understatement, so common in Bishop, gives words
their full weight. As the fact of her own contingency strikes the
child, "familiar" and "strange" become concepts which have
lost all meaning. "Mrs. Anderson's Swedish baby," says Ste-
vens, "might well have been German or Spanish." Carlos
Drummond de Andrade (whose rhythms perhaps suggested the
trimeters of "In the Waiting Room") says in a poem translated
by Bishop:

> Mundo mundo vasto mundo,
> se eu me chamasse Raimundo
> seria uma rima, não seria uma solução.

If one's name rhymed with the name of the cosmos, as "Raimundo" rhymes with "mundo," there would appear to be a congruence between self and world, and domestication of the world to man's dimensions would seem possible. But, says Drummond, that would be a rhyme, not a solution. The child of "In the Waiting Room" discovers that she is in no intelligible relation to her world, and, too young yet to conceive of domination of the world by will or domestication of the world by love, she slides into an abyss of darkness.

In "Poem" ("About the size of an old-style dollar bill") the poet gazes idly at a small painting done by her great-uncle and begins yet another meditation on the domestication of the world. She gazes idly—that is, until she realizes that the painting is of a place she has lived: "Heavens, I recognize the place, I know it!" In a beautiful tour de force "the place" is described three times. The first time it is rendered visually, exactly, interestedly, appreciatively, and so on: such, we realize, is pure visual pleasure touched with relatively impersonal recognition ("It must be Nova Scotia; only there / does one see gabled wooden houses / painted that awful shade of brown"). Here is the painting as first seen:

> Elm trees, low hills, a thin church steeple
> —that gray-blue wisp—or is it? In the foreground
> a water meadow with some tiny cows,
> two brushstrokes each, but confidently cows;
> two minuscule white geese in the blue water,
> back-to-back, feeding, and a slanting stick.
> Up closer, a wild iris, white and yellow,
> fresh-squiggled from the tube.
> The air is fresh and cold; cold early spring
> clear as gray glass; a half inch of blue sky
> below the steel-gray storm clouds.

Then the recognition—"Heavens, I know it!"—intervenes, and with it a double transfiguration occurs: the mind enlarges the picture beyond the limits of the frame, placing the painted scene in a larger, remembered landscape, and the items in the picture are given a local habitation and a name.

Heavens, I recognize the place, I know it!
It's behind—I can almost remember the farmer's name.
His barn backed on that meadow. There it is,
titanium white, one dab. The hint of steeple,
filaments of brush-hairs, barely there,
must be the Presbyterian church.
Would that be Miss Gillespie's house?
Those particular geese and cows
are naturally before my time.

In spite of the connection between self and picture, the paint-
ing remains a painting, described by someone recognizing its
means—a dab of titanium white here, some fine brushwork
there. And the scene is set back in time—those geese and cows
belong to another era. But by the end of the poem the poet has
united herself with the artist. They have both loved this unim-
portant corner of the earth; it has existed in their lives, in their
memories and in their art.

Art "copying from life" and life itself,
life and the memory of it so compressed
they've turned into each other. Which is which?
Life and the memory of it cramped,
dim, on a piece of Bristol board,
dim, but how live, how touching in detail
—the little that we get for free,
the little of our earthly trust. Not much.

Out of the world a small piece is lived in, domesticated,
remembered, memorialized, even immortalized. Immortalized
because the third time that the painting is described, it is seen not
by the eye—whether the eye of the connoisseur or the eye of the
local inhabitant contemplating a past era—but by the heart,
touched into participation. There is no longer any mention of
tube or brushstrokes or paint colors or Bristol board; we are in
the scene itself.

. . . Not much.
About the size of our abidance

> along with theirs: the munching cows,
> the iris, crisp and shivering, the water
> still standing from spring freshets,
> the yet-to-be-dismantled elms, the geese.

Though the effect of being in the landscape arises in part from the present participles (the munching cows, the shivering iris, the standing water), it comes as well from the repetition of nouns from earlier passages (cows, iris), now denuded of their "paint" modifiers ("two brushstrokes each," "squiggled from the tube"), from the replication of the twice-repeated early "fresh" in "freshets" and most of all from the prophecy of the "yet-to-be-dismantled" elms. As lightly as possible, the word "dismantled" then refutes the whole illusion of entire absorption in the memorial scene; the world of the child who was once the poet now seems the scenery arranged for a drama with only too brief a tenure on the stage—the play once over, the set is dismantled, the illusion gone. The poem, having taken the reader through the process that we name domestication and by which a strange terrain becomes first recognizable, then familiar, and then beloved, releases the reader at last from the intimacy it has induced. Domestication is followed, almost inevitably, by that dismantling which is, in its acute form, disaster, the "One Art" of another poem:

> I lost my mother's watch. And look! my last, or
> next-to-last of three loved houses went
>
>   . . .
>
> I lost two cities, lovely ones. And, vaster,
> some realms I owned, two rivers, a continent
>
>   . . .
>
> the art of losing's not too hard to master
> though it may look like (*Write* it!) like disaster.

That is the tone of disaster confronted, with whatever irony.

A more straightforward account of the whole cycle of domestication and loss can be seen in the long monologue, "Crusoe in England." Crusoe is safely back in England, and his long autobiographical retrospect exposes in full clarity the imperfection of the domestication of nature so long as love is missing, the exhaustion of solitary colonization.

> . . . I'd have
> nightmares of other islands
> stretching away from mine, infinities
> of islands, islands spawning islands,
> like frogs' eggs turning into polliwogs
> of islands, knowing that I had to live
> on each and every one, eventually,
> for ages, registering their flora,
> their fauna, their geography.

Crusoe's efforts at the domestication of nature (making a flute, distilling home brew, even devising a dye out of red berries) create a certain degree of pleasure ("I felt a deep affection for / the smallest of my island industries"), and yet the lack of any society except that of turtles and goats and waterspouts ("sacerdotal beings of glass . . . / Beautiful, yes, but not much company") causes both self-pity and a barely admitted hope. Crusoe, in a metaphysical moment, christens one volcano "*Mont d'Espoir* or *Mount Despair*," mirroring both his desolation and his expectancy. The island landscape has been domesticated, "home-made," and yet domestication can turn to domesticity only with the arrival of Friday: "Just when I thought I couldn't stand it / another minute longer, Friday came." Speechless with joy, Crusoe can speak only in the most vacant and consequently the most comprehensive of words.

> Friday was nice.
> Friday was nice, and we were friends.
> . . . he had a pretty body.

Love escapes language. Crusoe could describe with the precision of a geographer the exact appearances of volcanoes, turtles, clouds, lava, goats, and waterspouts and waves, but he is reduced to gesture and sketch before the reality of domesticity.

In the final, recapitulatory movement of the poem Bishop

first reiterates the conferral of meaning implicit in the domestication of the universe and then contemplates the loss of meaning once the arena of domestication is abandoned.

> The knife there on the shelf—
> it reeked of meaning, like a crucifix.
> It lived . . .
> I knew each nick and scratch by heart . . .
> Now it won't look at me at all.
> The living soul has dribbled away.
> My eyes rest on it and pass on.

Unlike the meanings of domestication, which repose in presence and use, the meaning of domesticity is mysterious and permanent. The monologue ends:

> The local museum's asked me to
> leave everything to them:
> the flute, the knife, the shrivelled shoes . . .
> How can anyone want such things?
> —And Friday, my dear Friday, died of measles
> seventeen years ago come March.

The ultimate locus of domestication is the heart, which, once cultivated, retains its "living soul" forever.

This dream of eternal and undismantled fidelity in domesticity, unaffected even by death, is one extreme reached by Bishop's imagination as it turns round its theme. But more profound, I think, is the version of life's experience recounted in "The Moose," a poem in which no lasting exclusive companionship between human beings is envisaged, but in which a series of deep and inexplicable satisfactions unroll in sequence, each of them precious. Domestication of the land is one, domesticity of the affections is another, and the contemplation of the sublimity of the nonhuman world is the third.

In the first half of the poem one of the geographies of the world is given an ineffable beauty, both plain and luxurious. Nova Scotia's tides, sunsets, villages, fog, flora, fauna, and people are all summoned quietly into the verse, as if for a last farewell, as the speaker journeys away to Boston. The verse, like the landscape, is "old-fashioned."

> The bus starts. The light
> grows richer; the fog
> shifting, salty, thin,
> comes closing in.
>
> Its cold, round crystals
> form and slide and settle
> in the white hens' feathers,
> in gray glazed cabbages,
> on the cabbage roses
> and lupins like apostles;
>
> the sweet peas cling
> to wet white string
> on the whitewashed fences;
> bumblebees creep
> inside the foxgloves,
> and evening commences.

The exquisitely noticed modulations of whiteness, the evening harmony of settling and clinging and closing and creeping, the delicate touch of each clause, the valedictory air of the whole, the momentary identification with hens, sweet peas, and bumblebees all speak of the attentive and yielding soul through which the landscape is being articulated.

As darkness settles, the awakened soul is slowly lulled into "a dreamy divagation / . . . / a gentle, auditory, / slow hallucination." This central passage embodies a regression into childhood, as the speaker imagines that the muffled noises in the bus are the tones of "an old conversation":

> Grandparents' voices
>
> uninterruptedly
> talking, in Eternity:

> names being mentioned,
> things cleared up finally
>
> . . .
>
> Talking the way they talked
> in the old featherbed,
> peacefully, on and on
>
> . . .
>
> Now, it's all right now
> even to fall asleep
> just as on all those nights.

Life, in the world of this poem, has so far only two components: a beloved landscape and beloved people, that which can be domesticated and those who have joined in domesticity. The grandparents' voices have mulled over all the human concerns of the village:

> what he said, what she said,
> who got pensioned;
>
> deaths, deaths and sicknesses;
> the year he remarried;
> the year (something) happened.
> She died in childbirth.
> That was the son lost
> when the schooner foundered.
>
> He took to drink. Yes.
> She went to the bad.
> When Amos began to pray
> even in the store and
> finally the family had
> to put him away.
>
> "Yes . . ." that peculiar
> affirmative. "Yes . . ."
> A sharp, indrawn breath,
> half groan, half acceptance.

In this passage, so plainly different in its rural talk and sorrow from the ravishing aestheticism of the earlier descriptive passage, Bishop joins herself to the Wordsworth of the *Lyrical Ballads*. The domestic affections become, for a moment, all there is. Amos who went mad, the son lost at sea, the mother who died, the girl gone to the bad—these could all have figured in poems like "Michael" or "The Thorn." The litany of names evoking the bonds of domestic sympathy becomes one form of poetry, and the views of the "meadows, hills, and groves" of Nova Scotia is another. What this surrounding world looks like, we know; that "Life's like that" (as the sighed "Yes" implies), we also know. The poem might seem complete. But just as the speaker is about to drowse almost beyond consciousness, there is a jolt, and the bus stops in the moonlight, because "A moose has come out of / the impenetrable wood." This moose, looming "high as a church, / homely as a house," strikes wonder in the passengers, who "exclaim in whispers, / childishly, softly." The moose remains.

> Taking her time,
> she looks the bus over,
> grand, otherworldly.
> Why, why do we feel
> (we all feel) this sweet
> sensation of joy?

What is this joy?

In "The Most of It" Frost uses a variant of this fable. There, as in Bishop's poem, a creature emerges from "the impenetrable wood" and is beheld. But Frost's beast disappoints expectation. The poet had wanted "counter-love, original response," but the "embodiment that crashed" proves to be not "human," not "someone else additional to him," but rather a large buck, which disappears as it came. Frost's beast is male, Bishop's female; Frost's a symbol of brute force, Bishop's a creature "safe as houses"; Frost's a challenge, Bishop's a reassurance. The presence approaching from the wood plays, in both these poems, the role that a god would play in a pre-Wordsworthian poem and the role that a human being—a leech-gatherer, an ancient soldier, a beggar—would play in Wordsworth. These human beings, when they appear in Wordsworth's poetry, are partly iconic, partly subhuman, as the Leech-Gatherer is part statue, part sea-beast, and as the old man in "Animal Tranquillity and Decay" is "insensibly subdued" to a state of peace more animal than human. "I think I could turn and live with animals," says Whitman, foreshadowing a modernity that finds the alternative to the human not in the divine but in the animal. Animal life is pure presence, with its own grandeur. It assures the poet of the inexhaustibility of being. Bishop's moose is at once maternal, inscrutable, and mild. If the occupants of the bus are bound, in their human vehicle, to the world of village catastrophe and pained acknowledgment, they feel a releasing joy in glimpsing some large, grand solidity, even a vaguely grotesque one, which exists outside their tales and sighs, which is entirely "other-worldly." "The darkness drops again," as the bus moves on; the "dim smell of moose" fades in comparison to "the acrid smell of gasoline."

"The Moose" is such a purely linear poem, following as it does the journey of the bus, that an effort of will is required to gaze at it whole. The immediacy of each separate section—as we see the landscape, then the people, then the moose—blots out what has gone before. But the temptation—felt when the poem is contemplated entire—to say something global, something almost allegorical, suggests that something in the sequence is more than purely arbitrary. The poem passes from adult observation of a familiar landscape to the unending ritual, first glimpsed in childhood, of human sorrow and narration, to a final joy in the otherworldly, in whatever lies within the impenetrable wood and from time to time allows itself to be beheld. Beyond or behind the familiar, whether the visual or the human familiar, lies the perpetually strange and mysterious. It is that mystery which causes those whispered exclamations alternating with the pained "Yes" provoked by human vicissitude. It guarantees the poet more to do. On it depends all the impulse to domestication. Though the human effort is bent to the elimination of the wild, nothing is more restorative than to know that

earth's being is larger than our human enclosures. Elizabeth
Bishop's poetry of domestication and domesticity depends, in
the last analysis, on her equal apprehension of the reserves of
mystery which give, in their own way, a joy more strange than
the familiar blessings of the world made human.

ROBERT PINSKY

The Idiom of a Self
Elizabeth Bishop and Wordsworth

I will begin with a couple of generalities about poetry, hoping that they are not too familiar to be useful.

Because prosody makes it the most consciously physical mode of language, poetry has a peculiar intimacy, like an inner penetration of the more external embodiment of words in actual song. It is in part a bodily experience. And because language (unlike paint or musical sounds) is handled daily by the world of people, serving the whole range of human motives from triviality to desperation, poetry's medium makes it peculiarly social. Its very formality is social.

This dual nature of the art, its physical reminder of our animal privacy and its formal reminder of our communal dealings, reaches its greatest emotional clarity and force, for me, in the poetry of Elizabeth Bishop. To put the idea a bit differently, her great subject is the contest—or truce, or trade-agreement—between the single human soul on one side and, on the other side, the contingent world of artifacts and other people.

Though that subject or preoccupation characterizes much of Bishop's work, it becomes most strikingly apparent, and even explicit, in her most recent book, *Geography III*. In that volume, the difference between what one learns, and what one is, emerges as a profound emotional focus, and a great poetic subject. To show what I mean, and to support the idea that poems like "In the Waiting Room," "Crusoe in England," and the earlier "At the Fishhouses" are great works of art, I will try to draw some terms from Wordsworth. Then, I will concentrate

First printed in *American Poetry Review* (January–February 1980), pp. 6–8.

on "In the Waiting Room" because in certain ways that poem seems to provide an entry into much of Bishop's work.

In turn, Bishop's work offers a special example of how a writer can find, in the most social or communal aspects of language, the means of a vehemently personal identity.

In Book XIV of *The Prelude,* the poet recalls hiking uphill, at night, ahead of his two companions out of sight, when suddenly "at my feet the ground appeared to brighten, / And with a step or two seemed brighter still." Then, there is a justly celebrated transformed landscape:

> The Moon hung naked in a firmament
> Of Azure without cloud, and at my feet
> Rested a silent sea of hoary mist.
> A hundred hills their dusky backs upheaved
> All over this still ocean; and beyond,
> Far, far beyond, the solid vapours stretched,
> In headlands, tongues, and promontory shapes,
> Into the main Atlantic, that appeared
> To dwindle, and give up his majesty,
> Usurped upon far as the sight could reach.
> Not so the ethereal vault; encroachment none
> Was there, nor loss; only the inferior stars
> Had disappeared, or shed a fainter light
> In the clear presence of the full-orbed Moon,
> Who from her sovreign elevation, gazed
> Upon the billowy ocean, as it lay
> All meek and silent, save that through a rift—
> Not distant from the shore whereon we stood,
> A fixed, abysmal, gloomy, breathing-place—
> Mounted the roar of waters, torrents, streams
> Innumerable, roaring with one voice!
> Heard over earth and sea, and, in that hour,
> For so it seemed, felt by the starry heavens.

The hills like whales; the sea of mist seeming larger than the Atlantic (in the 1805 text, "the Sea, the real Sea"); the earth brightening underfoot; the idea of "inferior stars"; the "meek" ocean—these impressive mutations are contrasted with two elements that are still more impressive, though they fulfill, rather than challenge, expectation: the penetrating voice of the ocean, and the cool gaze of the moon.

In the following passage, reflecting on that "vision" in "calm thought," Wordsworth chooses to consider it as:

> the type
> Of a majestic intellect, its acts
> And its possessions, what it has and craves,
> What in itself it is, and would become.
> There I beheld the emblem of a mind
> That feeds upon infinity.

He then chooses to consider the "vision" again, not as an emblem, but as an act of Nature, happening to imitate a certain kind of mind by "putting forth" a "mutual domination" upon the outward surface of things. When Nature thus imitates or resembles such human minds, by exerting this "interchangeable supremacy" upon the surfaces of things, even the dullest of us must be affected: "men, least sensitive, see, hear, perceive, / And cannot choose but feel." It is interesting to note that these duller spirits feel the power, but do not participate in the paradoxical "mutual domination" and "interchangeable supremacy" of Nature's transforming visions.

That same curious element of supremacy, power, freedom, even property ("its acts / And its possessions") appears also in the succeeding lines, those which I would like to bring most directly into comparison with Bishop's "In the Waiting Room." Wordsworth continues his argument by describing "higher minds" which not merely feel, but create "mutations" akin to those of Nature. Though built "from least suggestions," these acts of creation involve power, mastery, perhaps even embattled struggle; on the other hand, they also seem to involve something like social conversation—"fit converse":

> The power, which all
> Acknowledge when thus moved, which Nature thus
> To bodily sense exhibits, is the express

Resemblance of that glorious faculty
That higher minds bear with them as their own.
This is the very spirit in which they deal
With the whole compass of the universe:
They from their native selves can send abroad
Kindred mutations; for themselves create
A like existence; and when'er it dawns
Created for them, catch it, or are caught
By its inevitable mastery,
Like angels stopped upon the wing by sound
Of harmony from Heaven's remotest spheres.
Them the enduring and the transient both
Serve to exalt; they build up greatest things
From least suggestions; ever on the watch,
Willing to work and to be wrought upon,
They need not extraordinary calls
To rouse them; in a world of life they live,
By sensible impressions not enthralled,
But by their quickening impulse made more prompt
To hold fit converse with the spiritual world,
And with the generations of mankind
Spread over time, past, present, and to come,
Age after age, till Time shall be no more.

The passage is very exciting, with its gloriously suspended angels and, on a different level, the equally exciting plainness of "in a world of life they live."

To live *in* a world of life, yet not swallowed by it, not enthralled by sensory impressions, yet alert to them, seems to depend upon a "quickening impulse" whose outcome is "fit converse." Though that is perhaps not the main or only emphasis of the Wordsworth passage, it does suggest a striking paradigm: the individual mind in the "compass of the universe," defining its own separate powers, acts, possessions, by a constant vigilance to keep "domination" mutual, by being articulate. When we assimilate the idea that the earth is a globe immensely larger than the ground we can see around us, we are potentially lost in its vague enormity; as we map its parts, we restore ourselves by defining what we are not. In a world of life, the map is what we can say in our language.

Certainly, Bishop's "In the Waiting Room" begins with something more like a "least suggestion" than an "extraordinary call"; in the most ordinary of plain English, we are in the ordinary community:

> In Worcester, Massachusetts,
> I went with Aunt Consuelo
> to keep her dentist's appointment
> and sat and waited for her
> in the dentist's waiting room.
> It was winter. It got dark
> early. The waiting room
> was full of grown-up people,
> arctics and overcoats,
> lamps and magazines.

These remarkably flat three-to-five-word declarations culminate with a parenthetical one—"(I could read)"—the rift through which the transformation of tone and perception come flowing:

> My aunt was inside
> what seemed like a long time
> and while I waited I read
> the *National Geographic*
> (I could read) and carefully
> studied the photographs:
> the inside of a volcano,
> black, and full of ashes;
> then it was spilling over
> in rivulets of fire.

The invisible transition from "lamps and magazines" to "rivulets of fire" is an effect of Bishop's art, but it is also an exploitation of the flexible English idiom she speaks, and a phenomenon—she emphasizes—of the fact that people can read print and study photographs. The literate, industrial culture of the *National Geographic* reaches into the overheated room in Worcester, then into the child's brain, and transports her:

> Osa and Martin Johnson
> dressed in riding breeches,
> laced boots, and pith helmets.
> A dead man slung on a pole
> —"Long Pig," the caption said.
> Babies with pointed heads
> wound round and round with string;
> black, naked women with necks
> wound round and round with wire
> like the necks of light bulbs.
> Their breasts were horrifying.
> I read it right straight through.
> I was too shy to stop.

Of course, the child has read books before; this is no epiphany. The pleasing, funny line "I was too shy to stop," however, does call our attention to some of the peculiarities of the act of reading—peculiarities still fresh, vivid, and perhaps oppressive for a precocious child. (Some children fear *starting* a new book, because within a page or two one will care about some world not yet fully existent, like a bottled djinn.) Moreover, the phrase is important because the term "shy" reminds us of how social the act of reading is—if only by implication, like talking to oneself. The magazine, or the language, watches back, in mutual domination. It reminds one that one is connected to a whole, particular species of mammals, with their horrifying or inscrutable customs, their heavy adult bodies. One is connected to them not only through one's mother, but through one's language.

Still, "I was too shy to stop," like "(I could read)," is only part of the preparation. The revelation follows:

> Suddenly, from inside,
> came an *oh!* of pain
> —Aunt Consuelo's voice—
> not very loud or long.

I wasn't at all surprised;
even then I knew she was
a foolish, timid woman.
I might have been embarrassed,
but wasn't. What took me
completely by surprise
was that it was *me:*
my voice, in my mouth.
Without thinking at all
I was my foolish aunt,
I—we—were falling, falling,
our eyes glued to the cover
of the *National Geographic,*
February, 1918.

The innocent phrase "from inside" is one of the poet's characteristic timebombs. But what happens? A child of not quite seven has a dizzy spell in a hot, dull waiting room. Also, she suddenly sees the membrane between one's self and the rest of the world, between one's self and other people—the generations of mankind—as an idea. And, it is an idea made largely out of words:

I was saying it to stop
the sensation of falling off
the round, turning world
into cold, blue-black space.
But I felt: you are an *I,*
you are an *Elizabeth,*
you are one of *them.*
Why should you be one, too?
I scarcely dared to look
to see what it was I was.

This is amusing, and in some lights even genial, but it is also sad, and a crucial moment in the growth of a mind. And the surface geniality is partly a subtle disguise, rather like the ordinary gray clothing of Paul Valéry.

The language and observation that implicate the poet with

Aunt Consuelo, the magazine, "those awful hanging breasts," the people in the waiting room, the world, us her readers—the same language and observation are her weapons. "Ever on the watch," wrought upon by the world, she uses the same instruments "to work and to be wrought upon":

> I gave a sidelong glance
> —I couldn't look any higher—
> at shadowy gray knees,
> trousers and skirts and boots
> and different pairs of hands
> lying under the lamps.
> I knew that nothing stranger
> had ever happened, that nothing
> stranger could ever happen.

The knees and inert "pairs of hands," seen backlit from a seven-year-old's low perspective, become a little like a landscape of shadowy hills. They become transformed, somewhat eerily, both by the experience and by the slightly shifted language now applied to them. Transformed into terrain, the grown-up bodies are a little like the transformed landscape of hills become whales in *The Prelude*.

I don't know any other poet who has treated the contest between the individual, single consciousness and the world not itself with such depth and patient precision. This special subject or approach seems to have to do with a ferocity of quickening impulse, and a surface of enormous social control. It is ironic that Bishop is often praised, sometimes faintly, for having a loving eye toward the physical world; it is a matter of her mind, not her eye, and the process is equally as embattled or resistant as it is loving.

Nor is the space where the mind waits, "willing to work and to be wrought upon," necessarily comfortable:

> The waiting room was bright
> and too hot. It was sliding
> beneath a big black wave,
> another, and another.

Then I was back in it.
The War was on. Outside,
in Worcester, Massachusetts,
were night and slush and cold,
and it was still the fifth
of February, 1918.

The struggle to distinguish herself from the encompassing
world has entailed the reciprocal effort to come back from
"cold, blue-black space" by engaging that same world, until
finally "I was back in it." After all of that struggle and engage-
ment, the reference to the Great War has to suggest another,
more prolonged conflict, as well as the one in Europe. It is the
War of the soul to exist, as what in itself it is, and would be-
come. In somewhat less grand terms, it is the war of the poet to
work on the world of things and people as much as that world
works on her. Seeing and describing the world, and making her
own cartography from the English language, she makes the
world and language her own. From her native self, she sends
forth mutations.

The means for those mutations are somewhat unlikely. I
mean the kind of English spoken, and the kind of social observa-
tion, in the poems. Nothing is stranger, the poet tells us, than to
realize that one is an island in, but only partly of, the encompass-
ing ocean of social and physical entities. Because nothing is
stranger than that situation, "least suggestions" can bring one to
"greatest things"; because nothing is stranger than that geo-
graphical situation of the soul, the respectable, banal objects and
manners and language of the surface—lamps, pairs of hands,
"arctics"—are the strange, unlikely terrain upon which every-
thing rests. If the terrain exerts mastery over the individual, it is
also true that the terrain can itself be caught, perhaps momen-
tarily mastered, by means of geography. Naming and placing
things is an approach to genuine liberty. This is true even
though the very means of naming things—means such as the
word "unlikely," placed in quotation marks by the poet because
the seven-year-old still lacked command of it—are also part of
the terrain.

Thus, the deliberately somewhat old-fashioned and local term "arctics" is appropriate for those garments, because the term is both homely and strange. And thus, we have the characteristic Bishop idiom of English: the seemingly restrained, yet relaxed sentences, startlingly flexible in practice, framing the diction of a respectable, alert American tourist, educated but not pedantic, sophisticated but very quiet about its sophistication.

What a peculiar invention that idiom is: the formula of the normal as the "strangest thing there is" applies to this disguise or armor. In effect, the poet invents or exploits a whole dialect of English, creates out of the tongue's capacity for expressing shades of manners her remarkable steel instrument, that operates so quietly. Oppositions and qualifications are necessary to describe it, so that one can observe that it is cosmopolitan but too native for dandyism. It is humorous, but too modest—and too ready to reach heights—ever to be quite witty. And most essentially, it is utterly personal and individual, yet under a surface of detached, traveler-like anonymity. That anonymity of the tourist is a defense of the private self, allowing the self to work on things at least as much as it is wrought upon by them. Its neutrality, or simulacrum of neutrality, keeps us at a distance.

In this light, one notices the pronouns of "At the Fishhouses": if *you* should dip *your* hand into the briny cold water that "burns with a dark gray flame," then it is "your" hand that would burn at the touch, as the taste would burn "your" tongue. In contradistinction, "I" come closer to the seal who dwells in that water, "like me a believer in total immersion." Of course, the second-person pronoun here is mainly the impersonal "you," the informal American equivalent of "one"—but perhaps it is also a mannerly but unyielding truce with the reader, with other people, on the way to the poem's transcendent ending, and the way "we" imagine knowledge:

> It is like what we imagine knowledge to be:
> dark, salt, clear, moving, utterly free,
> drawn from the cold hard mouth
> of the world, derived from the rocky breasts
> forever, flowing and drawn, and since
> our knowledge is historical, flowing, and flown.

This lyrical passage, with its first-person plural, invites us to share the poet's knowledge of the world, and the poet's place in it, with her, in the first-person plural. But what knowledge it is—"bearable," as she says, "to no mortal."

Who speaks such strange, exciting, adamant lines? Not, simply, the detached and respectable tourist I have described above; it is hard to characterize entirely the complex garb that so many of Bishop's poems adopt. And by inventing the language in such a personal way, she seems at times, as at the close of "At the Fishhouses," to tap its entire, lyrical range. It is as if the child, in the space where one waits to be worked upon by the world, were confronted by the whole panoply of acquired experience at once—English language, middle-class manners, adult sexuality, bizarre customs, the volcanic being of the natural—and had decided to take it all on, to perfection, in order to use it as something separate from herself: all part of the terrain, and not of the geographer.

Perhaps my earlier term "disguise" is an overstatement. But there is a deceptive quietness of surface that helps define the sole self against the infinite—though it is the infinite in its quotidian, "strange" daily existence. I am thinking of such moments as when, on the bus journey of "The Moose," a woman seen from the window "shakes a tablecloth / out after supper," or when the "man carrying a baby" gets off another bus in "Cape Breton." The baby, supper, tablecloths, the man, the woman, their business at different times of day when they happen to be seen—no material could be less like an "extraordinary call." And yet there is not even a whisper of the corny, or the "sympathetic," about the way they are seen. For all the air of familiarity they are on the other side of something from the poet—if not on the other side of a war, then of a geographical division.

The only compromise of fellowship extended is perception itself—in effect the poem, its enormously perfected plain English, its knowledge: a burningly pure, harsh, cold, salt medium. It suggests that people are somewhat like islands in an infinite ocean; but, by saying precisely where one is in that ocean, it can be made more civil, as through a map of words. I think that is what Wordsworth means in the passage I began with when he speaks of minds that "feed upon infinity." "Hence endless occupation for the Soul, / Whether discursive or intuitive." The "endless occupation" of the active soul, "ever on the watch," suggests a stringent, daunting persistence of attention. And yet Wordsworth also declares that the reward—the freedom of identity—is supreme:

> the highest bliss
> That flesh can know is theirs—the consciousness
> Of Whom they are, habitually infused
> Through every image and through every thought.

DAVID LEHMAN

"In Prison"

A Paradox Regained

Traditionally, poets have dwelled in paradoxical prisons. To enter bonds of queen and country is to affirm one's freedom, Donne seductively argued; Lovelace, equally extravagant if less playful, insisted on liberty as a function of spiritual innocence. He denied not the actuality of stone walls and iron bars, just their right to cohere into prisons and cages, in a passage that schoolchildren were presumed once upon a time to know by heart:

> If I have freedom in my love,
>   And in my soul am free,
> Angels alone, that soar above,
>   Enjoy such liberty.
> "To Althea, from Prison"

If Lovelace could look upon imprisonment as "an hermitage," a time to rededicate himself to a courtly ideal, Hamlet's princely mobility could scarcely preclude a bout of claustrophobia. "Denmark's a prison," he announces, and follows with a characteristic verbal gesture, robust hyperbole collapsing into poignantly prosaic understatement:

> O God, I could be bounded in a nutshell and
> count myself a king of infinite space, were it not
> that I have bad dreams.
> [act 2, scene 2]

It is, as Hamlet acknowledges, a classic opposition of mind and matter. Whatever his present difficulties, he does not doubt the mind's supremacy over the world it beholds: "There is nothing either good or bad but thinking makes it so." As far as Hamlet is concerned, man's potential to breathe the infinite space of angels is, despite the narrow dimensions of his cell, still available, though not right here, not just now.

It would be interesting to determine when *despite* in that last clause turned into *because of,* when the emphasis shifted and poets actively sought a species of imprisonment because only there would the soul learn true freedom, or goodness, or the peace that passeth understanding. The argument, a recurrent one in medieval Christian theology, has in effect been rewritten, its paradox completed, by agents of the Romantic imagination. In the same spirit in which he commends duty as the "Stern Daughter of the Voice of God," Wordsworth solemnly wills a curtailment of his freedom, identifying form as a necessary jail in his sonnet on the sonnet:

> In truth the prison, unto which we doom
> Ourselves, no prison is: and hence for me,
> In sundry moods, 'twas pastime to be bound
> Within the Sonnet's scanty plot of ground;
> Pleased if some Souls (for such there needs must be)
> Who have felt the weight of too much liberty,
> Should find brief solace there, as I have found.
>
> "Nuns Fret Not At Their Convent's Narrow Room"

To Paul Pennyfeather, the beleaguered hero of Evelyn Waugh's *Decline and Fall,* prison ironically allows for the autonomy of the self, its independence from social pressures, its release from "the weight of too much liberty":

> The next four weeks of solitary confinement were among the happiest of Paul's life. . . . It was so exhilarating, he found, never to have to make any decision on any subject, to be wholly relieved from the smallest consideration of time, meals, or clothes, to have no anxiety ever about what kind of impression he was making; in fact, to be free . . . there was no need to shave, no hesitation about what tie he should wear, none of the fidgeting with studs and collars and links that so distracts the waking moments of civilized man. He felt

like the happy people in the advertisements for shaving soap who seem to have achieved very simply that peace of mind so distant and so desirable in the early morning.[1]

A comic gloss on Lovelace's "To Althea, from Prison," the chapter in which this passage appears has the title "Stone Walls Do Not A Prison Make"; not surprisingly, a later chapter is called "Nor Iron Bars A Cage."

As we proceed from *despite* to *because*, we move as well from a conception of the imagination as that which redeems reality to a conception of the imagination as, in the last analysis, sufficient unto itself. A clear statement of this last analysis is found in J. K. Huysmans' *À Rebours,* which develops the logic of the prison paradox into an aesthetic principle. The protagonist of that novel ingeniously devises a means by which to travel without ever having to leave his room, secure a passport, book passage, pack bags, or say farewell—without, in short, any of the inconveniences of actuality. "Travel, indeed, struck him as being a waste of time, since he believed that the imagination could provide a more-than-adequate substitute for the vulgar reality of actual experience."[2] Two poets upon whom Elizabeth Bishop has exerted a powerful influence, James Merrill and John Ashbery, offer inspired variations on this theme of the stationary traveler. More a *récit* than a short story, Merrill's "Peru: The Landscape Game" describes a trip to the land of the Incas; the poet plans to go there, but it is his anticipation of the place that he records, a Platonic reality too good not to be true. The imagination acts, as it were, in self-defense, as it spins out an eternal possibility, proof against the disappointment Wordsworth experienced when he saw Mont Blanc:

How to find the right words for a new world?

One way would be to begin, before ever leaving home, with some anticipatory jottings such as these. Then, even if the quetzal turns out to be extinct, if sure-footed grandmothers from Tulsa overrun the ruins, and Porfirio's baby has a harelip and there are cucarachas in the Hotel Périchole, the visitor may rest easy. Nothing can dim his first, radiant impressions.[3]

Such "jottings," intended for perusal on the ride down to Lima, give new meaning to the idea of flight insurance.

Ashbery too would seem to subscribe to Verlaine's notion that "every landscape is a state of mind." From his vantage point in an office building more than a thousand miles away, the speaker of Ashbery's "The Instruction Manual" takes us on a guided tour of Guadalajara, "City I wanted most to see, and most did not see, in Mexico!" The task of writing "the instruction manual on the uses of a new metal" serves as the launching pad for this mental flight, this enchanted product of an imagining. "How limited, but how complete withal, has been our experience of Guadalajara!" the speaker can exclaim upon his return to the desk he never had to leave.[4] Amusing as that statement is, it tells its sober truth about the poetic process. On paper the poet flies to Peru or Guadalajara not as places but as names, words, sounds; one arrives at "the imagination of the sound—a place." This is the conclusion reached by A. R. Ammons in his poem "Triphammer Bridge":

> *sanctuary, sanctuary,* I say it over and over and the
> word's sound is the one place to dwell: that's it, just
> the sound, and the imagination of the sound—a place.[5]

By delineating the progression from "wanted . . . to see" to "did not see" to "I fancy I see, under the press of having to write the instruction manual," Ashbery's poem makes a further point. It is as though a condition of absence were a prerequisite for the adventurous imagination. So we are directly told in another of Ashbery's early poems, "Le Livre est sur la table":

> All beauty, resonance, integrity,
> Exist by deprivation or logic
> Of strange position.[6]

The proposition that the imagination varies directly with deprivation and isolation, that imaginative need mothers invention, and that physical confinement is conducive to spiritual freedom, receives full treatment in Elizabeth Bishop's early and remarkably prescient short story (or *récit*), "In Prison."[7] This account of an ideal "life-sentence" contains the seed Ashbery would cultivate in "The Instruction Manual," even as it makes the case for creative misreading, for what Harold Bloom, like Miss Bishop a mapmaker, calls "misprision":

I understand that most prisons are now supplied with libraries and that the prisoners are expected to read the *Everyman's Library* and other books of educational tendencies. I hope I am not being too reactionary when I say that my one desire is to be given one very dull book to read, the duller the better. A book, moreover, on a subject completely foreign to me; perhaps the second volume, if the first would familiarize me too well with the terms and purpose of the work. Then I shall be able to experience with a free conscience the pleasure, perverse, I suppose, of interpreting it not at all according to its intent. Because I share with Valery's *M. Teste* the "knowledge that our thoughts are reflected back to us, too much so, through expressions made by others"; and I have resigned myself, or do I speak too frankly, to deriving what information and joy I can from this—lamentable but irremediable—state of affairs. From my detached rock-like book I shall be able to draw vast generalizations, abstractions of the grandest, most illuminating sort, like allegories or poems, and by posing fragments of it against the surroundings and conversations of my prison, I shall be able to form my own examples of surrealist art!—something I should never know how to do outside, where the sources are so bewildering. Perhaps it will be a book on the cure of a disease, or an industrial technique,—but no, even to try to imagine the subject would be to spoil the sensation of wave-like freshness I hope to receive when it is first placed in my hands.[8] [IP, 13–14]

In Miss Bishop's later work, a quite explicit echo of this passage occurs in "The End of March" where, in a tone more wistful than whimsical, the writer describes her "proto-dream-house," a "dubious" structure that tallies in a great many particulars with her earlier version of prison as paradise:

I'd like to retire there and do *nothing,*
or nothing much, forever, in two bare rooms:
look through binoculars, read boring books,

old, long, long books, and write down useless notes,
talk to myself, and, foggy days,
watch the droplets slipping, heavy with light.

[G, 43]

Indeed, for the way it prefigures attitudes and motifs that we
encounter not only in *Geography III* but throughout the poet's
career, "In Prison" commends itself to critical inspection over
and beyond its intrinsic merits, considerable though these are.
Here we find, at however ironic a remove, a defense of her
"mentality," her faith in "the power of details" as momentary
stays against confusion, her stance as a quiet non-conformist,
whose individuality of style is something subtle enough to flour-
ish within a regimented order. The insouciance of "One Art,"
the ironic process by which defeat turns into victory, is antici-
pated in the story; here is an initial statement of the dialectical
tension between autobiographical disaster and artistic mastery, a
tension central to the villanelle and one that lurks beneath the
surface of the prose poem "12 O'Clock News" with its military
metaphors for the act of writing. Moreover, "In Prison" con-
tains information helpful for us to understand the painterly dis-
position of a poet who continually derived inspiration, as well as
subject matter, from objects and apparitions, large bad pictures
and tiny ones ("About the size of an old-style dollar bill"), and
seascapes disguised as animated "cartoon[s] by Raphael for a
tapestry for a Pope" (CP, 46).

The strategy for reading that Miss Bishop proffers points to
the governing conceit of the story, "the pleasure, perverse, I
suppose, of interpreting it not at all according to its intent"—*it*
standing here for prison, which willful mis-interpretation ren-
ders to mean the inner life of the imagination, the "real life" of
the soul. The narrative starts with a flip reversal of Joseph K.'s
predicament in *The Trial:* like Kafka's protagonist, Miss Bish-
op's persona has committed no crime, but there the resemblance
ends. He positively wants what Joseph K. dreads; nor is it a case,
as it is for the latter, of irrational guilt seeking to justify its
existence. Once arrested, Joseph K. never doubts his guilt, even
while ostensibly seeking to prove his innocence; Miss Bishop's
nameless character runs no risk of arrest since, in order to attain

the imprisonment he "can scarcely wait for," he seems prepared to do precious little and certainly nothing criminal, unless criminality be defined in the singular way attributed to Edgar Degas in "Objects & Apparitions": "'One has to commit a painting,' said Degas, / 'the way one commits a crime'" (G, 47). But if the poet adopts this position, it is without political intent or fanfare. The pun on "sentence" in the phrase "life-sentence" may get us nearer the truth; from one point of view the writer may be said to serve successive "sentences." Be that as it may, the author of "In Prison" strikes the pose of a young Hegelian, wishing literally to make a virtue of necessity. Our hero has been chosen by prison, he would say; the will is needed not to act upon this destiny but to acquiesce before it, to accept what he conceives as "necessity." Given his definition of freedom, only an attitude of passive non-resistance will do, only the passive voice will be strictly accurate. Notice the grammatical ambiguity that closes the story:

> You may say,—people have said to me—you would have been happy in the more flourishing days of the religious order, and that, I imagine, is close to the truth. But even there I hesitate, and the difference between Choice and Necessity jumps up again to confound me. "Freedom is knowledge of necessity"; I believe nothing as ardently as I do that. And I assure you that to act in this way is the only logical step for me to take. I mean, of course, to be acted *upon* in this way is the only logical step for me to take. [IP, 16]

Justice is beside the point. It is clear we are talking metaphorically, not about guilt and punishment, but about the self and its need to make peace with the certitude of loss. To volunteer for prison is to plan a journey into the interior, confident that in the exchange of physical liberty for imaginative freedom one has, philosophically speaking, struck a good bargain, given up the apparent, embraced the real. Like Ashbery's dreary office building, prison affords both the opportunity and the motive for metaphor, but a far more urgent task also confronts the prisoner. It will be his audacious enterprise to establish an idealized dwelling place within the least likely, least congenial, of quarters; like Crusoe on his island, he will attempt to convert an alien landscape into one that responds to his humanity. It is almost as though he (or his author) were consciously designing a test for "one" art—singular, definitive of the poet's identity—an art that feeds on what might otherwise consume it, that thrives on loss, that welcomes limits in order to transcend them. We are, in sum, solidly within the walls of a conceit, a paradox regained, a cliché renewed in surprising ways. At one point at least, prison metaphorically dramatizes the situation of the writer, any writer conscious of his belatedness. Thus, referring to the "Writing on the Wall," our would-be prisoner announces his intention to "read very carefully (or try to read, since they may be partly obliterated, or in a foreign language) the inscriptions already there. Then I shall adapt my own compositions, in order that they may not conflict with those written by the prisoner before me. The voice of a new inmate will be noticeable, but there will be no contradictions or criticisms of what has already been laid down, rather a 'commentary.' I have thought of attempting a short, but immortal, poem, but I am afraid that is beyond me; I may rise to the occasion, however, once I am confronted with that stained, smeared, scribbled-on wall and feel the stub of pencil or rusty nail between my fingers" (IP, 14). The sense of postponement here as elsewhere in the piece reinforces our impression of it as an initial statement of purpose, a warm-up for the main event yet to come, the time of confrontation, pencil stub in hand, "with that stained, smeared, scribbled-on wall" of poetic tradition.

What makes "In Prison" work so well is that, having subtly and very quickly established the figurative nature of the writing, Miss Bishop ironically becomes a literalist of the imagination, specifying the exact dimensions of the cell, describing its walls and window and the view from the window with painterly precision, ruling out such surrogates for prison as monasteries. To live, in a shabby hotel room, "as if I were in prison"? No, the narrator says, that won't do. Nor will what we now call a country-club prison, the sort of place that has temporarily housed persons of a certain class convicted of wrongdoing with relation to the Watergate burglary and cover-up. Joining the navy is likewise eliminated from consideration, though on different grounds: not so much because it would parody "my real hopes," but for the telling reason that "there is something fundamentally uncongenial about the view of the sea to a person of my mentality" (IP, 15). Why? Because, we may infer, it is the very symbol of the lawless and limitless and as such must clash with the mentality that yearns for fixed borders; also because the sea's vastness and essential unity threaten to drown out all details, all the "slight differences" that strike the poet as inherently valuable. The sea's great expanse is a needless luxury, a point implicitly made in that portion of the story given over to a mock-review of the literature of incarceration. Oscar Wilde is rebuked for the self-pitying note that mars "The Ballad of Reading Gaol." " 'That little tent of blue, Which prisoners call the sky,' strikes me as absolute nonsense. I believe that even a keyhole of sky would be enough, in its blind, blue endlessness, to give someone, even someone who had never seen it before, an adequate idea of the sky" (IP, 11). The "romantic tunnel-digging" of *The Count of Monte Cristo* is also rejected by this early spokesman for Miss Bishop's views, this hard-liner impatient with sentimental formulae. What is desired, after all, is not an escape from, but an escape into, the unadorned cell of consciousness.

As in "Crusoe in England," it is a persona and not the poet who does the talking in "In Prison." To make sure we realize this, Miss Bishop takes pains to distinguish the speaker's gender from her own. (He has thought of enlisting in the armed services—and of playing on the prison baseball team.) The distance thus created between writer and text sets ironies in motion, but these seem otherwise directed than at the speaker's expense. Rather, they work to effect a delicate interplay between order and chance, limitation and space, determinism and free will, the philosophical dualities that energize the story. If one's reading consist of a single book, and that a boring one, one can multiply it by a theoretically infinite number of misreadings, magical as lies. If one's view be restricted to a bare cobblestone courtyard, framed by the window so that it takes on the aspect of a painting, its boundaries severely defined, its activity therefore rescued from disorder, it is nevertheless a series of paintings in one, and within its order there is plenty of room for chance; vagaries of weather ensure the possibility of variations galore, as Monet demonstrated with his cathedrals and haystacks, products of the changing light. The confinement, then, is meant not to eliminate dealings with the external world but to circumscribe the relations and, by doing so, to put them on an aesthetic plane. What one sees becomes an ever-changing picture, what one reads, an occasion for the imagination to roam free. If, for the aesthete's ends, what barely suffices ("a keyhole of sky") is deemed better than a surfeit, that is partially because it underscores an important truth about poetic knowledge. All that we can know are parts and fragments; by the same token, each part, each detail, acts as a synecdoche, pointing to a potential whole, a design the mind must intuit or invent. "I expect to go to prison in full possession of my 'faculties,'" the speaker says. "In fact," he adds, "it is not until I am securely installed there that I expect fully to realize them" (IP, 12–13). In short, the prison of his aspirations is nothing like a place of asylum, refuge from trouble, a rest cure; on the contrary, his sentence will tax, and reward, his powers of imagination. And one can go further: one can say too that he plots his prison itinerary for reasons similar to those that elsewhere impel Miss Bishop's "I" and fellow travellers to undertake journeys to unfamiliar places that call "home" into question. A fantasized excursion to prison can give rise to such "questions of travel" as Miss Bishop will pose in a memorable poem:

> "Is it lack of imagination that makes us come
> to imagined places, not just stay at home?
> Or could Pascal have been not entirely right
> about just sitting quietly in one's room?
>
> Continent, city, country, society:
> the choice is never wide and never free.
> And here, or there . . . No. Should we have stayed at home,
> wherever that may be?"

[CP, 109]

Such interrogations yield no answers, only suasions, and these subject to change. "In Prison" leans one way, *Questions of Travel* the other. But whatever the differences in their attitudes to travel, the restless geographer and the secluded inmate have an ultimate direction in common, an ultimate task in which their opposing inclinations will equally culminate—the making of the map of an identity.

As a theory of imagination which is necessarily a theory of absence, "In Prison" prepares us well for the projects of Miss Bishop's mature poetry. It is remarkable how often she turns to imagery of room, cell, cage, and box, and usually within the context of an aesthetic inquiry; she has a penchant for illustrating her sense of art by postulating constructions the shape of boxes or made of them. Take "The Monument," which traces the growth of a work of art from "piled-up boxes" to "a temple of crates." Its external appearance seems to some extent a subordinate value; it functions to safeguard "what is within," about which it is protectively reticent:

> It may be solid, may be hollow.
> The bones of the artist-prince may be inside
> or far away on even drier soil
> But roughly but adequately it can shelter
> what is within (which after all
> cannot have been intended to be seen.)
>
> [CP, 28]

A "crooked box," the dream house of "The End of March" is prison-like in more ways than one, a rough but adequate shelter with constraints enough to provide the stimulus, if not the necessity, for creative action. And in "Objects & Apparitions," Miss Bishop's translation of Octavio Paz's homage to the boxes of Joseph Cornell, the paradox of a nutshell's infinite space is immediately articulated:

> Hexahedrons of wood and glass,
> scarcely bigger than a shoebox,
> with room in them for night and all its lights.
>
> Monuments to every moment,
> refuse of every moment, used:
> cages for infinity.
>
> [G, 46]

Cornell's boxes have been characterized as "monumental on a tiny scale";[9] the phrase is not without relevance to Miss Bishop's art. The impulse toward this peculiar brand of monumentality combines with the conceit of the "enormous" room most notably, perhaps, in "12 O'Clock News," in which the writer's desk and the objects on it are magnified (and mis-translated), seen as through the eyes of a Lilliputian, with results at once humorous and touching.

Paradise, as Elizabeth Bishop with tongue-biting irony conceives it, has a precedent in "The Great Good Place" Henry James described, as these sentences from James's story make clear: "Slowly and blissfully he read into the general wealth of his comfort all the particular absences of which it was composed. One by one he touched, as it were, all the things it was such rapture to be without." The tone (and much else) is different, but the sentiment the same, in "One Art." There the disaster-prone are advised to "Lose something every day" and then to "practice losing farther, losing faster" (G, 40). The imperative seems at first purely ironic, a way to keep anguish and dread at bay, to avoid giving in to self-pity. But the ironist's supreme gesture is to mean just what she says, contrary to appearances as well as expectations. Miss Bishop does, at least in one sense, recommend that we go about losing things, not so much because this will prepare us for the major losses inevitably to follow, but because the experience of loss humanizes us; it shows us as we are, vulnerable, pathetic, and yet heroic in our capacity to endure and to continue our affirming acts amid conditions less than propitious. When Miss Bishop talks of losing as an art she does not mean losing well; it's not a matter of good sportsmanship or "grace under pressure." On the one hand, she means considerably less: it isn't hard to master what comes naturally to us: we are always losing things, from our innocence to our parents to our house keys: that is why *lose* was the perfect syllepsis for Alexander Pope. Yet "the art of losing" is a wonderfully ambiguous phrase, and the ability to reconcile its two meanings—to experience loss as itself a remedy for loss—constitutes a powerful poetic gesture, whose success may be measured by the poet's skillful handling of the villanelle's intricate form in the face of all that militates against order and arrangement.

In "The Poet," Emerson wrote that "every thought is also a prison; every heaven is also a prison." Not the least virtue of Elizabeth Bishop's poetry is that, from the start, it shows us the truth that remains when Emerson's terms are reversed.

1981

NOTES

1. *Decline and Fall* (Boston: Little, Brown, 1956), p. 229.

2. *Against Nature,* trans. Robert Baldick (New York: Penguin, 1977), p. 35. Characterized by Arthur Symons as "the breviary of the Decadence," *À Rebours* made a striking impression on the hero of *The Picture of Dorian Gray*—and on Paul Valéry. A strict translation of the title of Huysmans' book would give us "against the grain," "backwards," or "the wrong way."

In *Abroad: British Literary Traveling Between the Wars* (New York: Oxford University Press, 1980), Paul Fussell refers to W. H. Davies (in *The Autobiography of a Super-Tramp,* 1908), Anthony Powell's "Waring" (in *What's Become of Waring,* 1939), and Anthony Burgess as other examples of armchair travelers who needed to take no actual journey in order to arrive at an account of time spent abroad. Fussell, it must be noted, uses the term "stationary tourist" in a rather different sense from the one I intend in this essay.

3. *Prose* 2 (Spring 1971), p. 114.

4. *Some Trees* (New York: Ecco Press, 1978), pp. 14–18.

5. *Collected Poems, 1951–1971* (New York: Norton, 1972), p. 319.

6. *Some Trees,* p. 74.

7. Initially published in the *Partisan Review* (March 1938), "In Prison" was reprinted in *The Poet's Story,* ed. Howard Moss (New York: Macmillan, 1973), pp. 9–16. All page references are to the latter publication.

8. Compare with Kierkegaard's exposition of "the rotation method":

> The whole secret lies in arbitrariness. People usually think it easy to be arbitrary, but it requires much study to succeed in being arbitrary so as not to lose oneself in it, but so as to derive satisfaction from it. One does not enjoy the immediate but something quite different which he arbitrarily imports into it. You go to see the middle of a play, you read the third part of a book. By this means

you insure yourself a very different kind of enjoyment from that
which the author has been so kind as to plan for you.

Either/Or, trans. David F. Swenson and Lillian Marvin Swenson
(Princeton: Princeton University Press, 1971), vol. 1, p. 295.

9. John Ashbery, "Cornell's Sublime Junk," *Newsweek* (December
8, 1980), p. 111.

In an appreciation of Cornell published some years earlier, Ashbery
discerns in some of the boxes a version of the theme that informs his
own "The Instruction Manual." "It is likewise hard to believe that
Cornell has never been in France, so forcefully does his use of clippings
from old French books and magazines recreate the atmosphere of that
country. Looking at one of his 'hotel' boxes one can almost feel the
chilly breeze off the Channel at Dieppe or some other outmoded, out-
of-season French resort. But this is the secret of his eloquence: he does
not recreate the country itself but the impression we have of it before
going there, gleaned from Perrault's fairy tales or old copies of
L'Illustration, or whatever people have told us about it." "Cornell: The
Cube Root of Dreams," *Art News* 66 (Summer 1967), p. 58.

ABBREVIATIONS

In quoting from Miss Bishop's works, I used the following system of
abbreviations:

CP   *The Complete Poems* (New York: Farrar, Straus and Giroux,
      1970).

G   *Geography III* (New York: Farrar, Straus and Giroux, 1976).

IP   "In Prison," in *The Poet's Story,* ed. Howard Moss (New York:
      Macmillan, 1973), pp. 9–16.

Numbers following the abbreviations refer to page numbers in the
cited text.

PENELOPE LAURANS

"Old Correspondences"
Prosodic Transformations in Elizabeth Bishop

The bight is littered with old correspondences.
"The Bight"

When asked, in a 1966 *Shenandoah* interview, what she especially liked about George Herbert, whose poetry she said had influenced her own poem, "The Weed," Elizabeth Bishop explained that she admired "the absolute naturalness of tone." In the few reviews and critical pieces Bishop has written, she returns several times to spontaneity as a poetic quality she values. A pleasant but gently critical review of Wallace Fowlie's autobiographical book *Pantomime* concludes with the dry remark that Fowlie is "more spontaneous than he gives himself credit for." And it is for spontaneity, among other principal virtues, that she praises Marianne Moore in her early review of Moore's poems.[1]

Bishop's concern with tone is not surprising, since few aspects of composition have been more troublesome for that generation of poets following the great moderns. Most of them have tried for just that "naturalness" and "spontaneity" they learned to value from their Romantic progenitors, but the difficulty has been to define these qualities in mid-twentieth century terms. Bishop's own definition is suggested in the *Shenandoah* discussion where she describes her early discovery of an essay on seventeenth century baroque prose which "tried to show that baroque sermons . . . attempted to dramatize the mind in action rather than in repose."[2] The sense of the mind actively encountering reality, giving off the impression of involved, immediate discovery, is one of Bishop's links to the Romantics, as the recurrence of the word "spontaneous" in her critical vocabulary emphasizes.

This high valuation on the natural in Bishop's critical statements is especially interesting in light of the range of metrical variation and complicated versification in her poems.[3] For some

contemporary poets the "natural" has implied a certain dis-
respect for form. Bishop's poetry, on the contrary, has always
displayed a wide range of formal inventiveness. Yet, if one asked
a competent reader for an extempore comment on formal varia-
tion in Bishop's poetry, he might answer that he didn't remem-
ber much—it is that subtly done. The appearance of regularity in
the face of so much variation is partly evidence of Bishop's
technical versatility, but it is also directly connected with the
way formal qualities are related to thematic ones in her poetry. It
is consistent with Bishop's own preference for the natural that,
in her poems, form always yields to the exigency of what she is
trying to say. Her patterns are a result of her insistence that
formal structures adapt to the developing progression of the
poem, rather than predetermine that progression. Of course no
good poet allows form to dictate what he is going to say. But
many will let it guide them in making choices. Bishop, howev-
er, rarely seems to permit this to happen.

While it appears to be true that formal adaptiveness—the sub-
ordination of form to meaning—gives Bishop's poetry some of
that sense of spontaneity she admires, it also seems true, para-
doxically, that this same adaptiveness works to restrict the
meaning of spontaneity in her work quite narrowly. Thema-
tically, Bishop's poetry tends toward Romantic subject matter:
problems of isolation, of loss, of the quest for union with some-
thing beyond the self, press with dramatic force in her work.
These highly charged questions, however, are nearly always
countered by the way they are presented, which has earned for
the tone of her verse such critical characterizations as "matter-
of-fact and understated" and "flat and modest."[4] Indeed, it
seems to me that Bishop exercises her technical proficiency to
cut her poetry off from any of that "spontaneous overflow of
powerful feeling" so immediately central to the Romantic imag-
ination. Frequently it is this quality of restraint that keeps the
poetry from sentimental excess and gives it its elegantly muted,
modernist quality.

A well-modulated lyric like "The Armadillo" demonstrates
how the formal qualities of Bishop's poetry help to hold the
reader's emotional response in check. "The Armadillo" medi-
tates on the Brazilian custom of floating celebratory fire balloons

on saints' days and festival days. It depicts the almost unearthly beauty of these fragile, dangerous objects which rise in the night sky, seeming to imitate stars and planets, but which also sometimes fall flaming to earth, disrupting and destroying natural life. The animals in the poem, driven from their nests by a fallen balloon, emerge frightened and mystified, all, from the ancient owls to the baby rabbits, vulnerable in the face of this disaster. Even the ordinarily well-protected armadillo is defenseless before the incomprehensible and terrifying shower of fire.

The question for the critic of this poem is how Bishop shapes the reader's response to this beautiful and cruel event. One could say that the poem, by its factual presentation alone, asks us to recognize the chaos these illegal balloons generate. Yet, until the final stanza, there is little to indicate that Bishop's involvement in the scene is anything more than an aesthetic one. The dramatic beauty of the fire balloons and the vulnerable beauty of the animals are both described with equal power.

The distancing that goes on through most of "The Armadillo" is a way of keeping the poem free of a sentimentality that the depth of underlying feeling might generate. Although the beauty and delicacy of the finished work make this seem unlikely, less authorial control might well reduce it to moralizing (i.e. when men float fire balloons they may do violence to the natural life around them). Instead, Bishop exercises her command of the formal constituents of verse and her descriptive powers to hold the poem back from any easily paraphrasable "meaning" and to give it moral resonance.

The primary way Bishop manages this control is metrical variation. This form of variation is characteristic of Bishop's sure sense of herself: it shows her commanding tradition by apparently allowing her poems to develop spontaneously. At the same time that this variation gives the reader the impression that the poem is progressing naturally, however, it also carefully limits the intensity of response he can have to it. The habitually shifting rhythms of the poem do not allow the reader to lose himself in its lyric music; instead, they keep jolting him to recognition, thereby keeping him from "taking sides"—from becoming, that is, too caught up either in the beauty of the balloons or the terror of the animals.

The way this works is clear in these first stanzas:

> This is the time of year
> when almost every night
> the frail, illegal fire balloons appear.
> Climbing the mountain height,
>
> rising towards a saint
> still honored in these parts,
> the paper chambers flush and fill with light
> that comes and goes, like hearts.
>
> Once up against the sky it's hard
> to tell them from the stars—
> planets, that is—the tinted ones:
> Venus going down, or Mars,
>
> or the pale green one. With a wind,
> they flare and falter, wobble and toss;
> but if it's still they steer between
> the kite sticks of the Southern Cross

It would certainly not be true to say that these quatrains have no music. They do, but it is a distinctly variable one. The shift from two quatrains of three stress lines, each with a five stress third line that mirrors the appearance of the fire balloons and their flushing and filling with light, to the varying three and four stress lines of the next quatrains, keeps the reader constantly readjusting the meter in his head. Even in the first apparently regular stanzas there are examples of the roughness Bishop prefers: the first full sentence ends in the third, rather than in the fourth line of the opening stanza, countering the regular flow of the meter. And in the second stanza, the abab rhyme scheme shifts, retaining a hint of rhyme from the first stanza in "saint" and then picking up one of its full rhymes in "light," but setting the precedent for more variation in the following stanzas. Throughout the rest of the poem, the lines have either three or four stresses, but these stresses vary so from stanza to stanza that the poem projects a sense of constant shifting in spite of its recognizable lyric pattern.

With such extensive shifting it soon becomes clear that this is not simply the ordinary variation all good poets exercise to keep their poems from becoming too regular. Rather, it is variation that preserves a lyric quality while at the same time strictly delimiting lyric effusiveness. While reading this poem the reader is never allowed to forget himself and to be transported by the momentum of the verse. Instead, the metrical roughness keeps him detached, his attention concentrated on the complexity of the event the poet is describing.

Another characteristic technique Bishop uses to great effect in "The Armadillo" is that of drawing back from emotional intensity at just the point where a Romantic poet would allow such intensity to break through most completely. These stanzas from the center of the poem show something of how this works:

> Last night another big one fell.
> It splattered like an egg of fire
> against the cliff behind the house.
> The flame ran down. We saw the pair
>
> of owls who nest there flying up
> and up, their whirling black-and-white
> stained bright pink underneath, until
> they shrieked up out of sight.
>
> The ancient owls' nest must have burned.
> Hastily, all alone,
> a glistening armadillo left the scene,
> rose-flecked, head down, tail down,
>
> and then a baby rabbit jumped out,
> *short*-eared, to our surprise.
> So soft!—a handful of intangible ash
> with fixed, ignited eyes.

The medial pause of the final line of the first quatrain here, together with the series of enjambed lines following it, lead the reader to feel the fright and confusion of the owls, forced from their nest by the shattered balloon. But, typically, Bishop quickly draws back from this intensity. Just after this metrical excitement there is a change: the lines alter from the tetrameter of the former quatrains to three, four, and five stress lines, and the lines also become more end-stopped and more interrupted in their flow. This change mirrors the difference in the animals' response to their plight: the owls fly up shrieking, while the armadillo scurries away alone, and the baby rabbit jumps out, as if lost and mystified. Part of Bishop's achievement here is to catch the specific response of each animal and to convey it in the lyrical gesture of the verse as well as in the language.

But more important than the way Bishop catches the individual quality of each animal here is the way she controls the reader's response to the main event by choosing, just at this point, to reserve intensities and to begin patiently to *describe* the animals. The exactitude of the description determines the final meaning of the poem: it forces the reader to slow down and to visualize the particular vulnerability of each of these creatures when faced with this incendiary accident. Yet until the very end, Bishop directs the reader to the animals' trauma only obliquely, through the description itself, while the way she breaks and controls her verse holds him back from sympathizing with them too effusively. The italics which emphasize that the baby rabbit is "*short*-eared" physically stop the flow of the verse, obliterating much of the reader's momentary empathy for the animal by compelling him to focus on its physical uniqueness. And the exclamation "So soft!" to describe the rabbit is daring in another way. Its use of cliché is made to seem naive, as if Bishop were too unpracticed to find a more original way to describe the rabbit; but when followed by so subtle and exact a metaphor as "a handful of ash," the old cliché assumes renewed force, as if this direct simplicity were the only possible way to render the quality of the small animal. Again, the very fact of the exclamation keeps the reader from being spellbound by the ongoing impulse of the poetry.

After all this holding off, the final quatrain can be interpretive and dramatic without risking sentimentality:

> *Too pretty, dreamlike mimicry!*
> *O falling fire and piercing cry*
> *and panic, and a weak mailed fist*
> *clenched ignorant against the sky!*

All of the animals' panic and misery is conveyed in Bishop's own summation (italicized to separate it from the rest of the poem). In these final lines, their plight extends subtly to become our own. We, of course, understand the fire balloons. But, mailed as we are, with our own strength and intelligence, we cannot protect ourselves from the equally mystifying and terrible events that shake us. It is surely important to note, at this point, that Bishop dedicated this poem to Robert Lowell, who became a conscientious objector when the Allied command began fire-bombing German cities. Bishop's poem points directly to these fire bombings, which wreaked the same kind of horrifying destruction on a part of our universe that the fire balloons wreak on the animals. In the last quatrain, the "mailed fist," besides being a familiar figure of speech for threats of war making, represents the protective "armor" of a soldier which is suggested by the armadillo's carapace. The whole quatrain, with its exclamations and enjambed lines, leads upward in intensity to the expression of helplessness in the face of such terror. But because this intensity has been preceded by so much reticence, the emotion here seems earned. There is no sense of false moralizing about this poem; in fact, no sense of moralizing at all, although the moral dimension of the poem is inescapably present.

II

There are Bishop poems in which the proficiency apparent in "The Armadillo" gives the poetry not just the technical control, but also the special quality of reserve that is Bishop's hallmark. In an early poem like "Large Bad Picture" it seems as if Bishop uses her technical command to place ironic distance between herself and her subject. But the matter does not settle itself so simply as that. Bishop's poetry often concerns her quest to belong somewhere, to find a home. "Large Bad Picture" expresses both Bishop's desire to establish connection with a member of her family she never knew, and her recognition that she has moved beyond the point where this connection is possible. This complicated attitude is conveyed in a poem which never mentions these matters at all, one where meaning is controlled through description and through the formal composition of the poem itself, not through any direct expression of attitude or opinion.

The entire poem describes a scene painted by Bishop's great-uncle of points somewhat to the north of where Bishop grew up. The picture is primitive art at its most primitive, appealing but unsophisticated: the painted waves running along the bay are "perfect" as real waves never are; the spars of the little ships are "burnt match-sticks," like a child's naive depiction of spars; and the birds "hanging in n's in banks" are "scribbled," not rendered, but only approximated as well as the artist's talent allows.

Bishop's emphasis on the technical aspects of the picture, like the title of the poem itself, shows her distinct awareness of the limitations of her great-uncle's art. On the other hand, her involvement with the picture obviously goes far beyond any objective judgment of it. Whatever artistic sophistication her ancestor lacked, his picture captures the essential mood of the scene well enough to make Bishop recognize her own attraction for such a landscape, and to impel her imagination onward. By the sixth quatrain she begins to live in the scene deeply enough to hear sounds in it. Even though she characteristically uses the impersonal "one" instead of "I," the reader perceives that she is caught up enough to hear the crying of the birds in the awesome, eerie landscape, and to catch the mysterious sighing of some great animal of the deep:

> One can hear their crying, crying,
> the only sound there is
> except for occasional sighing
> as a large aquatic animal breathes.

Yet by the end of the poem there is a paradoxical sense in which

Bishop has both joined in the scene of the picture and remained separate from it:

> In the pink light
> the small red sun goes rolling, rolling,
> round and round and round at the same height
> in perpetual sunset, comprehensive, consoling,
>
> while the ships consider it.
> Apparently they have reached their destination.
> It would be hard to say what brought them there,
> commerce or contemplation.

This landscape is irresistible—anyone might be attracted by it. Those aboard the ships might well have been induced there by the same attractions that made Bishop's great-uncle wish to paint the scene, or that make Bishop herself admire it now. Seafaers, artist, and observer, in that case, are all linked in their shared appreciation. But this kind of Romantic merging, in which distant and separate people are brought spiritually close to one another, is countered by the technical limitations of the picture, which stop Bishop and do not allow her to go past a certain point in her interpretation of it. If the ships were more distinctly rendered by the painter it might indeed be possible to tell "what brought them there." But since they are not, the observer is necessarily kept at a distance from the scene.

What finally separates Bishop from her ancestor, however, and complicates the deep spiritual connection with him that the picture initiates, is Bishop's mastery of her craft. If the "large bad picture" is an example of naive art, the poem that describes it displays the technical command of an artist in such control that she makes her poem appear as simplistic as the picture, until a closer look reveals the difference. If there is condescension in the poem (and it seems to me there is a little), then it is not personal but artistic. It is not at all toward her uncle, with whom she clearly feels a deep kinship in spite of the fact she never met him, but toward the inherent technical limitations of the genre of art for which his talents suit him. The point is that her uncle loved the scene and was able to convey this love in an appealing but unsophisticated medium; but it is clear from the poem that if this is a medium Bishop appreciates, it is nevertheless one she has left far behind.

A closer look at "Large Bad Picture" shows how this is so. The poem looks at first as if it might be in regular ballad meter. In fact, however, the meter varies dramatically, and the poem as a whole cultivates a formal roughness that makes it seem the product of an artistically naive imagination. The poem begins with a quatrain in four stress lines that is made to look as if its pattern of rhyming might settle down to be aabb, if only the poet could manage it:

> Remembering the Strait of Belle Isle or
> some northerly harbor of Labrador,
> before he became a schoolteacher
> a great-uncle painted a big picture.

In the very next quatrain Bishop drops this playfully clumsy scheme, picking up alternating lines of four and three stresses and changing the rhyme to a true abcb:

> Receding for miles on either side
> into a flushed, still sky
> are overhanging pale blue cliffs
> hundreds of feet high

After two more quatrains that follow this pattern, the meter veers rapidly, changing four times in four stanzas and making the reader jolt and jog as he struggles to adapt to its changeable flow. The rhyme also occasionally augments this jolting, with such off rhymes as "ships" and "sticks" and "is" and "breathes."

Unlike the technical roughness of her great-uncle's picture, these jagged outcroppings are merely Bishop's imitations of roughness, which call attention to their creator's poetic refinement. And it is this refinement which finally separates Bishop from the great-uncle to whom the picture tantalizingly seems to offer access. In the uncle's picture, everything is cheerfully and awkwardly approximated, but in spite of the fact that the mood is caught exactly, the picture is limited by the attractive but narrow quality of the art. In Bishop's own poem, on the contrary, everything is unsaid, but in spite (or perhaps because) of its purposeful reticence and formal clumsiness, the reader is made to perceive a world of complicated emotion.

"Made to perceive" is a phrase worth emphasizing here, since the fact is that the formal strategy of the poem keeps the reader at a certain remove from Bishop's feelings. Still, it is this very remove that paradoxically makes the nexus of deep feeling at the poem's center more poignant to us. Bishop's unstated (perhaps not fully recognized) suffering is that she longs to be a part of that from which she has been cut off—not only by time and distance, but also by her gifts. The distance she has come as an artist is the distance she is removed from the uncle she never knew. She likes her uncle's picture, but while her personal feelings generate this affection, her artistic integrity forces her to judge the accomplishment, almost in spite of herself. Like many of us, she is nostalgic for a past she has gone beyond. The strength of the poem is that it allows us to share this longing and pain without either belaboring or sentimentalizing it. The reticence about the human emotion, all contained in what is unstated, makes the reader sense it more, not less, strongly. In the end, "Large Bad Picture" is a poem full of a nostalgic Romantic ardor, charged with Bishop's longing to be united with her past; but it is ardor in an unspoken dimension, countered by the poem's descriptive and technical accomplishment.

III

"The Armadillo" and "Large Bad Picture" are written in forms that Bishop adapted from traditional ones. Many of Bishop's major poems, however, like "The Man-Moth," "The Monument," "Over 2000 Illustrations and a Complete Concordance," "At the Fishhouses," "Brazil, January 1, 1502," and "Questions of Travel" are in free verse, or, as one might expect with Bishop, in her own version of free verse. In these longer poems Bishop often manipulates form in much the same way she does in her smaller lyrics. Her delicate exploitation of iambic pentameter in her free verse poems is an example of how she can use a regular meter to give intensity, and then shift the meter to pull it sharply back from this intensity.

One sees this technique at work in a rich and difficult poem like "The Monument." In the poem an admiring speaker seems to be describing an object to a second speaker, who resists seeing it as a work of art. Indeed, the monument is admittedly queer-looking, mysterious, and changeable in its form. The act of contemplating it occasions for Bishop the creation of a poetics, in which the monument becomes the symbol for that noble artistic presence which cannot be defined or explained, but is a product of knowledge, imagination, and faith.

The poem is constructed as a dialogue, predominantly in free verse. Bishop varies its progression several times, most pointedly in one of its important and difficult lines:

> The monument is one-third set against
> a sea; two-thirds against a sky.
> The view is geared
> (that is, the view's perspective)
> so low there is no "far away,"

> aňd wé | aře fár | ăwáy | wĭthín | tħe viéw.

In these lines, the speaker attempts to break down the barrier between the monument and the observer, implicating the observer in the structure of the work of art itself. Bishop underlines the importance of this implication by allowing the meter, at just this significant moment, to break into metrical regularity and to carry the poem along:

> A sea of narrow, horizontal boards
> lies out behind our lonely monument,
> its long grains alternating right and left
> like floor-boards—spotted, swarming-still,
> and motionless. A sky runs parallel,
> and it is palings, coarser than the sea's:
> splintery sunlight and long-fibred clouds.

After the pentameter has temporarily prevailed, the second speaker begins his prosaic questioning, and free verse again returns to deflect the flow of the poem and to keep the reader from losing himself in the first speaker's magical description.

This technique—of allowing the poem to break in and out of pentameter—is used in varying degrees and with varying effects in other major poems such as "Over 2000 Illustrations and a Complete Concordance," or "Brazil, January 1, 1502." In the latter, Bishop injects a line of pentameter here and there toward the end of the poem before she allows it to break fully into pentameter just before its intense conclusion. She even carries over this technique to a poem that has some five stress lines, but no pentameter at all, "At the Fishhouses":

I have seen it over and over, the same sea, the same,
slightly, indifferently swinging above the stones,
icily free above the stones,
above the stones and then the world.
If you should dip your hand in,
your wrist would ache immediately,
your bones would begin to ache and your hand would burn
as if the water were a transmutation of fire
that feeds on stones and burns with a dark gray flame.
If you tasted it, it would first taste bitter,
then briny, then surely burn your tongue.
It is like what we imagine knowledge to be:
dark, salt, clear, moving, utterly free,
drawn from the cold hard mouth
of the world, derived from the rocky breasts
forever, flowing and drawn, and since
our knowledge is historical, flowing, and flown.

Here at the magnificent end of her peom, Bishop twice deflects lyrical intensity. In the first instance, the anaphora which conveys the power of the sea ("the *same* sea, the *same*, / . . . swinging *above the stones,* / icily free *above the stones,* / *above the stones* and then the world") is countered by the mundane conditional clause ("*If* you should dip your hand in"). After bringing the reader down to earth this way, Bishop builds the verse again, and then once more ("If you tasted it") brings it down before she allows it to swing lyrically into its passionate conclusion. These interruptions do not permanently counteract the Romantic impulse of a poem which mystically identifies the cold northern waters of Nova Scotia as the source of an inexplicable power. But they do *curb* this impulse by metrically, as well as thematically, recalling the reader to the pragmatic expressions of everyday life, and by firmly keeping him from sentimentalizing the power of the primal source Bishop is conjuring.

IV

Bishop's recent book, *Geography III,* shows her using meter and versification to move even farther in the direction her earlier lyrics suggest. In these newer poems there is an increased tendency not just to pull back from a lyric intensity that might allow sentimentality, but sometimes to hold back from this intensity altogether. One way Bishop manages this is to make use of meters which have only two or three stresses to a line.

In the first poem of this book, "In the Waiting Room," Bishop describes going to the dentist's office as a small child with her aunt and sitting in the waiting room while her aunt's teeth are attended to. The experience of seeing pictures of naked African women, a shocking and frightening experience for a young North American girl, of sensing the unattractive presence of other patients around her, and of hearing her aunt's cry of pain from the inner office as if it were her own, gives Bishop an alarming sensation of the strangeness of her existence and of her uncomfortable connection with the rest of humanity. Since the poem is partly about a child's discovery of her own mortality, the waiting room becomes not merely a place where Bishop awaits her aunt, but, by extension, a place where she begins to await her death.

> I said to myself: three days
> and you'll be seven years old.
> I was saying it to stop
> the sensation of falling off

the round, turning world
into cold, blue-black space.
                    . . .
I knew that nothing stranger
had ever happened, that nothing
stranger could ever happen.
Why should I be my aunt,
or me, or anyone?
What similarities—
boots, hands, the family voice
I felt in my throat, or even
the *National Geographic*
and those awful hanging breasts—
held us all together
or made us all just one?

This moment of sudden awareness is obviously one of great
emotional intensity for Bishop, a "spot of time" that causes her
momentarily to lose ordinary consciousness and penetrate life
more deeply. Yet the verse that describes the experience holds
the reader back from immediately sharing it. Bishop's rather
awkward three stress lines here vary rhetorically, but they do
not otherwise bend or give—three stress lines in English simply
do not have that flexibility. The reader, then, is made to follow
this dramatic moment in a kind of flattened verse that leaves him
reflecting on, rather than immediately engaging in, the experi-
ence with the poet. It is not that the poem does not contain deep
feeling or that it does not have emotional impact; but the feeling
is tightly controlled by the formal configuration of the words,
which keep it from being either cheap or easy, and the impact is
deflected to give it subtler resonance.

It is a tribute to Bishop's technical excellence that she is able to
produce an important poem in such a meter. What stands behind
her achievement is the free verse movement, which taught poets
how to use what Williams called the "variable foot" to give
poems more flexibility of manner than stricter forms allowed. If
one scans a few passages of "In the Waiting Room," one finds
that, as in any good free verse poem, the feet vary from line to

line to keep the poem from monotony and to give it rhetorical scope:

> I knéw | that nóthing | stránger
> had éver | háppened, | that nóthing
> stránger | could éver | háppen.
>
> . . .
>
> Hów— | I dídn't | knów any
> wórd for it | —hów "un | líkely" . . .
> Hów had I | cóme to | be hére

Here the line break and meter in the first passage focus attention on the important word "stranger," and the variable feet in the second passage emphasize Bishop's existential puzzlement. But while the variable feet give the lines rhetorical latitude as they do in free verse lines, the actual three stress meter of the poem restricts the poem's direct emotional appeal more than might be true in a free verse poem of irregular line lengths. Once again Bishop has adapted tradition to her own ends: instead of using the variable foot to intensify the emotional appeal of a poem, she uses it to give rhetorical variation to a meter that limits this appeal.

Finally, in a poem like "The End of March," one is able to see how reluctant Bishop is to allow technical intensity and thematic passion to correspond in her work. She parcels out her poem's appeal to the reader's emotions charily, using prose passages to contradict what she expressly states, and lyric passages to imply what she is disinclined to make plain. Prose passages are hardly new in Bishop's poetry; they have been there almost from the beginning in poems like "The Bight," "At the Fishhouses," "Cape Breton," and "Manuelzinho." In *Geography III,* however, these passages grow more frequent, conveying the impression that as Bishop's security as a poet has solidified (Bishop has always shown great self-assurance in her writing) she has felt free to include more of these prose passages in her poems.

In "The End of March," for example, fully one third of the poem is prose arranged in verse lines. The poem concerns a walk along a Duxbury beach on a cold, windy, changeable day at the end of winter, and Bishop's desire to reach a rickety house she has spotted on her walk. The house represents a retreat and a release from a world where, as Bishop confides in "Five Flights Up," the final poem of the book, yesterdays are "almost impossible to lift." Living in such a place, one could occupy oneself merely by existing, enjoying the experience of life in its purest, most self-indulgent form. In fact, however, Bishop soon admits that such a dream is "impossible." The house is boarded up— one could not even get into it. And then the day is too cold to allow Bishop to get that far anyway.

Bishop calls the shack a "proto-dream-house," a "crypto-dream-house," and thematically presents it as an unattainable ideal to be approached but never reached. Yet, while the words say one thing, the metrical impulse of the poem communicates precisely the opposite to the reader. The passage in which Bishop describes the house and her wish to reach it contains far and away the most neutral, prose-like writing of the poem:

> I wanted to get as far as my proto-dream-house,
> my crypto-dream-house, that crooked box
> set up on pilings, shingled green,
> a sort of artichoke of a house, but greener
> (boiled with bicarbonate of soda?),
> protected from spring tides by a palisade
> of—are they railroad ties?
>
>   . . .
>
> There must be a stove; there *is* a chimney,
> askew, but braced with wires,
> and electricity, possibly
> —at least, at the back another wire
> limply leashes the whole affair
> to something off behind the dunes.

Everything in the diction and movement of the verse here—its ordinariness, its prosy, conversational sound and flow, as if Bishop were simply talking to the reader—works to diminish the excitement of the ideal she is imagining. Here is the "naturalness" Bishop likes, with a vengeance.

There is real verbal and metrical excitement in this poem, however, at its conclusion:

For just a minute, set in their bezels of sand,
the drab, damp, scattered stones
were multi-colored,
and all those high enough threw out long shadows,
individual shadows, then pulled them in again.
They could have been teasing the lion sun,
except that now he was behind them
—a sun who'd walked the beach that last low tide,
making those big, majestic paw-prints,
who perhaps had batted a kite out of the sky to play with.

Although in the poem Bishop leads the reader to believe she longs for life in the "crooked box" house, the beauty of the language and the movement of the verse show that she finds considerable pleasure in living in a world as vast and unknowable as the house is self-contained and intelligible. The forces she describes in this last passage seem beneficent ones: the great rocks come alive as playful beings, capable of "teasing" a receptive "lion sun," who like a small cub might take enjoyment in batting around a kite. But the energy behind all this playfulness is potentially tremendous and terrifying. The description here is of a universe where immense and dangerous power is contained but smouldering. The sun may act like a cub, but it is actually the "lion sun," a force of nature as capable of destroying men's kites (and men themselves) as it is of playing with them.

The quality of the sun as it is presented here is the quality of the end of March itself, a time when elemental forces first begin to seem friendly and contained, but are lurking dangerously in the atmosphere nonetheless. The dynamic way in which Bishop allows these lines to swing into a kind of lyric movement that is often rationed in her poetry shows that this is an energy Bishop values too much to make the other, more passive state her permanent ideal, no matter what she says directly. In fact, the final five lines of the poem make their own small, passionately lyrical stanza—two lines of pentameter, interspersed with two four stress lines, and completed by a long six stress line. Their climactic movement works to persuade the reader that, while Bishop says she longs for a rickety house on a hill, what she actually values is the large, dangerous universe where "all the untidy activity continues, / awful but cheerful."

The point here is that Bishop's daydream—the thing she says, however whimsically and momentarily, she desires—is described in the most flat, dead-pan verse, while a deeper, unspoken ideal is conveyed by the later momentum of the poetry. Significantly, Bishop releases her poem lyrically only at a moment which is not explicitly its thematic high point. Of course this moment becomes its high point, but that is another matter. The important fact is that Bishop seems reluctant to allow metrical intensity and plain-spokenness to correspond, as if she were afraid that the one might spoil or cheapen the other. In this case she uses this reluctance, craftily, to give the poem a more intricate resonance than it otherwise might have had.

V

What this essay has meant partly to address is the way that the reticence of Bishop's poetry is related to the intensity of feeling at its core. It is sometimes assumed that the cool surfaces of Bishop's poems reveal their lack of emotional depth; in fact, Bishop often uses such reticence as a strategy to make a deeper, more complex emotional appeal to the reader. Meter is one means by which she achieves this reticence, one technique she uses to circumscribe feelings so strong that their expression in unremittingly lyrical terms might make her poems seem easy or cloying to contemporary tastes. Such refined use of a technical aspect of poetry adds subtlety to utterance, and seems to me one of the less-recognized reasons that Bishop's poetry has retained its freshness and interest.

NOTES

1. The comment on George Herbert is reported by Ashley Brown in "An Interview with Elizabeth Bishop," *Shenandoah* 17 (Winter 1966), p. 10; the remark on Fowlie's book in "What the Young Man Said to the Psalmist," *Poetry* 79 (January 1952), p. 214; and the praise for Moore

in "As We Like It," *Quarterly Review of Literature* 4 (Moore Issue 1948), pp. 131, 134. I gratefully acknowledge the comprehensive bibliography in Lloyd Schwartz's 1976 Harvard dissertation on Bishop which helped me to locate these pieces. [All of the references in whole or in part are included in this volume.—Eds.]

2. Bishop, *Shenandoah,* p. 14.

3. Bishop is adept at regular meters like trimeter ("The Burglar of Babylon"), tetrameter ("Wading at Wellfleet"), and pentameter ("From Trollope's Journal") which she uses infrequently, and even then with some variation. She is equally at home with three stress lines ("The Fish," "In the Waiting Room,") and her much more frequent two stress lines ("Sunday, 4 A.M.," "A Summer's Dream," "Trouvée," "Song for the Rainy Season," "The Moose"). But she specializes in *borderline* meters: two stress, three stress, and four stress lines that might also be called modified dimeters, trimeters, and tetrameters, since they break back and forth between the two meters ("Jerónimo's House," "Night City," "First Death in Nova Scotia," "Manuelzinho," "Sleeping on the Ceiling").

Bishop likes as much fluctuation and variation in her poems as possible. Frequently, she will vary the meter within a poem as in "View of the Capitol from The Library of Congress" (where the meter remains constant until the final stanza, at which point each line varies), "Roosters" (stanzas of two, three, and four stress lines, where each stanza swells in intensity), or "The Unbeliever" (basically three stress lines, with occasional two stress variants and a resolving pentameter). In the end, it seems fair to say that Bishop finds loosened meters more congenial than strict ones, shorter lines more arresting than longer, and stanzas with variable meters more appealing than stanzas with a consistent pattern.

In rhyming, Bishop's practice is as variable and inventive as her meters. Besides endless permutations of slant and off rhymes, one meets, as a matter of course, such odd turns as the final word in one stanza rhyming with the final word in the next ("Wading at Wellfleet"); a final two stress line of a stanza rhyming with a final pentameter ("The Unbeliever"); or alternating pentameter and three stress lines rhyming in abc-acb ("Sleeping Standing Up"). Nor does Bishop ever feel compelled to stay with a rhyme scheme once she has established it. She is perfectly capable of beginning a poem in one scheme and then altering it several times within the course of the poem to suit her sense of the poem's development ("Argument" and "Night City").

Bishop also transmutes forms which traditionally are followed quite rigorously. Her one published sonnet, "Some Dreams They Forgot," written early and published late, and her one villanelle, "One Art," both show unusual variations of traditional forms.

4. Nancy McNally, "Elizabeth Bishop: The Discipline of Description," *Twentieth-Century Literature* 11 (January 1966), p. 191. David Kalstone, "Elizabeth Bishop: Questions of Memory, Questions of Travel," *Five Temperaments* (New York: Oxford University Press, 1977), p. 14. (See pp. 3–31.—EDS.)

ALAN WILLIAMSON

A Cold Spring
The Poet of Feeling

I

"Those who restrain desire, do so because theirs is weak enough to be restrained," William Blake wrote; but the same is not necessarily true of poets who handle feeling obliquely. It is increasingly evident that the force of Elizabeth Bishop's poetry is not altogether accounted for by that image of her so often put forward, in praise or blame: the heiress-apparent of Marianne Moore; the crowning glory of a canon of taste that emphasized surface exactitude, the elimination of the personal, and an arch, slightly inhibiting, self-consciousness about how the imagination works. I should therefore like to focus attention on Bishop's one sustained attempt at a passionately personal kind of lyric: the seemingly little-read, little-discussed, love poems of *A Cold Spring*. The very strangeness—and, occasionally, the failure—of these poems has much to teach us, not only about Bishop's reasons for reticence, but about the vision of life, the aura or under-feeling, that subtly animates her more reticent poetry (a poetry which also, paradoxically or not so paradoxically, assumed its most persistent shape, the travel narrative, in this same second volume).

My basic contention is that, if Bishop characteristically distanced emotion, it was partly because emotion for her—and especially feelings of despair, loneliness, apprehension—tended to become immense and categorical, insusceptible to rational or, in poetry, to structural counter-argument. There is a curious disproportion to many of the love poems in *A Cold Spring*, created by the tyrannical assertiveness, the refusal to engage in dialogue, of the darker feelings; and especially by a kind of

ground-conviction that reciprocal love is, almost metaphysical-
ly, impossible. Consider the conclusion of "Insomnia":

> So wrap up care in a cobweb
> and drop it down the well
>
> into that world inverted
> where left is always right,
> where the shadows are really the body,
> where we stay awake all night,
> where the heavens are shallow as the sea
> is now deep, and you love me.

The last line admits of two readings, neither very cheery: that
you "now" love me (but how deep is the sea, when compared
with the heavens?); or that the phrase "you love me" is one of a
series of impossible propositions, conceivable only in the nar-
cissist's mirror-world "where left is always right." But from the
reader's point of view, what is most shocking about this grim
assessment is the way he is led to it without the least hint that a
"you" is at issue in the poem; and then—as if the subject were
too painful to bear more than the briefest mention—suddenly
dropped. The naked emotion of the ending is pointed up by the
contrasting tone of jaunty insouciance, pretend-optimism, with
which the sentence begins.

Such an effect verges on melodramatic indulgence; for me,
the line is crossed in "Varick Street." There, the disproportion
lies in the juxtaposition of the three purely descriptive stanzas,
presenting the neighborhood where "our bed / shrinks from the
soot," with the thrice-repeated refrain:

> *And I shall sell you sell you*
> *sell you of course, my dear, and you'll sell me.*

Why?—the irritable voice of reason might ask—simply because
they live on an ugly industrial street? The inner eye, casting back
through the poem, might reply that the factories amount, from
the beginning, to a nightmare image of the human body and its
imperfections—

                    wretched uneasy buildings
                    veined with pipes
                    attempt their work.
                    Trying to breathe,
                    the elongated nostrils
                    haired with spikes
                    give off such stenches, too

—and that the definition of "certain wonders"—

                    Pale dirty light,
                    some captured iceberg
                    being prevented from melting

—suggests that the wonderful is something frigid, remote, self-sufficient (as in "The Imaginary Iceberg"), unnaturally half-preserved in the "dirty" glare and heat of physical contact. But such readings are strained and emblem-bookish, while the crying voice is commonplace, reasonless, shrill; a middle ground of normal human judgment cannot be established, and the poem fails to jell. One feels, as in "Insomnia," that the poet has been swept away by a monolithic, unarguable intuition of implacable fate.

Bishop was never guilty of such imbalances again; yet even *Geography III*—justly praised for its calm and direct treatment of personal themes—is ghosted with the same abruptness in the face of painful feeling. The jauntiness which insists on representing defeat as triumph (and which is not self-deception, but rather a peculiar exercise of pride: Anne Winters has compared it to the smile in the voice of a blues singer) is the basic premise of "One Art." The trick of turning the poem to an overwhelming personal sorrow in the last line—and then turning it off—reappears in "Five Flights Up," though here, perhaps wisely, only the force, and not the cause, of the sorrow is given:

               —Yesterday brought to today so lightly!
               (A yesterday I find almost impossible to lift.)

("One Art," too, waits until the last stanza to tell the reader that a lover's specific anxiety lies behind its general concern with "the art of losing.")

The love poems in *A Cold Spring* betray an immense anxiety about the adjustments between inner and outer worlds. The narcissistic emphasis of "Insomnia," the disbelief in reciprocal love, is one mode of this anxiety; a difficulty in distinguishing feeling from judgment is another. So far, we have been aware of the latter mainly negatively, as a weakness in the poems. Some poems, however, manage to make the confusion itself part of their manifest content. A playful, almost medieval, allegory underlines the speaker's inability to see the "Days and Distance" of a separation as neutral facts, and not as a malign "Argument" against love. Elsewhere, love itself is defined as the state in which "a name / and all its connotation are the same."

The happiest poem of the whole group, personally and artistically, is one involving both an interchange between people, and an interchange between feelings and realities, "Rain Towards Morning" (quoted here in its entirety):

> The great light cage has broken up in the air,
> freeing, I think, about a million birds
> whose wild ascending shadows will not be back,
> and all the wires come falling down.
> No cage, no frightening birds; the rain
> is brightening now. The face is pale
> that tried the puzzle of their prison
> and solved it with an unexpected kiss,
> whose freckled unsuspected hands alit.

All of the imagistic terms of this strange *aubade* have both an inner and an outer meaning. The "great light cage" of rain is also an intrapsychic cage, as the punning description already suggests: it is both substantial, a "cage" imprisoning "light"—as a "bear cage" imprisons bears—and insubstantial, gone in an instant, a "light cage." The literal birds soaring at dawn call up associations of romantic—basically orgasmic—release that go back, in poetry, at least as far as Bernard de Ventadour. But when the birds are seen as caged—as repressed impulses inside the psyche—they are suddenly re-seen as "frightening," the devouring birds or harpies of nightmare. Finally, the birds are tamed by being externalized once more, but not to as great a distance: they become the tremulous, frightened motions of the "unexpected," "unsuspected" lovers themselves, suddenly alighting on each other. The very fact that inward and outward things can be brought as close together as such imagery suggests; that an action, or another person, can "solve" an intrapsychic "puzzle," is greeted, in the poem, with a combination of joy, astonishment, and fear. "The face is pale" as after a struggle or a shattering revelation. And though the world is, indeed, lit up ("alit" has this punning double sense, I think), the old fear that love is evanescent, that dependence is already loss, can still be felt. It is there in the very image of birds finding a temporary perch; and in the seemingly inappropriate elegiac feeling about release itself—"will not be back." An impersonal despair is still very near the surface. But bounds have been set to it; the psychological nature of the impasse is partly acknowledged; and the result is at least one great, or near-great, poem of personal love.

II

For a poet so obsessed with the distance between human beings—and inclined to see the connections as illusory, muddling, transitory at best—the tourist's-eye view of life is not only comfortingly manageable but, in a fundamental way, *correct*. For the traveller, other people are necessarily remote, unknowable, almost interchangeable; the first flicker of attraction or interest toward an individual is already elegy. The multiplication in space of people doing almost the same things almost simultaneously—but utterly unknown to each other—has some of the annihilating effect of the multiplication in time, in a foreshortening of the centuries. The traveller, like Chaucer, knows that the earth is not home, but wilderness.

"Cape Breton" achieves such a vision simply by moving slowly across a landscape where all activities have been interrupted by an old-fashioned Sunday. From these interruptions is extrapolated a feeling of arbitrariness, of absurd or mysterious purposelessness, about almost anything being exactly where and as it is. The churches "have been dropped into the matted hills / like lost quartz arrowheads"; the road, like the bulldozers, looks "abandoned." On the cliffs "the silly-looking puffins all stand . . . in solemn uneven lines"; while sheep, frightened by the noise of airplanes, sometimes actually stampede into the sea and kill themselves. Even the sheen of the water seems to be "weaving and weaving" a Penelope's web, that disappears "under the mist equally in all directions." The one appealing human figure in the poem, a man carrying a baby, removes himself toward an "invisible house," through a meadow which, in a wonderful oxymoron, "establishes its poverty in a snowfall of daisies." Half-playfully explicit about its own effect, the poem suggests that

> Whatever the landscape had of meaning appears to have been
> abandoned,
> unless the road is holding it back, in the interior,
> where we cannot see

But all we find in the interior is

> miles of burnt forests standing in gray scratches
> like the admirable scriptures made on stones by stones

a vision of elaboration without intention almost as subversive of "scripture" itself as of the homiletic-pastoral of Shakespeare's "sermons in stones."

The same distrust of human readings of nature fills the title poem, "A Cold Spring"—a poem which also deserves our attention (again, structurally) as a kind of troubling middle ground between the poems of touristic detachment and the personal lyrics. It is basically a happy poem; but few happy poems are simultaneously so skeptical about the reasonless metonymies of happiness we are willing to accept. (Only the great opening section of Eugenio Montale's "Times at Bellosguardo" comes to mind.) Bishop begins by quoting Hopkins—"Nothing is so beautiful as spring"—but her uneasiness about the automatic affirmativeness of the season is quickly projected onto almost the entire natural order. "The trees hesitated," though "carefully indicating their characteristics"; "the violet was flawed on the lawn"; a newborn calf seems "inclined to feel gay," but its mother, eating the "wretched" afterbirth, quite clearly does not. There is a feeling—even as the weather finally warms up—of something mechanical, contrived about the whole process:

> Song-sparrows were wound up for the summer,
> and in the maple the complementary cardinal
> cracked a whip. . . .

Then the poem moves into the present tense and, rather wonderfully, relaxes, yields:

> Now, in the evening,
> a new moon comes.
> The hills grow softer. Tufts of long grass show
> where each cow-flop lies.
> The bull-frogs are sounding,
> slack strings plucked by heavy thumbs.

The concentration of long and short o's and u's makes the passage itself sound rather like a cello solo—slow, darkened, languorous. At the same time, there is just enough dissonance in the content to maintain a sense of limit, of uncertain grounding. The grass grows longer over cow-flops; the bull-frogs sound like "slack strings"; the fireflies rise only so high and no higher, "exactly like the bubbles in champagne." Yet the poem qualifies. "Later on they rise much higher"—thus leaving the growth of its own exhilaration, by implication, equally uncurtailed.

"A Cold Spring" becomes a problematic poem because of a teasingly absent-present further dimension: the question being whether, as so often in literature, the yielding to spring is itself a metonymy for the yielding to love. The word "your" occurs four times in the poem—always as an ascription of property, but still, often enough to call attention to itself. The first and last appearances of the word—"your big and aimless hills," "your shadowy pastures"—easily suggest an eroticized fusion of landscape and body. Perhaps the unresolved velleity of these hints has something to do with the curiously anticlimactic tone of the last three lines of the poem:

> And your shadowy pastures will be able to offer
> these particular glowing tributes
> every evening now throughout the summer.

The next-to-last line—redolent of the most formal occasions of congratulation, after-dinner speeches, blurbs—for a long time seemed to me a mere embarrassed stiffening at having to express joy, as wrong, and as telltale, as the abruptnesses of "Varick Street" or "Insomnia." Now, however, it occurs to me that Bishop may have intended such an effect from the moment she brought in the "champagne"; that she perhaps wished the reader to feel that something over-formal, and a little sad, occurs whenever we stand back and try to ratify how much "higher" we have risen or can rise—in a season, in our powers of feeling, or in love. The line between a defensive archness and a philosophically expressive one is peculiarly hard to draw here; for that very reason, we are left more sharply aware of the dangers Bishop faced, and of the nature of her success, in her more impersonal work.

The just balance between surface archness and detachment and subliminal emotional intensity is finally struck—as it will be again and again in the best of Bishop's later work—in "At the Fishhouses" and "Over 2000 Illustrations and a Complete Concordance." At the center of the latter (since I do not have space to discuss both poems in detail) is a vision of desolate accumulation comparable to that in "Cape Breton"—though this judgment will seem paradoxical as soon as I start to quote:

> And at St. Peter's the wind blew and the sun shone madly.
> Rapidly, purposefully, the Collegians marched in lines,
> crisscrossing the great square with black, like ants.
> In Mexico the dead man lay
> in a blue arcade; the dead volcanoes
> glistened like Easter lilies.
> The jukebox went on playing "Ay, Jalisco!"
> And at Volubilis there were beautiful poppies

splitting the mosaics; the fat old guide made eyes.
In Dingle harbor a golden length of evening
the rotting hulks held up their dripping plush.
The Englishwoman poured tea, informing us
that the Duchess was going to have a baby.
And in the brothels of Marrakesh
the little pockmarked prostitutes
balanced their tea-trays on their heads
and did their belly-dances; flung themselves
naked and giggling against our knees,
asking for cigarettes.

Desolate?—the reader may well ask. Surely, taken piece by piece—and in the brilliance of its modulations—this is one of the best, and most exuberant, poetic catalogues since Whitman. The careful contraction toward, and expansion away from, the minimal two-line unit; the hurrying, irregular, long-breathed march of the Collegians, marshalled along by their adverbs, set against the *andante* of Mexico; the "golden length of evening" which seems outside of time because it is spatial as well, the "length" of the moss-gilded hulks themselves . . . one could go on enumerating beauties indefinitely. And yet there is a terrible, and a touristic, detachment about this passage which is finally most un-Whitmanesque. The "dead man," so carefully paired with the beautiful "dead volcanoes," and given appropriate mood-music, becomes, inevitably, one *frisson* among many; the world in which the Duchess's baby is respectable before birth is blankly, without commentary, the same world in which some children are virtually born prostitutes. The world is everything that is the case; or, as Bishop puts it a few lines later, "Everything only connected by 'and' and 'and.'"

What saves this catalogue from a final coldness may be the slight "confessional" shock of the brothel scene. Because this is something one does not see without a choice, a choice that might arouse shame, and certainly arouses the reader's curiosity—yes, Miss Bishop went places she could not have taken Miss Moore, any more than Hart Crane could take his grandmother!—the speaker is suddenly, and vulnerably, part of the spectacle. Thus we are prepared for the more intimate, introspective voice that addresses us immediately thereafter: "It was somewhere near there / I saw what frightened me most of all. . . ."

What frightens the speaker is, in fact, a peculiarly striking emblem of the disintegration of vulnerable individuals into mere spectacle, mere phenomenon: "A holy grave, not looking particularly holy . . . open to every wind from the pink desert" and "half-filled with dust, not even the dust / of the poor prophet paynim who once lay there." That this unprotecting grave is "carved solid / with exhortation"—presumably from the Koran—is a further proof of human impotence, but also, of course, a critique *en abime* of the poem's own too solid effort to cover and preserve everything.

But the poem does not end on this vision of meaninglessness. In "our travels," we have, it goes without saying, failed to see the one thing that might really have mattered. (In the prototype of all voyage poems, Baudelaire observed that no real foreign city quite measures up to "ceux que le hasard fait avec les nuages.") For what is truly satisfying, we must return to the child's book where our desire to travel had its start:

> Open the heavy book. Why couldn't we have seen
> this old Nativity while we were at it?
> —the dark ajar, the rocks breaking with light,
> an undisturbed, unbreathing flame,
> colorless, sparkless, freely fed on straw,
> and, lulled within, a family with pets,
> —and looked and looked our infant sight away.

"The dark ajar" is, in its largest reverberations, an image of mystical revelation—"breaking" through the rocklike surface of phenomena to their permanent, essential being, sheltered in the "unbreathing flame" of eternal Mind. But it also suggests a poignant little story, of a stranger (or perhaps a child who has been sent to bed) peering in at the brightness of the family circle—the opposite of that final solitude which the brothel and the grave, in their different ways, represent. And it is, I think, from the tension between these poles of human and emotional, as well as ontological, experience that the poem gathers its seriousness and force. David Kalstone* has suggested how relevant Elizabeth Bishop's own experience of an essentially parentless childhood is here. And that relevance extends, surely, to many of the issues we have been concerned with throughout: the easy assumption of an uninvolved, spectator's stance toward life; the a priori pessimism about intimate relationships; the potentially monolithic despair. This is not the place to develop the biographical side of Kalstone's insight, since it is the literary consequences of this complex of attitudes that concern us here. But we might note that Bishop's last great voyage poem, "The Moose," follows the same trajectory as "Over 2000 Illustrations," from the traveller's atomized world back to a scene of familial enclosure, overheard by a half-included, half-isolated child. (The specification there, of "Grandparents" rather than parents, makes the child, more clearly than ever, Bishop herself.)

I have confined myself to *A Cold Spring* because, containing as it does such opposite kinds of poems, it seems to bring to a focus the problem of feeling in Bishop's work; and not because it seems to me (apart from "Over 2000 Illustrations" and "At the Fishhouses") her highest achievement as a poet. That distinction would have to go either to her first book, *North & South* (in which feeling keeps its intensity by a projection at times almost as visionary as Hart Crane's); or to her last, *Geography III* (in which feeling is meditated on, grandly, plainly, and in relative tranquillity, after being very slightly universalized). Let me then, in conclusion—and in lieu of the psychological speculations I have curtailed—turn back to one of the early visionary poems for Bishop's own portrait of herself as a rather special case of the poet of feeling.

In that fey creature, "The Man-Moth," are condensed several more and less familiar myths of the artist. He is *Pierrot lunaire,* the lover of the moon, of unattainable ideals and romantic strangeness; though this is a role he shares, a little, with mere ordinary Man, blindly "magnetized to the moon." On a more refined level, he suggests the Keatsian image of the artist with-

---

out personality, reducible to "a photographer's cloak" and a camera-eye. But finally and most importantly, he is the person who cannot take the outer world for granted, but must see it at the drastic extremes of process—the struggle to be born, or the menace of dying. Believing the moon to be "a small hole at the top of the sky, / proving the sky quite useless for protection," he tries, though it is "what [he] fears most,"

> to push his small head through that round clean opening
> and be forced through, as from a tube, in black scrolls on the
>   light.

(The image combines absorption into the external—photography—with self-expression—writing or painting—as it combines annihilation and birth.)

Further on, we find other metaphors for this inability to proportion the world to oneself. Motion (including, implicitly, the motion of time) becomes a nauseating vertigo: in the subway,

> the Man-Moth always seats himself facing the wrong way
> and the train starts at once at its full, terrible speed,
> without a shift in gears or a gradation of any sort.
> He cannot tell the rate at which he travels backwards.

Both actual life and the life of the psyche present themselves as a smooth, seamless, entrapping superficies ("artificial tunnels and . . . recurrent dreams"). Yet one absolute is ever-present: "the third rail, the unbroken draught of poison," which "he regards . . . as a disease / he has inherited the susceptibility to." Here, one can hardly help thinking of some of Bishop's later choices as a poet—her seamless, apparently depthless, cataloguing ("Everything only connected by 'and' and 'and'"), combined with the constant undercurrent of intimations of mortality.

Yet "The Man-Moth" ends with an extraordinarily charged and traumatic image for the expression of the inner self. As the Man-Moth, earlier, expected to be squeezed through the hole in the sky, so "one tear . . . slips" from his eye—"an entire night itself"—when a flashlight is held up to it. This tear is, in his orphaned perception, "his only possession," and, "like the bee's sting," presumably death to lose. The image can, I think, stand as our final emblem both for the peculiarly beleaguered mode of introversion or narcissism in Bishop's character, and for the way in which her feelingful self—never without some sense of trauma—entered the world in her poems. Bishop warns us that the Man-Moth will protect himself if he can: "Slyly he palms it" [the tear]

> and if you're not paying attention
> he'll swallow it. However, if you watch, he'll hand it over,
> cool as from underground springs and pure enough to drink.

Bishop did, in fact, sometimes "palm" the emotional dimension of her poems almost too successfully. But for those who knew how to pay attention, it was always there—an ambience, a *lacrimae rerum,* which, even as it presented a "pure," "cool" transparency toward things as they are, testified to the "underground" emotional personality of its creator.

1980

BONNIE COSTELLO

The Impersonal and the Interrogative in the Poetry of Elizabeth Bishop

In Elizabeth Bishop's poetry, geography is not for adventurers looking out from a center at the horizon, nor for imperialists seeking to appropriate that horizon. Rather, it is the recourse of those hoping to discover, out of the flux of images, where they are and how to get home again. Bishop's poetry accepts our uncertain relation to other times, places, and things, suggesting we have no "self" otherwise, and no home.

It is in this context that I would like to discuss the pervasiveness of the impersonal and the interrogative in her work. I want to show that, paradoxically, for Bishop, questions are assertions. However open-endedly, they structure experience and self-awareness. Like compasses, they point to something absolute we can neither see nor get to; yet in their pointing, they show us where we are. These questions, posed to an impersonal world, turn inward when it refuses to reply. Questions about the world become, then, obliquely, questions about ourselves. While the personal begins in assumptions about the self, the impersonal usually undermines or ignores the self. But in Bishop's poetry the impersonal is not depersonalized because its form is interrogative rather than negative.

These impersonal and interrogative modes tend to promote a feeling of disunity and disorientation, but for Bishop these are precisely the conditions conducive to discovery. Not surprisingly, travel is her major metaphor. Almost every poem treats the experience of travel ambivalently, for while finalities may be static or illusory, constant change is unsettling. Bishop does not resolve this ambivalence, but she eases it by offering her characters, and her readers, fleeting but calming moments of coalescence.

In discussing the significance of the impersonal and the interrogative, I will consider the entire scope of Bishop's poetic achievement. I will focus, however, on central poems from the recent volume, *Geography III,* which most fully express the positive value of these modes. The epigraph to *Geography III,* from *First Lessons in Geography,* begins with questions and answers; but the answers are soon dropped and only the questions continue. They are, we learn, firmer and more real than the answers. Bishop was always a student of geography, but her third level of geography steps back, slightly, from all the travelling, charting, and measuring, to consider the motives and impulses behind these activities. She still asks, Where is Nova Scotia? and Where is Brazil? but in the latest work she opens up previously implicit questions: *"What is a Map?"* and *"What is Geography?",* versions of: What am I doing? and What and where am I?

Such emerging self-consciousness is present in the very earliest poems, but less explicitly. "The Map" opens *North & South* with an assertion, but characteristically calls it immediately into question, into a series of questions, and these become the mode of attention throughout as Bishop looks at a printed map.

> Land lies in water; it is shadowed green.
> Shadows, or are they shallows, at its edges
> showing the line of long sea-weeded ledges
> where weeds hang to the simple blue from green.
> Or does the land lean down to lift the sea from under,
> drawing it unperturbed around itself?
> Along the fine tan sandy shelf
> is the land tugging at the sea from under?

Each observation leads to a new uncertainty and a new inquiry. These questions are never answered, but neither does the poem conclude as a personal complaint over the relativity and limitation of our interpretations. Instead, our curiosity persists. For all its ambiguity, the map engages our attention, draws us into a consideration of the world.

We can stroke these lovely bays,
    under a glass as if they were expected to blossom,
    or as if to provide a clean cage for invisible fish.

We are wrong, of course; the bays will not blossom, and the glass separates us from the object of our desire, but the imagination is not repelled by these facts. We affirm the printer's excitement, even if it does "exceed its cause." There is a pleasure in inquiry and conjecture for their own sake here; we feel no great pressure to resolve the questions posed, or to define a single perspective, a legend, by which the map can be consistently translated. The poem enjoys these very shifts of focus, from landscape to map, from map to words.

If anything, it is the imagination which is explored here, rather than the landscape. Questions put impersonally to an impersonal object turn inward. Indeed, the land is to the sea as we are to both.

    These peninsulas take the water between thumb and finger
    like women feeling for the smoothness of yard-goods.

The poem becomes, as it proceeds, an inquiry into the nature of perspective. Its conclusions are not about the land but about the map:

    Topography displays no favorites; North's as near as West.
    More delicate than the historians' are the map-makers' colors.

While the personal is initially preempted by the interrogative, questions do eventually lead us to an awareness of our situation.

The seven-year-old heroine of "In the Waiting Room," the first poem in *Geography III,* asks no questions at first, having little trouble knowing who or where she is:

            In Worcester, Massachusetts,
            I went with Aunt Consuelo
            to keep her dentist's appointment
            and sat and waited for her
            in the dentist's waiting room.

But wintery Worcester recedes into twilight, and the apparent hierarchy of time and space goes with it. Her aunt *seems* to be inside a long time, while she reads and studies the photographs of far-off places in the *National Geographic*. Then, the hinges of distance and duration come loose and the constructed self flaps precariously. The very layout of the magazine presses ordered differences into explosive proximity, forcing a violently widened definition of the human. The decorously English, well-protected "Osa and Martin Johnson / dressed in riding breeches, / laced boots, and pith helmets," stand side by side with the vulnerable and contagious "dead man slung on a pole," "babies with pointed heads," and "black, naked women" with "horrifying" breasts, creating a "perspective by incongruity" on humanity.

The child doesn't articulate her fascination, of course, but the very fact that she is "too shy to stop" implies that she is somehow brought home to herself here. She fixes her eyes on "the cover: / the yellow margins, the date" as a way of avoiding contact, but these form a fragile interface. The date, which should be a way of protecting boundaries, becomes rather, a sign of contact between this strange world and her own. She loses her balance over the side of the cover, and in a sudden moment of undifferentiation between Aunt Consuelo and herself, a cry "from inside" the dentist's office seems to come literally "from inside" her mouth. "I—we—were falling, falling, / our eyes glued to the cover / of the *National Geographic,* / February, 1918." She clings to the cover as to the rung of a ladder which has come loose from the structure supporting it. The bits and pieces of the personal ("three days / and you'll be seven years old") no longer have much meaning.

The intensity and strangeness of the experience derives not only from the slip into undifferentiation, but from the sense of difference preserved. This is not a pure moment of symbiosis, for there is always an emphasis on how "unlikely" this likeness is. The similarity between Osa and Martin Johnson and the "black, naked women" is never expressed except in the fact of juxtaposition, although the image of the volcano forces them together by its implied threat to human life. Similarly, the difference between the child and her "foolish, timid" Aunt is preserved even while it is denied by the cry of pain. This sense of differences is especially clear in the awkwardness of the child's attempts to come to terms with the experience: "you are an *I*, / you are an *Elizabeth*, / you are one of *them*." Making self both subject and predicate, she still preserves the difference.

A shocking experience of identification, as we have seen, creates a simultaneous loss of original identity, and this loss is never overcome. The inscrutable volcano, the inside of the child's mouth, the dentist's chamber, are all figures for the abyss the child has discovered, and as she peers into it she is full of questions, another and another—why? what? how?—until she is thrown back into the exclamatory "how 'unlikely'" and it is clear they will never be answered. But the transformation of question into exclamation does create a sense of recognition, even if it is the permanently strange that is recognized. We get only a "sidelong glance," not fulfillment or total recognition. Yet, for a moment, this glance does begin to organize the dualities toward some unutterable simplicity. The questions mediate between absolute difference and undifferentiation, between stillness and total flux, and in this way, however fleetingly, accommodate the self most. The experience in the dentist's office never attains a new, more genuine orientation. But in a fundamental way, the speaker is "brought home to herself" by moving through these questions, even while they are left unanswered. Indeed, many of Bishop's characters lose themselves to find themselves. Like the speaker in George Herbert's "Love Unknown," which Bishop has juxtaposed with this poem,[1] the young Elizabeth is made "new, tender, quick" through her sudden disorientation. It serves as a kind of baptism. In one sense, then, the child experiences a traumatic leap into the impersonal, the unfamiliar. But in a more profound sense, she discovers the personal. Somehow she would have been less herself, finally, if she had picked up *Dick and Jane,* a mirror of her own complacent sense of herself, rather than the *National Geographic.* Probably both were there for her on the waiting room table. But the inquisitive mind goes toward what is not obviously of the self, and it is clear that even then, Bishop was a traveller at heart.

In Bishop's poetry, such moments of confrontation, however powerful, are always transient. The pressure of the questioning pushes the room to a volcanic limit as it grows "bright / and too hot," and the child begins "sliding / beneath a big black wave, / another, and another," as if beneath a lava flow. But when the flow subsides, finally, the world is left ashen and silent. The adult vision, the dormant volcano that the child inherits, has none of the security of her childhood world of "grown-up people, / artics and overcoats, / lamps and magazines."

> Then I was back in it.
> The War was on. Outside,
> in Worcester, Massachusetts,
> were night and slush and cold,
> and it was still the fifth
> of February, 1918.

There is no stability in "night and slush and cold" and certainly none in war. In many ways the molten, self-annihilating questions are preferable to these dismally impersonal facts. For the adult narrator, memory is a way of reentering the charged moment of self-recognition, of escaping the bleak inheritance of certainty without security.

We have seen that Bishop constantly questions her surroundings, and inevitably in the process, questions her perspective. The usual comfort of home is, of course, that we can take it for granted, but for this very reason Bishop is never quite "at home." In the poem under discussion she is, in fact, in a "waiting room." There is certainly no place more impersonal. But precisely because she is not "at home," discovery is possible. A waiting room has very little definition as a place in itself—it is not a home or a destination, but only a transitional space where transitional time is spent. The object of those gathered there, what binds them, does not take place in the room they share but elsewhere, individually. And because it has no function in its own right, it is a place where anything can happen.

Most of the enclosed places Bishop describes are waiting rooms in one way or another (the most extreme being a wake). Her ports, islands, bights, are not microcosms of, or escapes from, history; they contain the tides of unity and discontinuity, of presence and absence, with much the same incompleteness as any wider experience of flux. But while they do not frame or displace the world, do not define us as a home does, they do become places to encounter the world in a focused way. In "The Bight" (from *A Cold Spring*), the speaker observes signs of an uncontainable amount of activity, crashing, soaring, scooping, all of it partaking in one way or another in an amorphous sky, shore and sea. The white boats are "not yet salvaged" and remind us of "unanswered letters." Pelicans dive "unnecessarily hard," "rarely coming up with anything to show for it." All the various efforts to grab hold of nature are "untidy," like the dredge which digs beneath what is seen and brings up not a neat bundle, but a "dripping jawful of marl." And yet Bishop seems to enjoy this messy business; it is "awful but cheerful." Like many of her poems this one finally affirms all endeavors to grasp and form and partake of the world, however insufficiently.

Bishop's characters never appear in places of origin or destination. Her poems are not without idealized dwellings, but these are only viewed from the outside, in a speculative attitude. The "cages for infinity" that Joseph Cornell created (described in a translation of Octavio Paz's "Objects and Apparitions") are seen from the outside, even in writing, for things "hurry away from their names." The proto-/crypto-dream-house of "The End of March" where otherness is happily contained in self-reflection, in the "diaphanous blue flame . . . doubled in the window," is "perfect" but "boarded up." The reality of the beach strollers is temporal, and so is their knowledge. Their vision of the house remains conjectural:

> a sort of artichoke of a house, but greener
> (boiled with bicarbonate of soda?),
> protected from spring tides by a palisade
> of—are they railroad ties?
> (Many things about this place are dubious.)
>   . . .
> There must be a stove; there *is* a chimney,
> askew, but braced with wires,
> and electricity, possibly

—at least, at the back another wire
limply leashes the whole affair
to something off behind the dunes.

The passage reveals the uncertainty with which the strollers ob-
serve this "dream house." They can only guess what it is made
of, what holds it together, or how to reconstruct it for them-
selves. There is always "something off behind the dunes," be-
yond the reach of sight and insight. It seems that the whole
world is "indrawn" this day, so that the possibility of contact is
minimal and the imagination must make much of very little. But
again, speculation is pleasurable. Since the world denies us final
access to its secrets, we are left with much speculative freedom,
not only about externals, but about ourselves as well. For the
self is as "indrawn" in the scene as everything else. The closest
the speaker gets to a stable image of herself is the house, and that
is, of course, "boarded up." Similarly, in trying to find the
"lion" that left the "lion-prints" on the beach, the strollers
imaginatively identify him with the sun, a kind of absolute, but
relative with respect to themselves, caught up in time.

Often Bishop's characters are not only displaced themselves,
but disarming to others by their conspicuous vagabondage. The
incorrigible Manuelzinho (in the poem of that name), "half
squatter, half tenant (no rent)" works on the imagination of his
mistress in spite of herself. His refusal to do as he is supposed to
do—his refusal, for instance, to call a dead man dead, to respond
to the conventional order of things—challenges the order she
works to preserve, suggesting that she too is in some fundamen-
tal way a squatter in a world that resists human interests. All the
boundaries of the personal are literally called into question. And
yet in trying to incorporate the beautifully bizarre reality of
Manuelzinho's gardens, his mistress' own world becomes more
appealing. Similarly, the "House Guest," the "sad seamstress,"
challenges the "home life" to which she won't subscribe, caus-
ing us to ask, "can it be that we nourish / one of the Fates in
our bosoms? . . . / and our fates will be like hers, / and our
hems crooked forever?" Disturbing as the presence of the house
guest is, her hosts are much more located in their sudden self-
consciousness than they ever were before, within rigid boun-

daries of property and propriety. The guest's identity is inscrutable, "her face is closed as a nut, / closed as a careful snail / or a thousand-year-old seed," but theirs have opened in her presence, partly because she is so impenetrable.

We have been dealing with the mode of the impersonal primarily in terms of theme, setting, situation. But of course the term is most applicable to a discussion of the speaker. Personal narration is precluded by Bishop's view that the self is amorphous in an amorphous world. Instead, we get a variety of distancing techniques, which bring order to the poems without belying their vision of flux, and without lending privilege to a single perspective.

Often these homeless figures are presented by a detached, third-person narrator, who sees their familiar structures foundering but can imagine a larger womblike mystery. The "Squatter's Children" "play at digging holes," at creating roots in the wider, mysterious world which is more meaningful than the "specklike house," the shelter from which their mother's voice, "ugly as sin," calls them to come in. The description repeatedly reveals their vulnerability. Their laughter, "weak flashes of inquiry," is not answered; their "little, soluble, / unwarrantable ark" will not sustain them far. And yet their questioning, digging natures are never really criticized. The narrator intrudes to affirm and reassure their "rights in rooms of falling rain." They are, in a sense, housed in the obscurity of the storm, even as the ark of their selves founders.

Above the mist, from where this impersonal narrator views the landscape, humans look as insignificant as Brueghel's Icarus. Among other things, the impersonal mode puts humanity in perspective. We are continually reminded of a reality that goes on quite aside from our human frame of reference. In "Cape Breton," signs of humanity are almost completely absorbed by the vaster landscape. A bus moves through the scene, but we never enter its frame, or follow the simple passenger who gets off and vanishes into the hills. In this deeply impersonal world, where the "thin mist follows / the white mutations of its dream" humanity looks slight and transient indeed. And yet, as in Brueghel's paintings, the human element is privileged, as a focus of interest if not power.

These detached narratives are among the most placid of Bishop's poems precisely because they put human confusion and loss, as well as human authority, "in perspective." By looking from above, they locate humanity in its wanderings. In a way they can be seen as acts of self-location. The tiny figures are our surrogates and thus soften our own pain in the midst of uncertainty. In "Squatter's Children" the narrator speaks directly out of a perspective from which obscurity no longer threatens. The children are safe in their unawareness, the speaker in a higher awareness. In a way all of these poems are "little exercises" through which we come to terms with our confusion by distancing ourselves from it momentarily. In fact, a poem like "Little Exercise" invites the reader directly into this special perspective. Everything in the scene is uneasy or precarious; but vulnerable as the "someone" is, his boat tied to a feeble mangrove root, he is "uninjured, barely disturbed." Little exercises like these give us a sense of ourselves in time which is much less threatening than immersion in a scene.

The impersonal, distanced narrator, then, admits a certain stability where experience is troubled. But Bishop never lets this perspective get complacently ironic. A "believer in total immersion," she continually returns to write poems from a more limited, more bewildered point of view. She enters the consciousness of characters lost in a world bigger than themselves or their ideas and lets them speak out of their limitations. We are invited into an intimacy with these speakers, but the impersonal mode is still doubly preserved. These are masks, not Bishop's own voice, or ours. And it is precisely the problem of the personal that these poems engage. In the dramatic monologues of "Rainy Season; Sub-Tropics" for instance, Bishop makes experience particular, while at the same time juxtaposing contradictory views in order to show the limits and errors of each.

"This is not my home," declares the Strayed Crab, much out of his element, not knowing how he got where he is. He has a very precise idea of his identity, but it is out of step with these new surroundings, and he is completely inflexible. "I admire compression, lightness, and agility, all rare in this loose world." For the Giant Toad and Giant Snail, too, the self is a source of both pride and discomfort. "I am too big. . . . Pity me," they cry. Each of these animals sings his own song to himself, re-marking on the personal beauty that he "knows" he possesses, but at the same time bemoaning his enormous hardship and disproportion, feeling his very nature a liability in a world that does not reflect or accommodate him. Isolated as these creatures are, they continually play back a sense of themselves, inquiring, recording, and tracing their own features and sensations. The external world brushes by them, but their relationship to it is defensive rather than adaptive or communicative. They with-draw into the personal rather than asking their way home. "I keep my feelings to myself," snaps the Crab. "Withdrawal is always best," mumbles the Snail. Partly because contact is so minimal, there is a good deal of discrepancy between how we perceive the animals and how they perceive themselves. Finally, they are not only lost, but self-deceived. Since we hear only the voice of each creature, our sympathy naturally goes out to him. And yet our judgment draws back at his inflexibility and defen-siveness.

We have seen how Bishop protects the reader from the disori-entation she depicts, first by impersonal narration and second by a series of masks from which we feel an ironic distance. But in *Geography III* these masks are dangerously familiar. The narra-tive distance of "In the Waiting Room" was not between a character and a creation simply, but between the poet and a memory of her past self. There, the problem of memory be-came, indirectly, another aspect of the instability of time and place. Crusoe of "Crusoe in England" is the most realized of Bishop's first person narrators, and here she allows us almost no ironic distance. Because he is human, because he is less certain in his delusions, because his is the only point of view presented, we are shipwrecked with him. Self-admiring but out of proportion, cut off from his surroundings, he is like the tropical creatures, but more aware of the relativity of his own dimensions. And his attempts to find himself are inquisitive and creative, even if they don't entirely succeed. This is the longest poem in Bishop's latest volume, one that brings together a great many of the themes, motifs, and images of her other work. Here again is the shipwreck, the self and its structures foundering in an impersonal-al reality of empty volcanoes, waves that close in (but never completely), mist, dry rock, inscrutable cries of goats and gulls. The island is an odd combination of elements from Cape Breton, scenes in the *National Geographic,* South America, all places where characters have earlier lost themselves in order to find themselves. Here again the speaker begins by putting questions to an outer world, but turns them inward from frustration. Like other characters, Crusoe tries to construct meanings "out of nothing at all, or air" when the world won't provide them; as before, such constructs fail to satisfy or protect. But more powerfully than before the experience is affirmed, despite discomfort and struggle, because of the creative, inquiring and self-reflective attitude it provides.

Defoe's Crusoe demonstrated civilized man's victory over the grandeur of nature. But Biship's Crusoe comes to land on an unresponsive, inscrutable but also uninspiring nature, in which he finds it impossible to place himself. The mist is not mysterious, but a confusion of "cloud-dump." The volcanoes are not majestic or threatening but "miserable, small" things, "dead as ash heaps." Crusoe, like the Giant Toad or Snail, feels his self to be an enormous burden, incongruous with his surroundings even while it is his solace. He can't seem to adjust his perspective to fit the proportions of the place, and he is left unsure whether the volcanoes are tiny or the goats grotesquely large.

What troubles Crusoe most about the place is its aridity, marked by the parched throats of the volcanoes. No rich "folds of lava" pour forth meaning. The most impressive features of the island, the "glittering" rollers, the "variegated" beaches, the "water spouts . . . sacerdotal beings of glass," invite no human association or romantic continuity. Seen as "glass," even water cannot be absorbed. All these features are "beautiful, yes, but not much company," pure abstract forms without sympathy. Even hostile otherness would be preferable to this inactive indifference, this monotonous world of white goats and gulls and oblivious lumbering turtles, of endless repetition:

> I still can't shake
> them from my ears; they're hurting now.
> The questioning shrieks, the equivocal replies
> over a ground of hissing rain

and hissing, ambulating turtles
got on my nerves.

Crusoe wonders if the goats think him one of their own kind, that they speak to him thus. But his mind cannot embrace these alien forms. He projects the structures of his own language onto theirs, imagining their cries as questions and replies. But they are never realized as such, for insofar as the cries are perceived in human terms, they are only echoes of his own questions, addressed only to himself. Similarly, Crusoe christens the volcano "*Mount d'Espoir* or *Mount Despair*," imposing positive and negative values on the landscape; but it will never verify any of this, as he is reminded by the blank, horizontal gaze of the goat, "expressing nothing" ("or a little malice" perhaps, since value is inevitable in human interpretation).

Crusoe tries to personalize an impersonal world, and of course his questions aren't answered. So he keeps coming back to the impersonal value-free "reality" of the landscape. But the mind cannot settle on such reductions; it seeks presence, and intersubjectivity. Since he cannot personalize his present surroundings, he infuses them with nostalgic feeling, converting the landscape to symbols of an elsewhere created more in his own image. But such symbolization remains mere simile or allegory where the distance between thing and sign is preserved. The turtles hiss like teakettles, but fail to be experienced as real teakettles just as they fail to be experienced as real turtles. The snail shells (empty vehicles) look like iris beds, and when the gulls fly up at once

they sounded
like a big tree in a strong wind, its leaves.
I'd shut my eyes and think about a tree,
an oak, say, with real shade, somewhere.

But the reality of the island keeps intruding on Crusoe's dream of home. The wish remains a pastoral one and fails as an act of self-location. Indeed, for Crusoe nostalgia adds a temporal displacement to the spatial one. Historic continuity is just as much disrupted as visual perspective. Crusoe "remembers" lines from

Wordsworth, written chronologically after his lifetime. His expectation that returning to England will set things right, that he can look it up when he gets home, ignores the fundamental displacement of his existence in time and space. There is no correlation between his internal sense of order and external reality.

The first theme of Crusoe, then, is that human order imposed on the landscape never "takes" as real presence. But neither does the landscape answer our questions about its objective order. (We hear in "Twelfth Morning; or What You Will": "Don't ask the big white horse, *Are you supposed / to be inside the fence or out?* He's still / asleep. Even awake, he probably / remains in doubt.") The second, related theme is that we must ask of ourselves the questions Crusoe asks: "'Do I deserve this? I suppose I must. / . . . Was there / a moment when I actually chose this? / I don't remember, but there could have been.'"

When the mind fails to find external objectifications it necessarily turns inward for its comfort. Bishop's position on such gestures is ambivalent. On the one hand they are surrenders to solipsism; on the other hand, they are all the meaning we can manage. From "Crusoe" it seems that self-explanation, achieved with self-awareness and humility, is justified. Like the Toad, Snail, and Crab, Crusoe begins explaining himself to himself; indeed, like the Snail he carries his own house around with him. But unlike the tropical creatures, he does more than complain or flatter himself; he attempts to construct a home out of the alien materials. Since his surroundings cannot be appropriated, and fail even to register his existence, he creates his own world to reflect himself in. Where love is not offered externally, he discovers self-love: "I felt a deep affection for / the smallest of my island industries." He rejoices over "home-brew" (imagination?) and his weird flute (poetry?).

But as a hero of self-consciousness, Crusoe sees the limits of his creations, and this in turn limits his ability to rejoice in them. The affection is based on an idea of free will and the autonomy and presence of the self which he cannot substantiate. "Reciting to my iris-beds," to his created, imagined correspondents (not even to the snail shells which gave rise to his metaphor), "'They flash upon that inward eye,'" he cannot finish the gesture; "'which is the bliss . . .' The bliss of what?" The iris beds never verify his inward existence since they are projections to begin with. They never fill in the blanks of the books he reads, precisely because the answers are fundamentally subjective: ". . . of solitude." The inward eye is precisely that blank center around which all questions are formed. And as long as that primary question of the self, of solitude, remains unanswered, so do all the others. The "smallest of my island industries," but that which gives all the others their efficacy, is a "miserable philosophy" about the authority and originality of the self. The awareness that the self, too, is created ("Home-made, home-made! But aren't we all?") limits the power of all other inventions. However frustrating this may be to Crusoe, Bishop does not finally negate these inventions: by confronting an impersonal world in an inquisitive attitude, we do not verify our own values or self-images, but neither do we replace these constructions with anything else. What we gain, what is missing without this experience of disorientation, is a clearer awareness of the relative nature of our identities and our creations. Such self-consciousness is positive, though it may be disturbing in that it disrupts our notion of the genuineness and discreteness of the self. Finally, to locate ourselves in the world, we need *both* to carve out definitions and to know their limitations.

Crusoe does, in a way, experience "the bliss of solitude," but not as Wordsworth might, in communion with nature, which reveals the truth of the subjective. Experiencing a harsh isolation of things from each other ("The island had one kind of everything"), Crusoe resorts to a kind of self-doubling, a dialogue with the self, the interior version of the charity he cannot acquire elsewhere.

> I often gave way to self-pity.
>   . . .
> What's wrong about self-pity, anyway?
> With my legs dangling down familiarly
> over a crater's edge, I told myself
> "Pity should begin at home." So the more
> pity I felt, the more I felt at home.

Bishop recognizes that narcissism is an essential aspect of self-definition. Dangling over the meaningless, strange crater,

Crusoe is the only familiar thing, so self-pity creates all the sense of home there is. Like "the moon in the bureau mirror" of "Insomnia," "by the Universe deserted, / *she*'d tell it to go to hell, / and she'd find a body of water, / or a mirror, on which to dwell."

Acts of self-creation go on throughout Bishop's poems, and though they are always incomplete, they are nevertheless affirmed steps toward self-consciousness, toward the questioning process. "Why didn't I know enough of something? / Greek drama or astronomy?" The self-splitting habit of "The Gentleman of Shalott" produces an "exhilarating" sense of "uncertainty." "He loves / that sense of constant re-adjustment." Bishop loves it too, as the structure of human experience. Self-knowledge remains tentative and incomplete at best, like the flow created in the divided heart of "The Weed." But that flow is vital and regenerative; the Toad, Crab, and Snail, for all their beauties, do not take a questioning or creative attitude, so they are simply lost in contradiction, stuck in the phase of self-pity.

Self-pity cannot provide a certain home for Crusoe, because finally it only perpetuates the echo, the greatest source of his anxiety. Self-repetition is not much more intimate, in the long run, than the rain's "echolalia," registered formally in the repetition of lines and phrases so frequent in Bishop's poetry. Musical in moderation, the "weaving, weaving," "glittering and glittering," can become a little eerie. The hermit in "Chemin de Fer" lives in a totally self-reflexive world, and thus lives perpetually in echoes. But Crusoe does not become so static in his self-pity. Even when his efforts to partake of the larger world fail, we admire them.

Many of Bishop's poems deal with love as a way of silencing the echo. Crusoe dreams of partaking of the external world, of "food / and love," when he is not having nightmares about the endless reproduction of experience, of "frogs' eggs turning into polliwogs / of islands." And when Friday comes there is even a moment of nearly realized love. Friday offers Crusoe his only access to the external world, for "at home" in the wilderness but also human, Friday is a kind of mediator. He almost promises to end difference without repetition. But it's not a productive love; the difference isn't adequate to create a new unity out of self and objective world. "If only he had been a woman!" Indeed, interpersonal love remains a pastoral ideal in Bishop just as much as solitude does. All of the poems that raise the question of love deal with separation and loss, destruction and attachment as equal impulses. Friday dies at the end, precisely because Crusoe has drawn him into his own world; he dies of measles, a European disease.

We do not find a permanent home, then, in dates and names, not in exalted strangeness, not in nostalgia, not in self-created surroundings, not in self-pity; not even in love. Questions persist past all these closures. And yet all these failed attempts at comfort seem preferable to the permanent home offered by despair or total withdrawal. The "rescuers" take Crusoe out of a situation which ultimately proves to be the source of vitality; for vitality, it seems, is one with the struggle to survive, to find oneself, or make a place for oneself.

At the time of the narration, Crusoe is, as the title indicates, "in England," home again. We would expect that homecoming to be the subject of the poem, and yet all but three stanzas deal with Crusoe's experience of shipwreck on a strange island. The point the title makes, of course, is that England is no more "home" than the place of miserable empty volcanoes. In this version of the Crusoe story, civilization is not exalted over nature. England, the object of Crusoe's nostalgia, is familiar and thus "real" enough, but nothing like his dreams of home. Like the narrator at the end of "In the Waiting Room," Crusoe knows where he is, but now he can barely inhabit that static, barren place. Here, he desires that continual struggle he so much hated before. Once he was tormented by the endless repetition of experience, having nightmares of islands, "knowing that I had to live / on each and every one, eventually, / for ages, registering their flora, / their fauna, their geography." Now, ironically, "that archipelago / has petered out," and he is bored and dismayed, longing again for the struggle. Nostalgia persists as part of the human character, transferred now to the former center of pain. He has moved from questions of place and purpose to questions of the past, as he tries to locate himself now in terms of his former hardships. In England the objects of his past have lost all the moisture of vitality; they are empty symbols. For

Crusoe the island is "un-rediscovered, un-renamable." He feels the failure of imagination to give presence to the past: "None of the books has ever got it right." And yet the story *he* tells does become authentic, even in reviving images of desire. For all his world-weariness, Crusoe does succeed in gathering a sense of self precisely *in* images of desire.

Clearly, Bishop does not believe in settling down. We never "find ourselves" in any stable location, but rather in transit. As all her critics point out, travel is her natural, dominant metaphor for the human condition. Even dreams, which we associate with wish-fulfillment, are, in Bishop's poetry, revelations of our homeless natures. The majority of Bishop's poems deal directly with the experience of travel, and none of them posit a secure home from which the characters have departed or an ideal destination toward which they move. Perhaps this is why it took the "prodigal" "a long time / finally to make his mind up to go home." The glorious images the explorers in "Brazil, January 1, 1502" look for are already out of fashion at home. Miss Breen of "Arrival at Santos" is a retired, seventy-year-old policewoman. "Home" no longer accommodates any of them, if it ever did. Indeed, Miss Breen's "home, when she is at home, is in Glens Fall / s New York" (with a hint of The Fall, by the dropping of the s). The travel poems reinforce the point that the search for origins and ideals is our way of structuring thought, of organizing experience and thereby locating ourselves. Like questions which have no answers but nevertheless give us a point of orientation, a concept of origins and destinations shapes our personal lives which would otherwise diffuse into impersonal landscapes.

Arrivals, for Bishop, are always starting points. Either a place does not excite us as we had hoped, or it dissolves or retreats on approach. In "From the Country to the City," for instance, the solidity of the endpoint becomes instead an array of tiny lights, as the road seems interminable. Arriving at Santos, two women find not the sublime nature they had imagined, but "self-pitying mountains," and "frivolous greenery," "feeble pink" warehouses and "uncertain palms," all drearily in between the comforts of home and an exotic wilderness. Their "quest" is "answered" with the same confusion they thought they had left behind.

> Oh, tourist,
>
> is this how this country is going to answer you
>
> and your immodest demands for a different world,
> and a better life, and complete comprehension
> of both at last, and immediately,
> after eighteen days of suspension?

The arrival immediately becomes a departure as the "tender," the "strange and ancient craft," comes and they prepare for "driving to the interior," literally and figuratively.

The poem expresses a fundamental ambivalence about this quest, since the ladies, while they want the "different world," are uneasy as they climb down the ladder backwards and hope that "the customs officials will speak English . . . / and leave us our bourbon and cigarettes." And yet the poem also accepts the essential ephemerality of all domesticities; all homes are in a way only waiting rooms, or in this case ports, which leave us in suspension, where experience is not grasped but used up, like "soap, or postage stamps— / wasting away like the former, slipping the way the latter / do when we mail the letters we wrote on the boat." In one sense this makes "driving to the interior" an idle impulse, since that completely comprehended "different world" is a fiction. And yet there does seem to be something attractive about the image of these two women moving with the natural drift of their lives, rather than resisting it.

In "In the Waiting Room," in "Crusoe," as in all the poems about travel, then, we discover not only that we are lost, but that there never *was* and never will be a home in any stable sense. Home is a fiction, a projection of an ideal state. In "Questions of Travel" Bishop both celebrates travel as leading to self-consciousness, and conversely declares there is no alternative to travel for the self-conscious person. The poem comes full circle to explain itself. In that sense it is not only a reflection on travel but a journey in its own right, like the other journeys Bishop has described.

In many ways at once, the poem "Questions of Travel" is central in Bishop's work, for it both comments on and repeats the structure of the other poems. It again deals with travel, and with the feeling of being lost, overwhelmed by change. It is structured in a series of observations that generate questions rather than answers. And again, the questions move increasingly inward, so that the quest for the external world becomes a quest for the self. The self-reflection at the end of the poem is affirmative in mood, even while it is interrogative in form.

The poem opens in complaint and regret, but as the questions push against the unfamiliar world they become more enraptured:

> What childishness is it that while there's a breath of life
> in our bodies, we are determined to rush
> to see the sun the other way around?
> The tiniest green hummingbird in the world?
> To stare at some inexplicable old stonework,
> inexplicable and impenetrable,
> at any view,
> instantly seen and always, always delightful?

It is not surprising that she turns to consider what has been gained rather than what was lost, or rather, what would have been lost if they'd stayed home, since loss faces them either way. What would have been lost is not contact with nature in its pure form, but (as the examples reveal) a glimpse of human history, however blurred and inconclusive. By the end of the poem she is celebrating the inevitable. It would have been a pity "never to have had to listen to rain." Choice is no longer an issue. And what she finds in the rain is not the rain itself, but a moment of awakened self-consciousness:

> two hours of unrelenting oratory
> and then a sudden golden silence
> in which the traveller takes a notebook, writes

and the poem comes around to its original questions, with the difference that it finally asks, not only: "Should we have stayed at home" but: Where is home? Home seems to be in question, or rather, in questioning.

But travel without pause is tiring and unsatisfying. The problem of these poems becomes how to present moments of rest and coalescence which nonetheless preserve the sense that our condition is inherently restless. Bishop's solution is to create places, objects, figures representing a unity around which we collect ourselves, but at the same time symbolizing our transience. The double function of these images satisfies our ambivalence about travel. The self is kept expansive even while it experiences a needed coalescence.

The "strangest of theatres" at which the characters of "Questions of Travel" arrive, for example, reflects their own condition of motion and confusion. The "streams and clouds keep travelling, travelling, / the mountains look like the hulls of capsized ships." The waterfalls even look like "tearstains." Surely the "strangers in a play" these travellers are watching are themselves. An early poem, "The Imaginary Iceberg," expresses this same sense of self-reflective destination especially well, for here an object in nature begins to correspond to the soul. This poem recognizes how a search for the most impersonal ideal is finally a search for the personal. Nothing could be less human than an iceberg, and yet it causes the "soul" to coalesce. We do not depart from the ship, from language, altogether at such moments, but like questions, these experiences let us look into a nonverbal center. The experience of travel toward a noncontingent endpoint is a kind of ideal condition, for the self is neither dispersed to total disorder, nor confined to static order. The imaginary iceberg, like Death, like Nature, like any absolute alterity, gives shape to the sailor's drift, just as the idea of the "Soul" gives shape to the self. Imagining an absolute other is always a way of imagining an absolute self. Perhaps this is why we are attracted in "Questions of Travel" to the "inexplicable old stonework, / inexplicable and impenetrable, / at any view, / instantly seen and always, always delightful." There is no limit here, but neither is there complete flux. Another poem, "The Fish," makes clear that these moments of sudden awareness depend upon the extension as well as the retention of difference. Here the narrator confronts, embodied in a fish she has caught, a universe of other parasitical life, and an infinite past of other similar encounters, thus locating herself in relation to other life and history.

All these are examples of the sudden feeling of home. The strange is suddenly familiar; history and change are brought into immediate focus and coherence. But of course, time and space cannot really be concentrated; the poems draw us back into extension. Though victory fills up the little rented boat in "The Fish," it is not properly ours, and we must let the fish go. "The power to relinquish what one would keep, that is freedom," wrote Marianne Moore, and it seems to be a maxim Bishop took to heart. The pain of loss and confusion is never trivialized in her poems, and yet it is overpowered by a sense of the value of process. "The art of losing's not too hard to master / though it may look like (*Write* it!) like disaster." In mastering the art of losing we master ourselves.

Possession is not the highest of goals for Bishop, but rather, engagement with the world and with one's self through inquiry, even when distance and difference result. The speaker of "Five Flights Up" may feel a certain envy for the bird or dog, without shame, without memory, their "Questions—if that is what they are— / answered directly, simply, / by day itself." In the human world distances are not so easily overcome; questions persist beyond all presences. And yet there is no preference for the nonhuman here. Acts of memory may indeed aggravate our losses, but they may also, like brief encounters with the strange, offer experiences of a sudden coalescence of feelings and associations.

"Poem" celebrates such an active concentration even while it fails to unite the self fully with the past or with others. We do not gain anything in such activities (the painting that here triggers memory may look like a dollar bill, but it is "useless and free") except perhaps self-location. The poem proceeds in a series of conjectures and questions, moments of identification and moments of separation. As a vessel of memory, the painting connects the speaker to a multiple past, not only to a scene but to those who have witnessed that scene, and even to those others through whose hands the picture has passed. None of these contacts is complete; each reach of the imagination beyond the present is curtailed by surface interruption. But at a certain juncture, the boundaries of the sign and the thing become obscure; we feel at once the retention and extension of difference. Representation fails to realize the world; thought remains in questions. And yet in questioning we briefly reach an ultimate question: "life and the memory of it so compressed / they've turned into each other. Which is which?" The poem never transcends the flux of things, the distances of time and space, but in the alternation of our thought in surface and depth, in pasts and presences, there exists a certain sudden feeling of well-being: "how live, how touching. . . ."

It is just such a feeling of well-being that the bus passengers experience in "The Moose." The poem brings together all the elements—disorientation, dream, travel, sudden strange appearances, memory—which the other poems, in various combinations, introduce. All are elements that help us lose ourselves in order to find ourselves. In "The Moose," the stability of the homeland is transformed into a locus of gentle flux, and the journey begins, travel in space corresponding here to travel in time, to memory. The passengers are again surrounded by fog, by a drowsy confusion, but as the distant narrator, looking sympathetically down on them, knows, it is a homey kind of confusion, softening the "hairy, scratchy, splintery . . . impenetrable wood[s]." Out of this oblivion we overhear a conversation "in Eternity," about pain and loss, where things are "cleared up finally," where an unqualified "yes" is possible. This is not the voice of the people on the bus, nor do they hear it except in a vague dream, and yet it belongs to them as their heritage. And as the moose emerges from the wood, simple in her otherworldliness, an emblem of all that the Grandparents have accepted, the passengers do not understand the relation they have to it, and yet they are moved by it. Strange as it is, it is also "homely as a house / (or, safe as houses.)" It offers them a sudden feeling of liberation but also of placement. They coalesce for an instant around this mystery. And like the experience in the waiting room, this one is never defined but only embraced in a question the travellers ask, a question about their own natures and identities:

> Why, why do we feel
> (we all feel) this sweet
> sensation of joy?

The impersonal and the interrogative are essential and pervasive characteristics of Bishop's style, linked by their common source in her uncertain, exploratory relation to the world. Inherent in them are certain aesthetic problems with which she has had to grapple. Since these poems lack the intimacy which urges our attention in other lyrics, they risk our indifference or our disbelief. In her early poetry, Bishop tries to surmount this problem by contriving a "we," "I" and "you" who interact, but only distantly. The impersonal requires that images speak for themselves, and at times in the early work, they are too reticent. But the details that introduce "The Moose" accumulate quietly, so that even while we are taken by surprise when events suddenly lift into dream, we are not disturbed because we have been guided by a silent ordering presence. Bishop does not falsify her sense of our situation by interpreting all the details she sets adrift towards us. But neither do we feel entirely alone in the wilderness she creates.

At its weakest, the interrogative mode seems a tic, as pat as any assertion it might overturn. In "The Map" and in "The Monument," some of the questions seem contrived. But in "Filling Station," "Faustina," and "First Death in Nova Scotia," the questions emerge from a change of consciousness; in *Geography III,* they always seem genuine. We come to poetry with the desire for wholeness and order, and the poet of the interrogative mode must somehow satisfy that need without reducing experience to simple answers. When it works, this is Bishop's greatest poetic achievement: to give us satisfaction even as she remains elusive and reticent, even as she reveals that the question is the final form. For through the impersonal mode she makes the questions our own, our most valued possessions, the very form of our identity.

1977

NOTE

1. Richard Howard, ed., *Preferences: 51 American Poets Choose Poems from Their Own Work and from the Past* (New York: Viking, 1974), pp. 27–31.

LLOYD SCHWARTZ

One Art
The Poetry of Elizabeth Bishop, 1971–1976

There is more continuity between *North & South,* Elizabeth
Bishop's first book, and the nine new poems of *Geography III,*
her latest, than the familiar and central image of travel. The new
poems dramatize even more painstakingly what is perhaps the
most fundamental issue in all of her poetry—seeing the ways
nothing about living in the human world is or can ever be sim-
ple: how isolation may be as necessary as communication; how
looking back may be as comforting—or as terrible—as looking
ahead, or around. We need to do what her Gentleman of Shalott
seems to enjoy so much—"constantly re-adjust" our vision of
the world and what we can get from it. That is what these
poems so poignantly and so powerfully do. And as they illumi-
nate, and consolidate, earlier interests and techniques, as they
insist on their *similarity* to the earlier works, they reveal *them* to
be more "felt," less "objective," more "serious" than we may
have assumed.

   The title *North & South* expressed both the literal and meta-
phorical implications of Elizabeth Bishop's most persistent im-
age. The world is full of differences, contrasts, and contradic-
tions—icebergs and burning decks, Wellfleet and Shalott.
"Half" may be "enough" for the Gentleman of Shalott, but it
doesn't seem to be sufficient for his author. For it is one world:
the civilized mechanical toy horse, with which the speaker in
"Cirque d'Hiver" identifies so poignantly, is as humanly rele-
vant as its opposite, the wild Dionysian landscape of "Florida"
(which it directly precedes in *North & South*). Her poems say
"North's as near as West" ("The Map," 1935); "Everything

First printed in *Ploughshares* 3, nos. 3 & 4 (1977), pp. 30–52.

[Newfoundland, Rome, Mexico, Morocco, Ireland] only connected by 'and' and 'and'" ("Over 2000 Illustrations and a Complete Concordance," 1948); any place is a starting point: *"Should we have stayed at home, / wherever that may be?"* ("Questions of Travel," 1956).

"In the Waiting Room," the first of the new poems to come out (July 1971), presents a disturbing answer to the disturbing questions raised in the earlier poems, as well as a consolidation of the issues themselves, in the most explicit and dramatic terms.

The connotations of the title are ambiguous, suggesting both a literal and a metaphorical situation. This is a poem of initiation, of a child, "an *Elizabeth,*" beginning to learn what it means to live in the world, to be a human being, to be an adult. She is literally in a dentist's waiting room, but she is also on a metaphorical threshold, and remains poised there at the end of the poem, having made discoveries that only the adult Elizabeth Bishop truly comprehends. Throughout the poem, a double perspective—the child's and the adult's—is subtly and consistently interwoven. It is an adult narrating, but an adult who is capable of reliving the point of view of the child, herself as a child.

Not unlike other poems by Elizabeth Bishop, "In the Waiting Room" opens with a scene, concretely visualized—a dentist's waiting room seen by a child waiting for her aunt:

> The waiting room
> was full of grown-up people,
> arctics and overcoats,
> lamps and magazines.

The voice is the child's—intelligent, perceptive, shy. She becomes engrossed in the *National Geographic,* also concretely described ("I looked at the cover: / the yellow margins, the date"), as are its contents—a volcano, cannibals, explorers. The perspectives here get very complex. The images in the *National Geographic* are pictures within a scene within a poem, descriptions *within* descriptions. Changes in levels of diction shift the point of view. There is the child's naivete and candidness ("grown-up people"; "I could read"; "I read it right straight through"). Even the similes suggest the homely comparisons a child might make ("black, naked women with necks / wound round and round with wire / like the necks of light bulbs"). And yet there are perceptions about the child's reactions only an adult could articulate ("Their breasts were horrifying"; "I was too shy to stop"), and the use of "grown-up" words like "arctics," or "pith helmets," or "rivulets of fire."

These shifting perspectives refuse to allow us to remain complacently satisfied with literalism. The "sense of constant re-adjustment" (as the Gentleman of Shalott would say), reminds us that all this both "really happened" and is "only a poem." Troilus says "this is and is not Cressid," and he is right. Nietzsche referred to the "Janus face" of every great insight: it is overwhelming to perceive how different, how "other," the exotic tribesmen and women are from the local, ordinary people in a waiting room—ourselves; and yet we are "all just one." What "happens" in the poem is how we get from one point of view to the other, how both of these perspectives are true.

The central event in the poem is almost a mystical experience, a kind of "ecstasy" in reverse. Instead of the girl's soul *leaving* her body, another's enters it, takes possession of it. The girl hears her aunt cry out "from inside"—"an *oh!* of pain . . . not very loud or long." She maintains her critical distance:

> I wasn't at all surprised;
> even then I knew she was
> a foolish, timid woman.
> I might have been embarrassed,
> but wasn't.

What takes her "completely by surprise" is that the cry is coming from within herself—"it was *me:* / my voice, in my mouth. . . . I was my foolish aunt." There is no explanation, no cause given. The two women, "I—we," have become one, confused, compounded, inseparable. The revelation is no comfort. Suddenly the child has lost her identity. This is dangerous, frightening—"the sensation of falling off / the round, turning world / into cold, blue-black space." The child tries to regain control of herself by concentrating on what is familiar—the date, her age. But soon the revelation arouses her curiosity; she begins to question:

> But I felt: you are an *I*,
> you are an *Elizabeth,*
> you are one of *them.*
> *Why* should you be one, too?
> I scarcely dared to look
> to see what it was I was.

Having an individual identity not only separates her from the others, it also does *not* separate her from others, who also have identities:

> I knew that nothing stranger
> had ever happened, that nothing
> stranger could ever happen.

The question of identity is more complicated yet. Why should we each have our own identity? Why should we exist?

> Why should I be my aunt,
> or me, or anyone?

The similarities go far beyond the perimeters of the family, or of the waiting room (which she begins to scrutinize with renewed interest). The grotesque, foreign beings in the *National Geographic* are also part of this bewildering unity. "What similarities . . . held us all together / or made us all just one?" There is something tense, something precarious in this unification. Could it all become *un*done, fall apart?

> How—I didn't know any
> word for it—how "unlikely" . . .
> How had I come to be here,
> like them, and overhear
> a cry of pain that could have
> got loud and worse but hadn't?

"How had I come to be *here*?" At this moment, the poet identifies totally with herself as a child. For an adult the question of pain, endurance, is a fundamental question—one of the very things that "makes us all just one." For the child, the questions are too hard—overwhelming. She can't get a grip on them. The waiting room seems to slide "beneath a big black wave, / another, and another," like the shores of the whole earth itself. The perspective changes again, to the poet herself, looking back in time at the specific place and date and details—so ordinary, so unique and memorable—the moment "in the waiting room" of her first questioning perception about the self and its relation to others and to the world, her first frightening awareness of her own individuality and the equally frightening awareness of her common humanity.

"Crusoe in England" contains similar issues in a vast metaphorical dramatic monologue. Just as the young "Elizabeth" can no longer feel at home either in the commonplace world of her hometown or in the terrifying one far from it, because there is no escape from either; so this latter-day Crusoe (he quotes Wordsworth, ironically unable to remember the word "solitude" in "I wandered lonely as a cloud"), is tormented by memories of his isolation, yet can no longer feel comfortable in the "real" world.

What seems most remarkable in this long poem is the complexity of feelings Elizabeth Bishop succeeds in conveying. The terror as well as the liberation of loneliness; pride; self-pity; self-irony:

> I felt a deep affection for
> the smallest of my island industries.
> No, not exactly, since the smallest was
> a miserable philosophy.

Contempt for the barren, exotic world of exile is sometimes inseparable from fascination with the bizarre natural phenomena—even awe:

> Well, I had fifty-two
> miserable, small volcanoes I could climb

with a few slithery strides—
volcanoes dead as ash heaps.

. . .

I'd think that if they were the size
I thought volcanoes should be, then I had
become a giant;
and if I had become a giant,
I couldn't bear to think what size
the goats and turtles were . . . .

Nostalgia and loathing—like the two names he had for a volcano, "*Mont d'Espoir* or *Mount Despair!* / (I'd time enough to play with names)"—there are infinite possibilities, infinite variety, "the island had one kind of everything." But the piquant irony is that there is only one of each kind, no partners: beauty—"yes, but not much company." Each possibility contains its own limitation. There is a kind of proprietary interest—he is the sole historian of the god-forsaken place:

my poor old island's still
un-rediscovered, un-renamable.
None of the books has ever got it right.

But he also dreams of the horror of "infinities / of islands, islands spawning islands" and "knowing that I had to live / on each and every one, eventually, / for ages, registering their flora, / their fauna, their geography." Being the historian of a microcosm, or rather the cartographer ("More delicate than the historians' are the map-makers' colors," Elizabeth Bishop wrote at the end of "The Map"), provides the main interest, the *raison d'etre* for keeping alive, both on the island and back in civilization. But the responsibility, the inescapability of the effort is, literally, a nightmare.

Crusoe finds a partner, Friday; but though great, it is only a limited affection they can share:

If only he had been a woman!
I wanted to propagate my kind,
and so did he, I think, poor boy.

Yet when "one day they came and took us off," there is still no mention of marriage. "England" is just "another island." The island itself was real, but it was also a metaphor—for exile, isolation, independence, loneliness, self-contemplation. In England, even Friday has died.

Elizabeth Bishop usually writes in her own voice—there are few personae (the "Riverman," the "Colored Singer," "Jerónimo"). "Crusoe" is one of the exceptions to the particularly and emphatically personal voice of the recent poems; so the implications of the choice of this mode are especially revealing. First of all, though most of her poems are not "spoken" by other characters, she often presents herself in a dramatic situation or scene—"The Fish," "The Weed," "Roosters," "Faustina"— these among her masterpieces. "Crusoe" more clearly, more fully than any of the other "character" poems illustrates how useful it is to think of the personal lyrics as metaphorical monologues. These poems are no more simply confessions or self-defensive anecdotes than is "Crusoe"; they are moments of revelation, and models of the process of revelation.

The "fiction" of a "Crusoe" also provides another vantage point from which to see the more directly personal poems. When in "One Art," for example, Elizabeth Bishop writes of losing "two cities, lovely ones. And, vaster, / some realms I owned, two rivers, a continent," she has already indicated, in "Crusoe," that this can also be true of another person. Crusoe's final stoical reticence at his loss of Friday is a paradigm reflected again in "One Art," the only other poem in this group to deal with the loss of a person. Losing "the joking voice, a gesture / I love," like losing Friday, may seem a "disaster," but may be endurable nevertheless. Creating a fiction may have even allowed her to make the kinds of statements she makes in "One Art," to say something that is true of herself because she has already said it is true of someone else. The fictional monologue becomes both a useful parable against which we can measure "truth," and a way of suggesting (as a parallel to it) how a poem in which something "really happened" may function as a parable. In either case, "Crusoe in England" is the most emotionally exhaustive study of a single character in all of Elizabeth Bishop's poetry—even more impressive because it is the result of a capacity for total empathy. And it is all the more moving because the concerns of the character, of "Crusoe," are so directly connected to the concerns Elizabeth Bishop expresses in her own voice.

One of the many ironies of "Crusoe in England" is the way one may become nostalgic about what was essentially painful. "In the Waiting Room" has this kind of painful nostalgia—for the exciting and terrible moment when the child first perceived the tragic "complexities" she will eventually have to deal with. In these poems this nostalgia is not self-deception, but an awareness of the profound dilemma created by the question of how much pain we require, how trapped we need to be, to find the fullest life.

> I'm old.
> I'm bored, too, drinking my real tea,
> surrounded by uninteresting lumber.
> The knife there on the shelf—
> it reeked of meaning, like a crucifix.
> It lived.

The nostalgia of "The Moose" is of a different order. No less aware of herself, the poet looks back to her origins, her roots— as she is both literally and figuratively moving away from them, moving south from Nova Scotia, from the "narrow provinces / of fish and bread and tea." "Home-made, home-made! But aren't we all?" Crusoe says. "*Home, / wherever that may be,*" is the final question of travel.

The entire first half of "The Moose" is the movement of "goodbye," the movement away from "home," "home of the long tides," "red, gravelly roads," "rows of sugar maples," "clapboard farmhouses / and neat, clapboard churches." It is "goodbye to the elms, / to the farm, to the dog," as "a lone traveller" bids farewell to "seven relatives" while "a collie supervises." It is a leisurely journey, with plenty of opportunity to observe the passing scene—the villages, the people, the natural setting,—especially the natural setting. The first three stanzas are largely concerned with the "long tides"—the bay meeting the river "coming in," "not at home"; or the sun "silted red," creating a "red sea," giving the "lavender, rich mud" veins of "burning rivulets." There is something primordial about this scene, elemental, existing before villages, houses, people—the ultimate "home."

The names of the Nova Scotia towns—"Bass River," "the Economies— / Lower, Middle, Upper; / Five Islands, Five Houses"—have a homely sound, humorous in their literalness. The tone changes gradually with the change in the quality of light. In the "moonlight,"·the woods of New Brunswick feel like slightly sinister homespun and firewood, "hairy, scratchy, splintery." Inside the bus, passengers have begun to fall asleep:

> Snores. Some long sighs.
> A dreamy divagation
> begins in the night,
> a gentle, auditory,
> slow hallucination. . . .

In this state of trance, the night-voices of the people on the bus blend into the voices of the past in the poet's mind, her Grandparents—everyone's grandparents—talking simultaneously "in the old featherbed" and "in Eternity." They are detached—they share the detachment of the gods—commenting on what is past, or passing, or to come; births, marriages, illnesses, deaths:

> half groan, half acceptance,
> that means "Life's like that.
> We know *it* (also death)."

The hallucination is comforting—"it's all right now / even to fall asleep"—a vision, all-knowing, of protection and peace. One can become a child again, regain innocence, believe in God, safety, comfort; life and death can be accepted, because they fit into the scheme of things.

It is at this moment the bus stops, "suddenly . . . with a jolt." The dream of the past is interrupted by the unexpected present. A huge she-moose "has come out of / the impenetrable wood" and, like an apparition, "looms . . . in the middle of the road." Potentially dangerous, it turns out to be "perfectly harmless . . .", similar to things we find familiar, comfortable:

> high as a church,
> homely as a house
> (or, safe as houses).

But it is also mysteriously similar to the hallucination: "grand, otherworldly" on the "moonlit macadam." It too like the Grandparents in their featherbed, seems beyond time.

> Why, why do we feel
> (we all feel) this sweet
> sensation of joy?

This confrontation—in some ways like the poet's confrontation with the huge, venerable, ancient fish in "The Fish"—with the past, with natural innocence, with the timeless is both comic and touching. It's funny to think of the moose investigating the bus, sniffing at the hood as if at one of its own kind. But the one thing the moose is *not* like is the bus, the vehicle carrying us away from home, from childhood, from protection, from grace. It is this difference with which we are left:

> a dim
> smell of moose, an acrid
> smell of gasoline.

The bus leaves the moose behind on the "moonlit macadam."

The "dream of protection and rest" of "Faustina" might define the sense of sweetness, freedom, protection, comfort, and rest that the Grandparents, the moose, the primeval landscape of Nova Scotia offer. In "Faustina," this dream poses a "cruel black / coincident conundrum," for it may also mean for the white woman "the unimaginable nightmare"—the horror of entrapment, or death. In "The Moose" the attractiveness of the dream is less ambiguous, but less possible as anything we can live with. We are ineluctably drawn away from the dream; confrontation with it is momentary grace. It is sweet, and necessary, to remember where we are from; but home is also the place we have to leave.

It is with ambivalence that the poet greets what she leaves *for* and goes *to*. This ambivalence is what both "Night City" and

"12 O'Clock News" are concerned with. One of Elizabeth Bishop's earliest poems (1937) was "From the Country to the City," developing an elaborate conceit in which the topography of a highway approaching a city is compared to a harlequin, "wickedest clown." The clown's "brain," the city, "shines through his hat / with jeweled works," flashing at the environs, projecting dreams. But in an alternating current of messages, the country, "from the long black length of body," responds with the repeated plea to "subside." "Night City" is another fantastical landscape. Seen "From the Plane," it seems a vast furnace, burning "broken glass, broken bottles"; "tears"; "guilt." The city is no longer seen merely as a gilded harlequin; though still beautiful, with its molten "clots of gold" and "green and luminous / silicate rivers," it is Hell:

> The city burns guilt.
> —For guilt-disposal
> the central heat
> must be this intense.

The only peace lies in rising above the glamorous inferno—literally. "Careful" creatures (airplanes) "walk" through the "dead" sky, lighting their own way, modulating "green, red; green, red."

"12 O'Clock News" also develops techniques of surrealism used much earlier. "Sleeping on the Ceiling" (1938) metamorphosed the image of a room into an allegorical topography, "the Place de la Concorde." Thirty-five years later the landscape is more intimate, more personal, more complex. In this poem in prose, the focus is tighter: the top of a writer's desk—typewriter, manuscripts, paper, lamp, ashtray. We are given a guided tour of the paraphernalia of writing—as if it were an *archaeological* discovery. "The Monument," a poem dealing with the mysteries of the creation and the effect of a work of art, also employed the voice of some sort of guide; so does "The Man-Moth," which deals with what Yeats might characterize as a "subjective," lunar figure, at least on one level an image of the artist. In the witty and sinister surrealism of "12 O'Clock News" we get closer than ever to Elizabeth Bishop's view of herself as a writer.

Once again, but in a new way, we face a double tone—the

dramatic irony of a speaker who doesn't fathom the full implications of what he reports, and the poet's own voice, laconically indicating her own capacity for perception. This is done simply by indicating in the margin what "real" object is being described by the "imaginary" speaker. This is a game, we are told, that is not just a game: the "answer" is given in advance. We are prevented from *guessing* (the reverse of "The Monument," where the subject itself is essentially mysterious); we are compelled to examine how deeply clever the questions are.

The *typed sheet,* for example, is perceived by the speaker as "a large rectangular 'field,' hitherto unknown . . . obviously man-made." Ironically, every descriptive detail is more literally true than we had expected. The final speculation about the "dark-speckled" page is more disturbing: "An airstrip? A cemetery?" Unlike the others, these words can *not* be literally true. The puns ("hitherto unknown," "man-made"), essentially comic, turn into something more serious—allegory. And with the images posed as questions, we find ourselves teased onto a roller coaster of shifting levels of diction. Images, and words themselves, are revealed in all their power to alter perceptions.

Much of the piece is playful: the typewriter eraser is taken to be a "unicyclist-courier" with "thick, bristling black hair"; the grim heap of dead soldiers "in hideously contorted positions" are only cigarette butts. Some of the humor lies in the grandiose language the speaker uses for the commonplace objects: the typewriter as "escarpment," the eraser as one of "the indigenes," the ink-bottle as either a "great altar" or "some powerful and terrifying 'secret weapon'." Among other things, "12 O'Clock News" is a canny satire on archaeological guesswork and socio-scientific jargon.

But the poem functions in ways more complex than parody. Even when comic, the atmosphere is undeniably eerie—with a "moon" that "seems to hang motionless in the sky. . . . it could be dead." What is observed is essentially painful: "endless labor," crude "communications," soil of "poor quality," the "people" in a state of "superstition and helplessness," hoping to be rescued from their "grave difficulties." Their "soldiers" are "all dead"—they have lost a war. They seem to have been the "opponents" of the speaker's party. He explains their defeat by calling them childish, hopelessly impractical, and inscrutable, and "their leaders" in a "sad" state of "corruption." The irony is mordantly directed at the author's own sense of insurmountable odds, being resigned to rely on recalcitrant machines and inanimate objects, but also to the inescapable difficulty and possible pointlessness of the creative process itself. The writer, in his accustomed surroundings, at "home," though he may potentially have "some powerful and terrifying 'secret weapon'" at his command, is essentially a figure of pathos and irony, a figure of "childishness and hopeless impracticality," "superstition and helplessness." His work is either an "airstrip" or a "cemetery." He flies, or dies.

In "Poem," Elizabeth Bishop again consolidates a nexus of issues that have always been of serious interest to her. Like "The Moose" and "In the Waiting Room" it looks back to a place and a time in her own earliest experience; like "Large Bad Picture" and "The Monument" it is a detailed description and a meditation on a work of art, finally dealing with the implications of its own existence; like "Crusoe in England" it is also a monologue, more a dramatic scene than a lyrical discourse. The frequent intrusions of qualifying and parenthetical remarks are not only subsidiary explanations as in "The Monument," but sudden *new* insights, *new* revelations. We are presented with, and compelled to examine, the *process* of the poet's discoveries.

The value of "this little painting," "about the size of an old-style dollar bill," ironically has nothing to do with dollars and cents: it "has never earned any money in its life." It is not exactly an heirloom, rather casually handed over "collaterally" from one relative to another. A "minor family relic," hardly noticed, it is "useless and free." The value, and the price, of its being free will emerge later in the poem.

The poet's attempt to "place" the picture is dramatized:

> It must be Nova Scotia; only there
> does one see gabled wooden houses
> painted that awful shade of brown.

She is not uncritical. She also takes delight in examining the painter's technique: "that gray-blue wisp" seems meant to be "a thin church steeple"—"or is it?" Is there a "specklike bird" or is it "a flyspeck looking like a bird?" Some "tiny cows" are painted with only "two brushstrokes each," but "confidently"; a "wild iris" is only "white and yellow, / fresh-squiggled from the tube."

While she is scrutinizing the painting, she suddenly feels an excited shock of recognition:

> Heavens, I recognize the place, I know it!
> It's behind—I can almost remember the farmer's name.
> His barn backed on that meadow. There it is,
> titanium white, one dab.

The poet has lived through the scene in the painting—but at a different time from the painter.

> Those particular geese and cows
> are naturally before my time.

She never knew the artist—all they have in common is this scene, or "the memory of it"; but they are united because their "visions coincided—'visions' is / too serious a word—our looks, two looks."

Both Elizabeth Bishop and her "great-uncle," Uncle George, "an R.A.," took the scene in the painting from life and committed it to memory. Creating the work of art becomes the equivalent of *memorizing*:

> art "copying from life" and life itself,
> life and the memory of it so compressed
> they've turned into each other. Which is which?

Memory, "on a piece of Bristol board" and in the mind of the poet (*and in her poem*), is what allows the original place, the "small backwater," to be "still loved," since the present place "must have changed a lot." It is loved not only because it is pretty, but because it is alive:

> dim, but how live, how touching in detail.

These "details" are what we have—"the little that we get for free, / the little of our earthly trust. Not much. / About the size of our abidance. . . ." The painting, with its living details, is a true gift—"useless and free": merely the image of cows, an iris, spring pools, trees, geese—in the mind, in a painting, in a poem. Art, the equivalent of memory, has the capacity to keep things—even little things, *especially* little things, things we love, things that die—alive. The elms in the painting are "yet-to-be-dismantled." The memory of them is the memory of life that no longer exists in the world of time and practical values, trust funds and price tags. What is "free" may be a small thing, but its life is essential to ours; and in fact, because we die, identical to ours, "our abidance," "our earthly trust."

The ultimate irony is the initial one—the title. When we think back to the title, it ceases to function as a mere generic indicator. "Poem" is about what it means to be a poem—whatever the particular incarnation. It is the preservation of perception and emotion—the perception of details, the details that "touch" us—the maintenance of the ability to see and love whatever is alive, through a coalescence of empathies, the artist's and the viewer's. This poem provides the human and moving definition of its title.

If we learn anything from a reading of all these poems so far it is that even at their most highly artificial, Elizabeth Bishop's poems have never been manufactured out of nothing. Her interest in small things, in "details," if we hadn't noticed before, is—as "Poem" reveals—not a mannerism, but part of a profound vision (*not* "too serious a word"). The wonderment that some squiggles of paint can make an iris or cows expresses what life-giving possibilities lie behind technical ability. As "12 O'Clock News" suggested, though with a different emphasis, a work of art has the potential to soar (if it doesn't die). These attitudes towards her work have always been present, but never before so clearly articulated. The remaining three new poems turn more directly to her personal life. In their various ways they indicate how much of her personal life energizes all her poems.

"Five Flights Up" is an ironic and painful *aubade*. Elizabeth Bishop has written before of her ambivalent feelings about the morning: the daily ceremonies of "Anaphora," the urban daybreak of "Love Lies Sleeping," the mixed blessings the sunrise brings in "Roosters"—the ambiguous sunrise following the "unimaginable nightmare" with the fidelity of an "enemy, or friend." It is even one of the subjects of her recent translation of Octavio Paz's "January First."

The strategy of the poem resembles that of "Cirque d'Hiver." Both poems seem at first to be about what is being observed—a mechanical "little circus horse" with "glossy black" eyes in "Cirque d'Hiver"; in this poem, a "little black dog" next door and "unknown bird." It is not until the end of both poems that we are made aware that the poet has been implicitly seeing herself in these creatures. She poignantly reveals how similar her life has been to that of the mechanical toy:

> Facing each other rather desperately—
> his eye is like a star—
> we stare and say, "Well, we have come this far."

The comparison in "Five Flights Up" is one of contrast rather than similitude. The questioning inquiries of bird and dog, even the stern voice of the owner trying to calm the dog ("You ought to be ashamed!") are resolved for the animals "directly, simply, / by day itself." The dog "has no sense of shame." Each new day is a new beginning. This is where animals are enviably different from human beings. "—Yesterday brought to today so lightly!" For human beings the morning is "enormous," "ponderous." If "Poem" is about the possibilities of preserving what dies, "Five Flights Up" is about the burden of memory, of the past.

Up to the very last line the contrast between human and animal feelings has been understated, implicit, apparently general. There is no reference whatsoever to the first person. The last line, in its directness and explicit personal application, is a shock:

> (A yesterday I find almost impossible to lift.)

The sense of shame, of guilt is overwhelming. In the least directly personal of these new poems, "Night City," we were told that the city "burns tears" and "burns guilt." "Five Flights Up" is a "city poem," too. But in the suddenness, simplicity, and the off-handed matter-of-factness of the parenthesis in the last line, we are confronted with the most direct statement of personal despair in the works of Elizabeth Bishop.

We don't know exactly what happened to cause that despair. We didn't know in "Roosters" how the night "could . . . have come to grief" or precisely what had been lived through in "Cirque d'Hiver," though we certainly feel the enormity of the suffering. When this kind of explanation has been offered to us, as in "Faustina" or "Crusoe," it has been information about others, alter egos, personae; never directly about the author. But directness, frankness have been characteristic of these recent poems, and the most recent, "The End of March" and "One Art" (March 1975, April 1976), are among Elizabeth Bishop's most specifically autobiographical poems.

If "Five Flights Up" presents a contrast to "Poem," "One Art" is a kind of corollary to it. In "Poem" loss is implicit: inherent, inevitable, but pending, "yet-to-be." In "One Art" loss is all pervasive. "Poem" only implied what is stated here as fact: "so many things seem filled with the intent / to be lost. . . ." The poem, with its unexpected self-irony, tells us "how to" deal with loss, to "master" the "art of losing." It is a kind of lecture by an expert, a master, an artist.

The opening remark is more ambiguous than it seems—

> The art of losing isn't hard to master . . .

—for mastering the art of losing can mean two things, both learning not to mind and learning to lose more. Though the latter may be easier than the former, the "expert" ironically suggests practice:

> Lose something every day . . .

> Then practice losing farther, losing faster . . .

If, as she says, loss is implicit, then when loss occurs it is only fulfilling an expectation. If we are used to dealing with loss, we can learn to accept it; acceptance is the prevention of disaster. Thus the ironic rationale for courting disaster, like Mithridates and his poison, in order to survive it. The art of losing, then, is the art of survival.

At the approximate half-way point in the poem, the expert presents us with her credentials, the list of losses. Each succeeding item increases in magnitude, from her mother's watch, a house she loved, to "some realms I owned, two rivers, a continent." These are what she has, with the assertion of ease, survived. But the survival of loss is not altogether as casual as the ironic persona would have us believe. She is still capable of saying of her losses, "I miss them." Nevertheless, nostalgia, the pained awareness of loss, is not the equivalent of "disaster." Anything less than total defeat is victory.

But the crisis in the poem is not in the past, it is in the present. In the growing list of things loved and lost the last and greatest is revealed to be "you," the poem's apparent audience of one.

> —Even losing you (the joking voice, a gesture
> I love) I shan't have lied. It's evident
> the art of losing's not too hard to master . . .

The refrain is changed slightly from "the art of losing isn't hard to master"; it is now more tentative, more understated, more negative, more ironic. This loss is the closest to "disaster"; she must force herself to say just how close:

> though it may look like (*Write* it!) like disaster.

The real audience at this lecture on the bearability of loss, it turns out, is the expert herself—she has been trying to convince herself that any loss can be endured. And finally, she is forced to admit that she was right; she really may not have believed it, or wanted to believe it, before. Apparently, any loss, no matter how great—even *this* loss—*can* be lived through.

"One Art" is a villanelle, one of Elizabeth Bishop's rare excursions into a complex, pre-existent verse pattern (only her two sestinas and the double sonnet of "The Prodigal" come to mind). Perhaps—without the fiction of a character like Crusoe, who experiences similar losses—the framework of a formal pattern was a necessary structure for the use of so many personal details (details corresponding especially to the image of travel, which has been so central to her work for so long). Certainly the formality of the structure contributes to a universalizing element in this poem. But the repetitions of the villanelle also heighten the dramatic immediacy of the poem. As we learn at the end that the poet has tried to persuade herself that her losses can be survived, the repetitions, with their slight but suggestive variations, emerge as the principal vehicle by which the lesson can be drummed not only into our ears but her own. The formality of the verse increases the emotional pitch and, paradoxically, contributes to the sense of personal pain.

Unlike "Dover Beach," where being "true to one another" may stave off the disaster of the collapse of the civilized world, "One Art" denies the possibility of Matthew Arnold's final option. Elizabeth Bishop's only faith seems to be in loss, or at least in her desperate refusal to be defeated by it; not in "one another" but in oneself, one's art. The "one art" is the need to "write it"—recognizing, and naming, the loss itself and finding the form that will arm one against all the disastrous losses.

Many of these new poems dramatize some sort of conflict between the past and the present: the passing of time, the pain of loss, the nature of what endures, the need to remember, the need to forget. "The End of March" has a kind of reverse nostalgia, a mellower resignation to the limitations of the future ("the opposite of History," as she writes of Joseph Cornell in her translation of Octavio Paz's "Objects & Apparitions").

The tension in the poem is between what is actually there and what can only be imagined. There is a "long beach," Duxbury; it is cold; there is a wind; the tide is out, far out; there are seabirds. The description tells us what is there—seen, felt, heard, tasted: the sky darker than the water, which "was the color of mutton-fat jade." The poet and her friends (to whom she has dedicated the poem) are wearing rubber boots. These are all facts. They follow "a track of big dog-prints." But these tracks are mysterious, "so big / they were more like lion-prints." They lead to more things that can be examined, but not explained:

>   Then we came on
> lengths and lengths, endless, of wet white string,
> looping up to the tide-line, down to the water,
> over and over. Finally, they did end:
> a thick white snarl, man-size, awash,
> rising on every wave, a sodden ghost,
> falling back, sodden, giving up the ghost. . . .

It could be a kite string—a logical guess; but there's "no kite." The mystery remains unsolved.

The poet, we soon learn, had a destination in mind: "my proto-dream-house, / my crypto-dream-house." It seems she has secretly fantasized about living in a mysterious green-shingled house on the beach. "Many things about this place," she reminds us, "are dubious." The fantasy is very complete and detailed. It is almost a Robinson Crusoe fantasy of independence and isolation, contented self-containment:

> I'd like to retire there and do *nothing,*
> or nothing much, forever, in two bare rooms:
> look through binoculars, read boring books,
> old, long, long books, and write down useless notes,
> talk to myself, and, foggy days,
> watch the droplets slipping, heavy with light.

Back in 1938 Elizabeth Bishop wrote a Kakfa-esque story called "In Prison," in which the narrator's obsessive ideal for himself, where he foresaw his maximum possibility for freedom, was in the narrowest, sparest possible confinement, almost solitary confinement. Every demand he anticipated in his own mind. Here, too, future necessities are carefully foreseen—a stove, a chimney, electricity, books, binoculars. A vivid romantic scene is imagined, drinking grog alone on a cold night. This isolation is a self-removal from the "acrid" problems of the "round, turning world," the possibilities of pain and loss that result inevitably from human contact. Yet it provides a means not only of meditation, but of observation. It is ideal, "—perfect! But—impossible." The poet, unlike the narrator of "In Prison," has too much self-irony to be taken in by her dream.

She *knows* she has to take the real world into account. Reality, however painful, is too strong: "that day the wind was much too cold / even to get that far." Romantic isolation, however desirable, is possible only in the imagination. People are needed, the world must be contended with, illusions cannot be maintained—"and of course the house was boarded up." The house is not reached.

As they walk back they feel the wind freezing the other side of their faces; it's *there*. But there is a moment of beauty and mysterious revelation. The sun comes out. "For just a minute . . . the drab, damp, scattered stones / were multi-colored, / and all those high enough threw out long shadows, / individual shadows, then pulled them in again." Everything is alive with an individual life of its own (this is what was so frightening in "In the Waiting Room," and so important to remember in "Poem"). Beauty is possible, if momentary. Myth or illusion or fantasy are never far removed from the real world. The shadows could be "teasing the lion sun," the mythical March lion,

> —a sun who'd walked the beach the last low tide,
> making those big, majestic paw-prints,
> who perhaps had batted a kite out of the sky to play with.

"Perhaps." Elizabeth Bishop is too much a realist to give herself completely to the fantasy; she also has too much imagination to ignore its presence. In these new poems, each side of these profound and central issues is observed, explored. A myth can be created if necessary; if necessary the painful facts of autobiography—past, present, or future—can be touched on or dramatized. The fear of isolation and the desire for it are seen in their equal power; the need to escape and the desire to explore are recognized as equally powerful motivations; the value of holding on to the past and the need to forget it are both understood with clarity and compassion. Human understanding and the refusal to sentimentalize are always present, have always been present. The richness of her earlier poems is still present, with a new confidence and broader vision. These new works, each in itself and all together, develop those very qualities which have always been the source of Elizabeth Bishop's real greatness.

WILLARD SPIEGELMAN

Elizabeth Bishop's "Natural Heroism"

In her genial invitation to Marianne Moore to come flying over the Brooklyn Bridge one fine morning for a *fête urbaine*, Elizabeth Bishop conjures up an image of Miss Moore borne aloft like the good witch of Oz, shoes trailing sapphires, cape full of butterflies, hat decked with angels. Defined by fey and glittering objects, and not quite a part of this world, Moore rises "above the accidents, above the malignant movies" of profane life, while listening to "a soft uninvented music," like Keats's spiritual toneless ditties. She floats up, "mounting the sky with natural heroism."[1] This is a curious phrase, since we are likely to think of the hero as one set apart in his superiority or struggle, and of his status as one not easily achieved. If anything, heroism and nature are antithetical. In Bishop's work, however, the "natural hero" occupies a privileged position which is unattainable by the super- or unnatural exploits of masculine achievement which the poetry constantly debunks. For Bishop, as for Stevens, "the man-hero is not the exceptional monster." This, in itself, is nothing new: ever since Wordsworth attempted to democratize the language and the subjects of poetry, his Romantic heirs have focused on ordinariness and on the self-conscious meditative habits which turn heroism inward. But Bishop goes even beyond Wordsworth's radical break with the past.[2] Her hero replaces traditional ideas of bravery with a blend of domestic and imaginative strengths. The highest value in Bishop's work is a politely skeptical courage which neither makes outrageous demands on the world nor demurely submits to the world's own.

To understand Bishop's natural heroism, and her kinship

First printed in *Centennial Review* (Winter 1978), pp. 14ff.

with, yet movement beyond, Wordsworth, I wish to look at three types of poems, all tinged with her qualifying skepticism. First, there are those which trace the outline of heroic situations or devices and then negate or undercut them; second, those which internalize an encounter or conflict and, in the manner of a Romantic crisis lyric, make the act of learning itself a heroic process, but which also dramatize the avoidance of apocalypse that Geoffrey Hartman has located at the heart of Wordsworth's genius[3]; and finally those in which the *via negativa* of denial or avoidance implies Bishop's positive values, poems where a dialectical struggle between two contestants is resolved by an assertion of heroic worth.

At her most playful, Bishop insinuates heroic, mythological allusions, often with a tentative, amused tone, so that their full impact is softened. In "House Guest," she wonders, "Can it be that we nourish / one of the Fates in our bosoms?" but Clotho is only an inept seamstress. Eros (in "Casabianca") is reduced to the obstinate boy standing on the burning deck, trying to recite Mrs. Hemans' "The boy stood on the burning deck." Hyperion-Apollo, the Romantics' fair-haired youth of morn, becomes some "ineffable creature" whose daily appearance and fall (in "Anaphora") are purposely rendered by a series of effects on his beholders, as if Bishop is too modest to describe or even name the god himself.

More important in Bishop's habitual tactic of diminution or undercutting is the way certain ideas of masculine greatness are filed down or eroded to their essential littleness. "The Burglar of Babylon" deprives its eponymous hero of his glory by recounting, in childlike ballad quatrains, his life as a petty criminal sought by a whole army of police who finally, and unceremoniously, kill him. As Ezra Pound is revealed through the expanding stanzas (modeled on "This is the house that Jack built") of "Visits to St. Elizabeths," his simple nobility is smothered by the weakness, fragility, and insipidity of the other inmates. The stanzas enlarge, and as Pound is seen in a setting (the literal one of the hospital, the figurative one of the syntactic, grammatical units of increasing complexity) he moves from "tragic," "honored," and "brave," to "cranky," "tedious," and "wretched."

The clichés of masculine conquest are also exploded in "Brazil, January 1, 1502," and in the first half of "Roosters." In the first poem, the Portuguese invaders are no better than aroused, predatory jungle lizards. Their "old dream of wealth and luxury" provokes them to the attempted rapacious destruction of landscape and native women. In "Roosters," virility and combativeness, "the uncontrolled, traditional" virtues that create "a senseless order," are mocked by the image of the roosters as pompous, puffed-up military dictators ("Deep from protruding chests / in green-gold medals dressed") and as colorful metallic map-marking pins (the lizards and Christians in the previous poem were also hard, glinting, metallic): "glass-headed pins, / oil-golds and copper greens, / anthracite blues, alizarins, / / each one an active / displacement in perspective; / each screaming, 'This is where I live.'" Like Stevens' Chief Iffucan, Bishop's roosters virtually squawk "Fat! Fat! Fat! Fat! I am the personal," and she witnesses the "vulgar beauty" of their iridescence as well as their lunatic, pseudo-heroic fighting swagger. Even the unmilitary Gentleman of Shalott, who has been domesticated (as if Sir Lancelot, originally seen in the mirror in Tennyson's poem, has come indoors to replace the lady who died for love of him), and who is reflected in profile by the mirror, is only a shadow of his total self. Resigned and uncertain, "he loves / that sense of constant re-adjustment. / He wishes to be quoted as saying at present: / 'Half is enough.'" His partner in Bishop's first volume is the Man-Moth, a curious creature from an imaginary bestiary, the inspiration for whose creation (a newspaper misprint for "mammoth") epitomizes Bishop's metamorphosizing and whimsical imagination. As mammoth, he is literally extinct, as man-moth, confected and precarious.

It is tempting to write off these playful inhabitants of Bishop's world as cousins of Moore's fanciful animals and flowers. But even the most fragile bear weightier implications. The bravado, false heroics, and metallic sheen of the cocks, for example, as well as the speaker's scorn and patronizing amusement, are replaced in the second half of "Roosters" by a new perspective and a softer voice. No longer mock-warriors, the roosters become emblems of human sin and the promise of Christian forgiveness. Peter's denial of Christ at the cock's crowing is sculpted in stone as a tangible reminder of his weakness and his master's love. Even the little rooster is "seen / carved on a dim column in the travertine." If you look hard enough, in other words, the fighting cock of the first part of the poem can be seen anew. Peter's tears and the cock's call are bound together, both in action and its symbolic representation: "There is inescapable hope, the pivot; / / yes, and there Peter's tears / run down our chanticleer's / side and gem his spurs." As Peter was long ago forgiven, so we still learn that "'Deny deny deny' / is not all the roosters cry." Spurs encrusted with tears mark the transformation of militancy into humility.

In the poem's last section, Bishop returns to her opening picture of daybreak, and the difference in her imagery alerts us to the distance between braggadocio and the roosters' subsequent Christian meekness. The opening was a military fanfare:

> At four o'clock
> in the gun-metal blue dark
> we hear the first crow of the first cock
>
> just below
> the gun-metal blue window
> and immediately there is an echo
>
> off in the distance,
> then one from the backyard fence,
> then one, with horrible insistence,
>
> grates like a wet match
> from the broccoli patch,
> flares, and all over town begins to catch.

The final view moves us to a slightly later stage of the dawn, gentler and tamed, as the roosters have literally ceased to crow, their threat having been figuratively replaced by the promise of forgiveness and natural harmony:

> In the morning
> a low light is floating
> in the backyard, and gilding

from underneath
the broccoli, leaf by leaf;
how could the night have come to grief?

gilding the tiny
floating swallow's belly
and lines of pink cloud in the sky,

the day's preamble
like wandering lines in marble.
The cocks are now almost inaudible.

The sun climbs in,
following "to see the end,"
faithful as enemy, or friend.

Moving as it is, "Roosters" is not typical of Bishop's work. For one thing, the vocabulary of Christian belief appears only rarely in her poetry, and her imagination is more secular than religious (in "A Miracle for Breakfast," there are mysterious hints of communion, or of the miracle of the loaves and fishes, but these are never clarified). For another, the studied symmetry, the juxtaposition of opposing views which augment one another seems too easy. More typical is "Wading at Wellfleet," a short, early lyric which encompasses the tensions I've discussed and diminishes or deflects heroic action more subtly than "Roosters":

In one of the Assyrian wars
a chariot first saw the light
that bore sharp blades around its wheels.

That chariot from Assyria
went rolling down mechanically
to take the warriors by the heels.

A thousand warriors in the sea
could not consider such a war
as that the sea itself contrives

but hasn't put in action yet.
This morning's glitterings reveal
the sea is "all a case of knives."

Lying so close, they catch the sun,
the spokes directed at the shin.
The chariot front is blue and great.

The war rests wholly with the waves:
they try revolving, but the wheels
give way; they will not bear the weight.

The poem is deceptively simple; even its playfulness shows Bishop's ability to take a natural event (named in the title), establish it within a larger metaphoric context, and then surprise us by defusing the bomb she herself has lit. As in "Roosters," glittering danger—here in the opening military details—is evoked like a "false surmise" and then reduced, but unlike "Roosters," "Wading at Wellfleet" avoids simple dualisms. It is, instead, both neatly divided into three parts and, at the same time, seamless in its verbal repetitions and unity. The three pairs of stanzas are isolated by rhyme and subject matter. In the first, we have a backward historical glance at biblical battles (with, I suspect, a whispered reminder of Byron's "The Destruction of Sennacherib"); in the second, the central image of the beach on Cape Cod; and in the third, a dialectical synthesis which paradoxically unites and separates the terms of the first two. The first section introduces the poem's major concept (danger) in the guise of military activity, and its first important image (sharp light) in the off-handed pun of line 2. The same wit is present in lines 5 and 6, where "rolling" sets us up for the last stanza ("revolving") and "heels" reminds us of the title ("Wading"). The second section explicitly combines the light and dazzle of the first with this day's water, and brings the Assyrian warriors into an imaginary relationship with the speaker (they become *any* warriors). The pivotal image is conditional and deliberately vague: we want to know whether any sea has ever put into action its threat, or whether the Atlantic, this particular ocean on this particular day, has been withholding its power. As it surprisingly turns out, the sea is a paper tiger, like the roosters, because it is constitutionally incapable of making real the threat which the human observer has imagined (like the paranoid speaker in Frost's "Once by the Pacific," who supposes that the waves "thought of doing something to the shore / That water never did to land before"). The dialectical synthesis of the last stanzaic pair, then, is imagistic only (the sea–chariot–light configuration). The waves reflect, but can never duplicate, the knifelike sharpness of the sun, itself an image of the chariot wheel (the pun in Herbert's "case of knives" suggests the same weakening of the military motifs); their revolution is their destruction as they roll over and past the feet of the wader.

The frequency with which Bishop attacks and transforms military formulas, forays, and glory shows her grappling with received values and ideas, and struggling towards new ones. In "Roosters," the replacement is clear and easy, while in "Wading at Wellfleet" it is cunningly avoided by disarming the military apparatus, which is the poem's unifying force, without filling the void it leaves. In their dealings with large themes, these poems are relatively minor when compared with others which bring us to the very edge of imaginative revelation and then hold back. Skepticism, an unwillingness to approve either major conflicts or major revelations, is common to both groups. If heroism is undercut in the first poems, we should not be surprised to learn in the next group, that even meditative, epistemological problems (i.e., encounters between a speaker and a natural scene or object) can be subjected to the same deflating treatment. The dangers and traumas of knowledge are posed and then removed. This is, as Geoffrey Hartman has shown, the standard strategy of Wordsworth, who first plunges into some shadowy terrain within the heart or mind of man and then, when scared by what he might learn there, withdraws and calls it "nature." To raise a threat and then to dissipate it, not so much out of fear or cowardice as out of ontological skepticism (which, in "Wading at Wellfleet" and other poems, is disguised as polished lightheartedness) is Bishop's way as well.

"Cape Breton" and "The Moose," two of her longer poems, sustain the anxieties of the shorter lyrics and build towards larger statements.[4] Masquerading as a description of a natural scene, "Cape Breton" is a glimpse into a heart of darkness. Indeed, Bishop's vision is to Conrad's as Marlow's is to Kurtz's:

He had made that last stride, he had stepped over the edge, while I had been permitted to draw back my hesitating foot. . . . perhaps . . . all truth, and all sincerity, are just compressed into that inappreciable moment of time in which we step over the threshold of the invisible.

Throughout, descriptive data are balanced by suggestions of absence, disappearance, and vacancy: "Cape Breton" is more about what is not there than what is. The opening images are negated: we see an uneven line of birds, but their backs are toward us; we hear sheep whose fearfulness, we are parenthetically told, causes them occasionally to stampede over the rocks into the sea. Water and mist are the salient features of this world, melting into each other, "weaving . . . and disappearing," and "the pulse, / rapid but unurgent, of a motorboat" is incorporated into the mist, while the boat's invisible body is obliterated.

The delicate beauty enfolded within and by the secret ministry of mist evinces both dissipation ("like rotting snow-ice sucked away / almost to spirit") and erosion ("the ghosts of glaciers drift / among those folds and folds of fir . . . dull, dead, deep peacock-colors"). Having set the scene in a primal, almost Gothic chill, the speaker proceeds to human, domestic details, but with the same plan of taking away with one hand what the other offers. There is a road along the coast with "small yellow bulldozers" but no activity: "without their drivers, because today is Sunday." There are "little white churches" (all the human details are deliberately dwarfed) in the hills, but they too are vestiges of some unknown past, "like lost quartz arrowheads." The central revelation comes now, and as we might expect, it is one of human and epistemological emptiness:

The road appears to have been abandoned.
Whatever the landscape had of meaning appears to have been
    abandoned,
unless the road is holding it back, in the interior,

where we cannot see,
where deep lakes are reputed to be,
and disused trails and mountains of rock
and miles of burnt forest standing in gray scratches
like the admirable scriptures made on stones by stones—

The disappointment is double: the evidence of the eye leads us to nothing (we see no meaning), and the possibility of hidden truth is buried beneath hearsay ("reputed to be") and the geological palimpsests which can be seen and read only by the Kurtzes of the world. All that the speaker is able to hear these regions "say for themselves" is the song of the small sparrows, themselves too fragile to last, sustain meaning, or provide comfort: "floating upward / freely, dispassionately, through the mist, and meshing / in brown-wet, fine, torn fish-nets."

The next verse paragraph looks as if it will announce a major turn in the poem, but we learn that Bishop's singular devotion to painting emptiness here deceives us with apparently human images. A bus, packed with people, comes into view, but once again a parenthetical afterthought reduces fullness to relative emptiness:

(On weekdays with groceries, spare automobile parts,
    and pump parts,
  but today only two preachers extra, one carrying his
    frock coat on a hanger.)

Passing a closed roadside stand, a closed schoolhouse ("where today no flag is flying"), the bus finally emits two passengers, a man with a baby, who immediately vanish in "a small steep meadow, / which establishes its poverty in a snowfall of daisies," to return "to his invisible house beside the water." The human dimension is teasingly put into, and then erased from, the picture where even natural details are muted, softened, and so delicately and charmingly miniaturized that we might almost forget the accumulated horror that they are surely meant to convey. Indeed, as the bus itself pulls off, the birds keep on singing, normal activity, such as it is, resumes, and the poem ends like a surrealistic movie (e.g., *Blow-Up*) where, in a field, a man stands and then quite simply vanishes, as if he were never there. There remains only the mist which covers and swallows all:

> The thin mist follows
> the white mutations of its dream;
> an ancient chill is rippling the dark brooks.

Who has been dreaming, really: the mist which encompasses everything, or the human viewer who thought she saw a man on a bus? Both the landscape and its meaning have been abandoned in a cinematic sleight-of-hand that calls into question the very grounds of our knowing.

Though not as chilling in its implications, "The Moose" follows a similar course of isolating the speaker, and presenting her with the potential dangers of encounter with the unknown; but here, instead of remaining uncertain and tantalizing, the threat is destroyed. A heart of darkness, in "Cape Breton," is implied but experientially unknowable; in "The Moose," the midnight danger is tamed and domesticated, its sting removed. The poem begins as a series of farewells, as a bus moves west and south in late afternoon, from Nova Scotia to Boston. The light darkens, the fog gathers round, "a lone traveller" says goodbye to family and dog. Moonlight surrounds the bus as it enters New Brunswick's forests, and the passengers sink together into their private dreams, divagations, and conversations, some overheard by others ("—not concerning us, / but recognizable, somewhere, / back in the bus"). Two-thirds of the way through the poem, as a sense of comfort enables the travellers to succumb finally to sleep, the bus stops with a jolt, halted by a creature from the deep, dark interior:

> A moose has come out of
> the impenetrable wood
> and stands there, looms, rather,
> in the middle of the road.

But the moose is no memento of the inner depths, nor a visitor from the heart of the night. The only revelation is of the beast's harmless, almost personable, curiosity as she sniffs the bus. And yet the very plainness of the beast, an emblem of the plainness of the experience of confronting it, provokes a question which Bishop refrains from answering directly:

> Taking her time,
> she looks the bus over,
> grand, otherworldly.
> Why, why do we feel
> (we all feel) this sweet
> sensation of joy?

Grand but "awful plain," the moose becomes an occasion for a shared experience, a common sense of surmounting a momentary fright (which in this case is hardly heroic) followed by the reunion, in separate contentment, of the passengers with one another.

Habitually, then, we see Bishop constructing situations in which disaster is averted, or at worst insinuated gently enough so as to appear harmless. We can go even further, however, to discover in a third group of poems that active confrontation with physical or intellectual danger may yield lessons of wisdom and strength of purpose to narrators and characters.

Bishop's "natural" (i.e., either automatic, "in the nature of things," or common, "universal") heroism becomes clear in many of these poems, among them the terrifying "In the Waiting Room," the only one in which her own name appears. The seven-year-old Elizabeth, waiting while her aunt is in the dentist's chair, learns two primal lessons: of human pain and mortality, as she hears her aunt scream; and of unity in spite of human differences as she looks at African pictures in a *National Geographic,* and sinks into a confused semiconsciousness. She speaks her name ("you are an *I,* / you are an *Elizabeth*"), asserting her essential individuality, while simultaneously entertaining a nightmare vision of the universal sameness of all people: herself, Aunt Consuelo, the native African women, and the other patients in the office. This crisis lyric describes both a revelation and the joint horror and acceptance it provokes in the girl who has now, irrevocably, entered into her rational maturity. For all its differences in tone and language, it is Bishop's "Immortality" ode, where we see the light of common day begin its irreversible movement in the child's consciousness. For Wordsworth, years bring the philosophic mind to the adult who is, at the same time, borne down by the accumulated baggage of deadly custom and stale imitation. But where Wordsworth's manic willingness to be cheerful in the face of frost ("We in thought will join your throng") is the key to his own heroism, Bishop tentatively accepts continuity and community as bulwarks against separateness. Hence the circular structure of the poem which nakedly returns to the opening details of time and place, relocating the child, after her momentary blackout, in this very world, "which is," in Wordsworth's phrase, "the world of all of us." The "sweet sensation of joy" which unites the riders in "The Moose" is now replaced by an awful wonder at the fact of unity when one feels most alone:

> Why should I be my aunt,
> or me, or anyone?
> What similarities—
>
> held us all together
> or made us all just one?
> How—I didn't know any
> word for it—how "unlikely" . . .

The unlikely but perfectly natural realization that we have all of us one human heart is the crucial beginning, in Bishop's view of the self, of a transformation of isolation into community (on the egoism of the child, cf. Wordsworth's remark, "I was often unable to think of external things as having external existence"). In maturity, as opposed to childhood, it is joy that brings the separate travellers together.

It is no surprise that Bishop should instinctively be a poet of *places,* because the conditions of placement—stasis, domesticity, routine, community—compensate for her natural humility in the face of the greater "world" where she often feels estranged. The attractions of travel are its dangers ("Questions of Travel" presents the philosophical dimensions of the debate between movement and rest): hence poems like "Cape Breton" and "The Moose," which depict the avoidance of revelation of which I've written (significantly, the passengers in the bus are united by joy when the bus is stopped; when it starts up again, it leaves behind "a dim / smell of moose, an acrid / smell of gasoline"). Conversely, the domestic coziness of Bishop's Brazilian poems invokes traditional pastoral ideas of rest and also the relief that accompanies a sense of belonging in a harmonious community. In this context, the apparent oxymoron in "natural heroism" is erased: the heroic self does not stand apart from his tribe by virtue of either suffering or action (nor is he isolated like Man-Moth, Portuguese invaders, or Pound); rather, by synecdoche, he exemplifies his community.

Since he does not stand alone, the hero is usually presented as part of a group, or especially a pair. The confrontations between people in Bishop's work are sometimes ambivalent and tricky: high and low, victor and victim, master and servant, are likely to change places. The relationship of patron and tenant-farmer in "Manuelzinho" turns upon the seeming inequality between them and upon their reversal of roles, when "superior" and "inferior" lose all meaning. Manuelzinho, a blessed fool, magical and hexed, can grow nothing, and the frustrations of his employer, affectionately but exasperatingly listed, proclaim the distance between his childlike wonder and her mature sensibleness. But this distance is reduced by love, first the patronizing affection of adult for child, then, gradually, the accumulated sense of dependence on Manuelzinho for more than mere amusement. Figurative exaggerations become statements of fact, just as fancy begins to assume solidity:

> Account books? They are Dream Books.
> In the kitchen we dream together
> how the meek shall inherit the earth—
> or several acres of mine.

Colorful harlequin, aged child, and useless necessity, Manuelzinho, without his knowing it, occasions humility and warmth in his patron, so that at the poem's end, their positions have been reversed. In this quasi-feudal relationship, propriety demands courteous generosity from both, especially from the patron whose plea for understanding and forgiveness is one of those gestures in Bishop's work that reaffirm human community between equals and prove that heroism need be neither grandiose nor excessive. Having mocked Manuelzinho's ridiculous, painted hats, the speaker doffs her own to him in a kind act of homage:

> One was bright green. Unkindly,
> I called you Klorophyll Kid.
> My visitors thought it was funny.
> I apologize here and now.
>
> You helpless, foolish man,
> I love you all I can,
> I think. Or do I?
> I take off my hat, unpainted
> and figurative, to you.
> Again I promise to try.

"I could have laughed myself to scorn to find / In that decrepit Man so firm a mind," Wordsworth's surprised response to his leech-gatherer, is equivalent to the sustenance which this speaker derives from Manuelzinho. Where Bishop surpasses Wordsworth, however, where her egoism is simply less intense, is in her continual insistence on the need for symbiosis: mutual support, rather than epiphanies wrought by otherworldly visitors, is the key to natural polity, as well as piety. Her other long poem about master and servant ("Faustina, or Rock Roses") also dramatizes "service," but through images that reflect and complement one another, it turns hierarchy into a bizarre democracy. Here it is difficult to know who is master—the white woman, shrivelled and dying, or Faustina, the black servant whose own freedom is imminent but whose current status is ambivalent. The uncertainty of the human relationship is depicted in the opening stanza:

> Tended by Faustina
> yes in a crazy house

upon a crazy bed,
frail, of chipped enamel,
blooming above her head
into four vaguely roselike
  flower-formations,

the white woman whispers to
herself.

We must infer an initial ellipsis ("The rock roses are . . .
tended by Faustina") to grasp the full, functional ambiguity of
the lines: the servant is caretaker of sculpted flowers (which
metamorphose into a visitor's gift of real flowers at the end of
the poem) and of the white woman, equally "frail" and
"chipped," lying in "white disordered sheets / like wilted
roses," beside a crooked table littered with chalky powder,
cream, and pills, in a room where each rag contributes "its /
shade of white, confusing / as undazzling." The poem is a still
life, a study in desiccated whiteness, with a human analogue.
Faustina's "terms of . . . employment" ("terms" suggesting
both time and condition) are complained of, and explained to,
the visitor. Her "sinister kind face" poses an unanswerable rid-
dle of her own feelings about the mistress' approaching death
and her own survival; the ambiguous antecedent of "it" is both
the señora's *and* the servant's conditions:

Oh, is it

freedom at last, a lifelong
dream of time and silence,
dream of protection and rest?
Or is it the very worst,
the unimaginable nightmare
that never before dared last
  more than a second?

"There is no way of telling" is the closest thing to a response as
mistress and servant, polar opposites, one dying and one living,
converge in the ambivalent haze of this syntax.

We do not normally think of Bishop as a poet of struggle; the tension in her poems is mostly internalized, and confrontations, when they occur, are between the self, traveling, moving, or simply seeing, and the landscape it experiences. But in "Manuelzinho" and "Faustina" we have two pairs of agonists, locked in relationships of affection and struggle from which there is no release in life. In fact, Bishop's most anthologized poem, "The Fish," is more typical of its author than we might suspect. It depicts external and internal conflict, and a heroic action which is perfectly "natural" in its motivation and accomplishment. It follows the pattern I have traced for all of Bishop's poems so far, thus making it a paradigm of her work: an action is intimated and then undercut; next, a mild revelation, hardly heralded, occurs, and then a positive reaction proves the speaker's heroism. The simple experience literally surrounds the reasons for it: "I caught a tremendous fish" (line 1), "and I let the fish go" (line 76). We first see deflation: the tremendous fish is caught with no struggle whatsoever, and, like the moose, turns out to be anything but dangerous: "He hung a grunting weight, / battered and venerable / and homely." It is not for the absence of a good fight, or as a testimony to the grim veteran who has struggled in the past, that the speaker releases her catch. More important to her action are the accumulated details of her revelation. These involve an anthropomorphizing of the adversary (as in "Roosters" and "The Moose") and, as a result of a camaraderie, an aesthetic epiphany which preempts and therefore obliterates the military antagonism hinted at earlier in the poem.

The description of the fish (the bulk of the poem) domesticates him (his skin is like wallpaper; there are rosettes of lime and rags of seaweed on him; the swim-bladder is like a peony), while not omitting reminders of his potential danger ("the frightening gills . . . that can cut so badly," "his sullen face, / the mechanism of his jaw"). Stressing the fish's familiarity *and* otherness, the speaker transforms him into a veteran fighter, a survivor of many contests who wears the remnants of old fish-lines in his lower lip like battle scars or "medals with their ribbons / frayed and wavering, / a five-haired beard of wisdom / trailing from his aching jaw."

The revelation has two parts: first, the new picture which the speaker's imaginative perception has created; and second, the way this new image of the fish colors and alters her environment. For an analogue to the heroic dimension of the poem we have only to look at Wordsworth's encounters with spectral, ghastly figures (leech-gatherer, beggar, discharged soldier) who are shocking, at first, because of their subhumanness, but who subsequently chastise and instruct Wordsworth in the "unlikely" connections among us all. In his famous description, the leech-gatherer is changed from a rock into a giant sea-beast before finally assuming his full human identity. Likewise, Bishop's fish undergoes a series of revisions which build to create his final symbolic weight.

The aesthetic nature of this experience, by which the fish is literally *seen* and metaphorically tamed, is the final cause of the speaker's release of him. Looking hard at her opponent, Bishop moves beyond military conquest to a "victory" in which both contestants have a part: "I stared and stared / and victory filled up / the little rented boat." The last twelve lines return us to the model of the Wordsworthian nature lyric,[5] first in their insistence on a mesmerizing vision (cf. "I gazed and gazed" in "I Wandered Lonely as a Cloud"), next in the metaphoric "wealth" which this show brings, and last, in a muted reminder of the covenant and the natural piety emblemized by a rainbow, inspiring confidence and joy through a feeling of connection with the world (it is a nice detail that this feeling comes in a "rented boat," where the speaker is a natural outsider):

> I stared and stared
> and victory filled up
> the little rented boat,
> from the pool of bilge
> where oil had spread a rainbow
> around the rusted engine
> to the bailer rusted orange,
> the sun-cracked thwarts,
> the oarlocks on their strings,
> the gunnels—until everything
> was rainbow, rainbow, rainbow!
> And I let the fish go.

Victory, then, comes with neither the catching of the fish (almost accidental) nor its release (virtually automatic) but with the conjunction of two antagonists, heroic by virtue of their endurance (the fish, like the leech-gatherer, is admirable for merely surviving), their embodiment or perception of natural beauty, and the harmony of visual detail which reflects their personal connections. For Bishop, natural heroism becomes not the elimination, or conquest, of the enemy, but the embracing, subsuming, and internalizing of him. In the largest sense, separateness is denied, and victory is earned: another word for her heroism is love.

NOTES

1. References are to Elizabeth Bishop, *The Complete Poems* (New York: Farrar, Straus and Giroux, 1969); and to Elizabeth Bishop, *Geography III* (New York: Farrar, Straus and Giroux, 1976).

2. For a discussion of Bishop's connections with the Romantic nature lyrics of Wordsworth and Coleridge, see my "Landscape and Knowledge: The Poetry of Elizabeth Bishop," *Modern Poetry Studies* 6 (1975), pp. 203–24. The present essay is in some ways a continuation of certain ideas suggested and presented there.

3. Geoffrey Hartman, *Wordsworth's Poetry 1787–1814* (New Haven: Yale University Press, 1964), pp. 40–60 and *passim*.

4. One could as well examine other poems, such as "Questions of Travel," "The Imaginary Iceberg," "Over 2000 Illustrations and a Complete Concordance," or, for the pain of knowledge, "At the Fishhouses," and "In the Waiting Room." I deal with all of these in my earlier Bishop essay; see note 2.

5. The best analysis of this kind of poem is still M. H. Abrams, "Structure and Style in the Romantic Nature Lyric," in Frederick W. Hilles and Harold Bloom, eds., *From Sensibility to Romanticism* (New York: Oxford University Press, 1965), pp. 527–28.

PART TWO   *A Chronology*

MARIANNE MOORE

Archaically New

In trying to reveal the clash of elements that we are—the intellectual, the animal; the blunt, the ingenious; the impudent, the imaginative—one dare not be dogmatic. We are a many-foliaged tree against the moon; a wave penetrated by the sun. Some authors do not muse within themselves; they "think"—like the vegetable-shredder which cuts into the life of a thing. Miss Bishop is not one of these frettingly intensive machines. Yet the rational considering quality in her work is its strength—assisted by unwordiness, uncontorted intentionalness, the flicker of impudence, the natural unforced ending.

Mere mysteriousness is useless; the enigma must be clear to the author, not necessarily to us.

> Such curious Love, in constant innocence,
> > Though ill at ease,

has the right air, and so has this:

> —Sure of my love, and Love; uncertain of identity.

The specific is judiciously interspersed with generality, and the permitted clue to idiosyncrasy has a becoming evasiveness. We are willing to be apprised of a secret—indeed glad to be—but technique must be cold, sober, conscious of self-justifying ability. Some feminine poets of the present day seem to have grown horns and to like to be frightful and dainty by turns; but distorted propriety suggests effeteness. One would rather disguise than travesty emotion; give away a nice thing than sell it; dis-

---

Trial Balances, ed. Ann Winslow (New York: Macmillan, 1935), pp. 82–83.

member a garment of rich aesthetic construction than degrade it to the utilitarian offices of the boneyard. One notices the deferences and vigilances in Miss Bishop's writing, and the debt to Donne and to Gerard Hopkins. We look at imitation askance; but like the shell which the hermit-crab selects for itself, it has value—the avowed humility, and the protection. Miss Bishop's ungrudged self-expenditure should also be noticed—automatic apparently, as part of the nature. Too much cannot be said for this phase of self-respect.

We can not ever be wholly original; we adopt a thought from a group of notes in the song of a bird, from a foreigner's way of pronouncing English, from the weave in a suit of clothes. Our best and newest thoughts about color have been known to past ages. Nevertheless an indebted thing does not interest us unless there is originality underneath it. Here, the equivalence for rhyme, achieved by the coming back again to the same word, has originality; and one feels the sincerity, the proportionateness, and the wisdom of superiority to snobbery—the selectiveness.

One asks a great deal of an author—that he should not be haphazard but considered in his mechanics, that he should not induce you to be interested in what is restrictedly private but that there should be the self-portrait: that he should pierce you to the marrow without revolting you. Miss Bishop's sparrows ("Valentine I") are not revolting, merely disaffecting. It is difficult, moreover, not to allow vigilance to fluctuate; an adjective or an "and" easily eludes one, and a mere shadow of the unintentionally mechanical deflects interest. Some phrases in these pieces of Miss Bishop's work are less live than others, but her methodically oblique, intent way of working is auspicious; one is made aware of the kind of refraction that is peculiar to works of art, that is in accordance with a good which is communicated not purveyed.

MARIANNE MOORE

A Modest Expert
North & South

Elizabeth Bishop is spectacular in being unspectacular. Why has
no one ever thought of this, one asks oneself; why not be accu-
rate and modest? Miss Bishop's mechanics of presentation with
its underlying knowledges, moreover, reduces critical cold
blood to cautious self-inquiry.

The adornments are structural, as with alliteration, contrast,
and the reiterated word as a substitute for rhyme. And rhyme,
when used, outshines restraint. Miss Bishop says, "icebergs be-
hoove the soul," "being self-made from elements least visible
. . . fleshed, fair, erected indivisible"; and of "snow-fort"
"sand-fort" Paris at 7 A.M.,

> . . . It is like introspection
> to stare inside, or retrospection,
> a star inside a rectangle, a recollection:

One notes the difficult rhyme-scheme of "Roosters," sustained
through many stanzas: "Peter's sin was—"

> of spirit, Peter's
> folly, beneath the flares
> among the servants and officers. *

The Nation (September 28, 1946), p. 354.
*In *North & South* these lines read:

> of spirit, Peter's
> falling, beneath the flares,
> among the 'servants and officers.'

Several of these quotations differ somewhat from the versions in *North & South*.
—Eds.

Among the many musicianly strategies is an expert disposition of pauses; and the near-rhymes are impeccable, as in "Wading at Wellfleet," "The sea is 'all a case of knives'"

> Lying so close, they catch the sun,
> the spokes directed at the shin.

One has here a verisimilitude that avoids embarrassingly direct descriptiveness; when journeying from the Country to the City, for instance: "flocks of shining wires seem to be flying side-wise"; and direct description is neat, never loose, as when the asphalt is said to be "watermelon-striped, light-dry, dark-wet," after the water-wagon's "hissing, snowy fan" has passed. We find that enumerative description—one of Miss Bishop's specialties—can be easy and compact:

> Now can you see the monument? It is of wood
> built somewhat like a box. No. Built
> like several boxes in descending sizes
> one above the other.
> Each is turned half-way round so that
> its corners point toward the sides
> of the one below and the angles alternate.

The wake of the barge is foliage with "Mercury-veins on the giant leaves," always the accurate word; and sensation, yet more difficult to capture than appearance, is objectified mysteriously well:

> Alone on the railroad track
> I walked with pounding heart.
> The ties were too close together
> or maybe too far apart.

Miss Bishop does not avoid "fearful pleasantries," and in "The Fish," as in the subject of the poem, one is not glad of the creature's every perquisite; but the poem dominates recollection; "Anaphora" does; and "The Weed" has so somber an authority, surrealism should take a course in it.

Dignity has been sacrificed to exactness in the word "neatly": "The mangrove island with bright green leaves edged neatly with bird-droppings like illuminations in silver"; and in "Songs for a Colored Singer," where impulsiveness is the verbal machinery, has every phrase the feel of the rest of the words—the auxiliary verb "will" for instance? "And if I protest Le Roy will answer with a frown." Like Pyramus and Thisbe, however, ardor in art finds a way, and apostrophe *s* is the deft spelling for "is": "All we got for this dollars and cents / 's a pile of bottles by the fence." The omission of three poems which appeared in *Trial Balances* is a loss—"The Reprimand," and "Valentines I" and "II."

Art which "cuts its facets from within" can mitigate suffering, can even be an instrument of happiness; as also forgiveness, symbolized in Miss Bishop's meditation on St. Peter by the cock, seems essential to happiness. Reinhold Niebuhr recently drew attention in *The Nation* to the fact that the cure for international incompatibilities is not diplomacy but contrition. Nor is it permissible to select the wrongs for which to be contrite; we are contrite, we won't be happy till we are sorry. Miss Bishop's speculation also, concerning faith—religious faith—is a carefully plumbed depth in this small-large book of beautifully formulated aesthetic-moral mathematics. The unbeliever is not ridiculed; but is not anything that is adamant, self-ironized?

> . . . Up here
> I tower through the sky
> For the marble wings on my tower-top fly.

With poetry as with homiletics, tentativeness can be more positive than positiveness; and in *North & South,* a much instructed persuasiveness is emphasized by uninsistence. At last we have a prize book that has no creditable mannerisms. At last we have someone who knows, who is not didactic.

RANDALL JARRELL

On *North & South*

The best poems in Elizabeth Bishop's *North & South* are so good that it takes a geological event like *Paterson* to overshadow them. "The Fish" and "Roosters" are two of the most calmly beautiful, deeply sympathetic poems of our time; "The Monument," "The Man-Moth," "The Weed," the first "Song for a Colored Singer," and one or two others are almost, or quite, as good; and there are charming poems on a smaller scale, or beautiful fragments—for instance, the end of "Love Lies Sleeping." Miss Bishop is capable of the most outlandish ingenuity—who else could have made a witty mirror-image poem out of the fact that we are bilaterally symmetrical?—but is grave, calm, and tender at the same time. It is odd how pleasant and sympathetic her poems are, in these days when many a poet had rather walk down children like Mr. Hyde than weep over them like Swinburne, and when many a poem is gruesome occupational therapy for a poet who stays legally innocuous by means of it. The poet whom the poems of *North & South* present or imply is as attractively and unassuming good as the poet of *Observations* and *What Are Years*—but simpler and milder, less driven into desperate straits or dens of innocence, and taking this Century of Polycarp more for granted. (When you read Miss Bishop's "Florida," a poem whose first sentence begins, "The state with the prettiest name," and whose last sentence begins, "The alligator, who has five distinct calls: / friendliness, love, mating, war, and warning," you don't need to be told that the poetry of Marianne Moore was, in the beginning, an appropriately selected foundation for Miss Bishop's work.) Miss Bishop's poems are almost

Poetry and the Age (New York: Farrar, Straus and Giroux, 1972), pp. 234–35. Originally published as a part of the essay, "The Poet and His Public," *Partisan Review* 13, no. 4 (Sept.–Oct. 1946), pp. 488–500.

never forced; in her best work restraint, calm, and proportion are implicit in every detail of organization and workmanship.

Instead of crying, with justice, "This is a world in which no one can get along," Miss Bishop's poems show that it is barely but perfectly possible—has been, that is, for her. Her work is unusually personal and honest in its wit, perception, and sensitivity—and in its restrictions too; all her poems have written underneath, *I have seen it.* She is morally so attractive, in poems like "The Fish" or "Roosters," because she understands so well that the wickedness and confusion of the age can explain and extenuate other people's wickedness and confusion, but not, for you, your own; that morality, for the individual, is usually a small, personal, statistical, but heartbreaking or heartwarming affair of omissions and commissions the greatest of which will seem infinitesimal, ludicrously beneath notice, to those who govern, rationalize, and deplore; that it is sometimes difficult and unnatural, but sometimes easy and natural, to "do well"; that beneath our lives "there is inescapable hope, the pivot," so that in the revolution of things even the heartsick Peter can someday find "his dreadful rooster come to mean forgiveness"; that when you see the snapped lines trailing, "a five-haired beard of wisdom," from the great fish's aching jaw, it is then that victory fills "the little rented boat," that the oil on the bilgewater by the rusty engine is "rainbow, rainbow, rainbow!"—that you let the fish go.

LOUISE BOGAN

On *North & South*

It is a hopeful sign when judges unanimously and with enthusi-
asm make an award to a young, fresh book of verse instead of to
an old, stale one. Last year, the three judges of the Houghton
Mifflin Poetry Prize Fellowship did that in the case of Elizabeth
Bishop's *North & South,* now published by Houghton Mifflin.
Miss Bishop's poems, moreover, are not in the least showy.
They strike no attitudes and have not an ounce of superfluous
emotional weight, and they combine an unforced ironic humor
with a naturalist's accuracy of observation, for Miss Bishop,
although she frequently writes fantasy, is firmly in touch with
the real world and takes a Thoreaulike interest in whatever
catches her attention. She can write descriptions of New En-
gland and of Florida seascapes, of a mechanical toy, of boats and
leaves in the Seine, of a city dawn, or of a mysterious pile of old
boxes. And she has unmistakably her own point of view, in spite
of her slight addiction to the poetic methods of Marianne
Moore. Like Miss Moore, Miss Bishop, thoroughly canvassing
all sides of a central idea, will make a poem out of one extended
metaphor (as in "The Imaginary Iceberg"). Or she will bring
into imaginative relation with one central theme a variety of
subjects, making a poem out of a list of things or attributes
related to a title (as in "Florida"). She often starts with a realistic
subject, which, by the time she has unravelled all its concealed
meaning, turns out to be the basis for a parable—the poem
"Roosters," for example, contains all manner of references to
war and warriors. Miss Bishop is a natural lyricist as well, but
she does not use her lyrical side as often as she might. None of
these thirty poems gives up its full meaning at once, so it is a

New Yorker (October 5, 1946), p. 113.

pleasure to read them repeatedly. Miss Bishop has evidently put in eleven years on their composition; the first appeared in print in 1935. It is to be hoped that we shall get thirty more, equally varied, unexpected, and freshly designed, in rather less than another decade.

OSCAR WILLIAMS

North but South

Elizabeth Bishop is the deserving winner of the Houghton Mifflin Poetry Award for which almost 800 poets contended. Her unquestionable talent produces such fresh unostentation as this from "The Imaginary Iceberg":

> The wits of these white peaks
> spar with the sun. Its weight the iceberg dares
> upon a shifting stage and stands and stares.
>
> This iceberg cuts its facets from within.
> Like jewelry from a grave
> it saves itself perpetually and adorns
> only itself, perhaps the snows
> which so surprise us lying on the sea.

She has, however, possibly overeducated herself in what is, or rather was, going on in the best circles, and hasn't trusted enough in her own psyche. She has listened every once in a while to certain cliques which are trying to palm off academic composition as poetic perception.

Miss Bishop has real perception but it is struggling with her angel in a too fashionable apartment. It is to her credit that the angel got by the Big-Bosomed Gold-Buttoned Footman of Academe. She has a keen eye for small physical detail: of roosters she writes, "plus all the vulgar beauty of iridescence"; of turtles, "their large white skulls with round eye-sockets / twice the size of a man's" /; of a caught fish, "a five-haired beard of wisdom / trailing from his aching jaw." Such poems as "The Imaginary Iceberg" and "Roosters" are not only full of this exquisite detail, but are emotional wholes, and therefore successful.

New Republic (October 21, 1946), p. 525.

But Miss Bishop does not break away from the purlieus of the fashionable. She apologizes subtly to the academic powers when she writes (this is her complete statement): "Most of these poems were written, or partly written, before 1942." Since the world's greatest literature was written before 1942, she should know she is on the right side of the fence. The present book whose publication has been rumored for a decade is, one senses, out a bit too soon in spite of such magnificent hesitation. For there are poems that are Audenary and Wallace Stevensish, and socially conscious poems that have not shaken off the ferment and not-so-fine frenzies belonging to others. I feel that such poems of class consciousness as the one on Cootchie, Miss Lula's servant, and "Songs for a Colored Singer" are a bit too easily on the expected side, charming little stained-glass bits here and there not saving the poems from a charge that the poet is defending the oppressed because it's the thing to do.

All in all, however, this is a good book. Its failures seem more prominent because the author is making such a to-do about having a book at all. The free verse is delicate and not too free, the preciosity is not unpleasant, the sestina is modern, competent and digestible, the influences from a half-dozen sources are handled with gloves, any thumb-prints have been wiped from the shining legs of the poetic furniture at least twice in every other poem.

I have always considered it rather mean for reviewers to pick lines from a poet's work in order to criticize that work, but Miss Bishop has written such a real poem in her "A Miracle for Breakfast," ending

> We licked up the crumb and swallowed the coffee.
> A window across the river caught the sun
> as if the miracle were working, on the wrong balcony

that I cannot resist saying of her work, in not uncomplimentary summation, that it is as if the miracle were working, on the wrong balcony.

ROBERT LOWELL

From "Thomas, Bishop, and Williams"

Nothing more unlike what I have been reviewing could be imagined than the unrhetorical, cool, and beautifully thought out poems of Elizabeth Bishop. To some readers, and to all readers at first, their inspiration will appear comparatively modest. Her admirers are not likely to hail her as a giant among the moderns, or to compare anything that she will ever write with Shakespeare or Donne. Nevertheless, the splendor and minuteness of her descriptions soon seem wonderful. Later one realizes that her large, controlled, and elaborate common-sense is always or almost always absorbed in its subjects, and that she is one of the best craftsmen alive. Thomas has greater moments and fewer successful poems. At their best, they are about equal.

On the surface, her poems are observations—surpassingly accurate, witty and well-arranged, but nothing more. Sometimes she writes of a place where she has lived on the Atlantic Coast; at others, of a dream, a picture, or some fantastic object. One is reminded of Kafka and certain abstract paintings, and is left rather at sea about the actual subjects of the poems. I think that at least nine-tenths of them fall into a single symbolic pattern. Characterizing it is an elusive business.

There are two opposing factors. The first is something in motion, weary but persisting, almost always failing and on the point of disintegrating, and yet, for the most part, stoically maintained. This is morality, memory, the weed that grows to divide, and the dawn that advances, illuminates and calls to work, the monument "that wants to be a monument,"* the

Sewanee Review 55 (Summer 1947), pp. 497–99.
*Some of these quotations differ from the versions in North & South.—EDS.

waves rolling in on the shore, breaking, and being replaced, the echo of the hermit's voice saying, "love must be put in action"; it is the stolid little mechanical horse that carries a dancer, and all those things of memory that "cannot forget us half so easily as they can forget themselves." The second factor is a terminus: rest, sleep, fulfillment or death. This is the imaginary iceberg, the moon which the Man-moth thinks is a small clean hole through which he must thrust his head; it is sleeping on the top of a mast, and the peaceful ceiling: "But oh, that we could sleep up there."

The motion-process is usually accepted as necessary and, therefore, good; yet it is dreary and exhausting. But the formula is mysterious and gently varies with its objects. The terminus is sometimes pathetically or humorously desired as a letting-go or annihilation, sometimes it is fulfillment and the complete harmonious exercise of one's faculties. The rainbow of spiritual peace seen as the author decides to let a fish go, is both like and unlike the moon which the Man-moth mistakes for an opening. In "Large Bad Picture," ships are at anchor in a northern bay, and the author reflects, "It would be hard to say what brought them there / Commerce or contemplation."

The structure of a Bishop poem is simple and effective. It will usually start as description or descriptive narrative, then either the poet or one of her characters or objects reflects. The tone of these reflections is pathetic, witty, fantastic, or shrewd. Frequently, it is all these things at once. Its purpose is to heighten and dramatize the description and, at the same time, to unify and universalize it. In this, and in her marvelous command of shifting speech-tones, Bishop resembles Robert Frost.

In her bare objective language, she also reminds one at times of William Carlos Williams; but it is obvious that her most important model is Marianne Moore. Her dependence should not be defined as imitation, but as one of development and transformation. It is not the dependence of her many facile contemporaries on Auden, but the dependence of Herrick on Jonson, the Herberts on Donne, or of Pope and Johnson on Dryden. Although Bishop would be unimaginable without Moore, her poems add something to the original, and are quite as genuine. Both poets use an elaborate descriptive technique, love exotic objects, are moral, genteel, witty, and withdrawn. There are metrical similarities, and a few of Bishop's poems are done in Moore's manner. But the differences in method and personality are great. Bishop is usually present in her poems; they happen to her, she speaks, and often centers them on herself. Others are dramatic and have human actors. She uses dreams and allegories. (Like Kafka's, her treatment of the absurd is humorous, matter of fact, and logical.) She hardly ever quotes from other writers. Most of her meters are accentual-syllabic. Compared with Moore, she is softer, dreamier, more human and more personal; she is less idiosyncratic, and less magnificent. She is probably slighter; of course, being much younger, she does not have nearly so many extraordinarily good poems.

Bishop's faults leave her best poems uninjured, and I do not need to examine them at length as I did with Thomas. A few of the shorter poems seem to me quite trivial. On rereading them, one is struck by something a little pert, banal, and over-pointed—it is as though they had been simplified for a child. Occasionally the action seems blurred and foggy especially when she is being most subjective, as in "Anaphora." In others, such as "The Map," "Casabianca" and "The Gentleman from Shallot," she is self-indulgent, and strings a whimsical commentary on an almost non-existent subject.

Few books of lyrics are as little repetitious as *North & South*. It can be read straight through with excitement. About ten of its thirty poems are failures. Another ten are either unsatisfactory as wholes, or very slight. This leaves "Roosters" and "The Fish," large and perfect, and, outside of Marianne Moore, the best poems that I know of written by a woman in this century. The first of her "Songs for a Colored Singer" is serious light verse; it is of the same quality as MacNeice's "Bagpipe Music" and Auden's wonderful "Refugee Blues." In roughly descending order, "The Monument," "The Man-Moth," "The Weed," "Cirque d'Hiver," "Large Bad Picture," "Sleeping on the Ceiling," the second "Song for a Colored Singer," "Jeronimo's House," "Florida," "Seascape," and "Quai D'Orléans" are all wonderfully successful and good. Bishop's poems are so carefully fitted together, her descriptions give such body to her reflections, and her reflections so heighten her description, that it is hard to

indicate her stature and solidity by quotation. I will give a few
stanzas from a poem published since her book. Faustina is a
negro servant, and her mistress is dying:

> Tended by Faustina
> yes in a crazy house
> upon a crazy bed,
> frail, of chipped enamel,
> blooming above her head
> into four vaguely rose-like
>   flower-formations,
>
> the white woman whispers to
> herself. The floor-boards sag
> this way and that. The crooked
> towel-covered table
> bears a can of talcum
> and five pasteboard boxes
>   of little pills,
>
> most half-crystallized.

Then as Faustina bends her "sinister kind face" over the white
woman, the poet reflects:

> Oh, is it
>
> freedom at last, a lifelong
> dream of time and silence,
> dream of protection and rest?
> Or is it the very worst,
> the unimaginable nightmare
> that never before dared last
>   more than a second?

ARTHUR MIZENER

New Verse
North & South

Miss Bishop's mind is as dramatic and anagogical as the best, but
it has an unusually acute respect for fact and sense, observations
of which run through her poems like the crumbs "those clever
children placed by day / and followed to their door / one night,
at least." This is the quick awareness which is wise enough to
know that brilliant sensitivity is not enough, that the love which
does not, in Auden's words, "Leave the North in place / With a
good grace" is not satisfactory. Miss Bishop is always trans-
forming facts, making us see their meaning and elegance, till the
"bright green leaves edged neatly with bird-droppings" are
"like illumination in silver," and the lights on the Navy-Yard
aerial are "Phoenixes / burning quietly, where the dew cannot
climb." But we never forget that the bird droppings and the
lights are what they are. The meaning and the elegance, the
colors the mind gives things are enormously important, heaven
knows, but not more important than the topography of things,
which "displays no favorites"; "More delicate than the histo-
rians' are the map-makers' colors." Miss Bishop has little respect
for the mind which cannot tell a hawk from a heronshaw and is
not as sane north and south as it may be mad north-north-west.

> This celestial seascape, with white herons got up as angels,
> flying as high as they want and as far as they want side-wise
> in tiers and tiers of immaculate reflections; . . .
> it does look like heaven.

We are never allowed to forget that fancy is fancy or that what
heaven may know as "immaculate reflections" we know as
herons. The will "to cherish something," "to commemorate"

Furioso (Spring 1947), pp. 72–75.

what the consciousness may linger over does so by producing a monument "built somewhat like a box" out of common materials. Either the everyday fact itself is elegant or miraculous as is the city in early morning "made delicate by over-workmanship," or the assertion of these conditions is mere sentimentality.

> My house, my fairy
>   palace, is
> of perishable
>   clapboards with
> three rooms in all,
>   my gray wasps' nest
> of chewed-up paper
>   glued with spit.

Miss Bishop's poems are like the ships at rest in the harbor in her great uncle's large bad picture:

> It would be hard to say what brought them there,
> commerce or contemplation.

All this is to say, as critics have remarked, this Miss Bishop makes her poems the way Miss Moore makes hers, by making imaginary gardens with real toads in them. Miss Bishop is not, however, merely imitating a manner, and there is an important respect in which the two are not alike. Miss Moore always describes an object. A proper description of the Jerboa may involve Scipio Africanus and Jacob's dream and the Bedouin flute and Chippendale, but however much what she has to say about him is the definition of an attitude which may well have other applications, Miss Moore is always talking about the Jerboa, not about the attitude. But Miss Bishop's poems are primarily accounts of states of mind, not of objects about which they crystallize, much as she respects these objects and insists on their importance. "Paris, 7 A.M." for instance starts with a trip around her apartment to look at all the clocks' faces. "Time," she remarks, apparently at random, "is an Etoile," and "Winter lives under a pigeon's wing, a dead wing with damp feathers." Then she looks out the window at the courtyard:

> It is like introspection
> to stare inside, or retrospection,
> a star inside a rectangle, a recollection.

And with that the scene is transfigured:

> —The childish snow-forts, built in flashier winters,
> could have reached these proportions and been houses.

But something is wrong:

> Where is the ammunition, the piled-up balls
> with the star-splintered hearts of ice?
> This sky is no carrier-warrior-pigeon
> escaping endless intersecting circles.
> It is a dead one, or the sky from which a dead one fell.
> The urns have caught his ashes or his feathers.
> When did the star dissolve, or was it captured
> by the sequence of squares and squares and circles, circles?
> Can the clocks say; is it there below,
> about to tumble in snow?

This summary does much less than justice to Miss Bishop's poem, but I think it shows that the real heart of the poem is in the two images of a star and a pigeon, and that these images are being used to elucidate a state of mind. The apartment with its clocks, the courtyard with its mansard-roofed houses and its urns, these are perfectly concrete and never disregarded; but they are not the prime concern, the interest which ultimately determines the poem's form. For this reason Miss Bishop writes poems about "Sleeping on the Ceiling" and a "Gentleman of Shalott" who, like a character from some limerick, is only half a man with a mirror "down the edge." These are not subjects for Miss Moore, though Miss Bishop knows how to retain Miss Moore's virtues in speaking of them, as when the gentleman of Shalott reaches a conclusion characteristic of them both:

> He wishes to be quoted as saying at present:
> "Half is enough."

We have waited a long time for these thirty poems, seeing that Miss Bishop was writing good verse when she was a senior at Vassar in 1934 (at least one of these poems was written then). It is easy to say they are well worth having waited for; they are. It is not so easy to say why, to say how honestly they use, without abusing, the rhetorical resources of verse, how perfectly they balance devotion to fact and to memory and desire, how beautifully they combine toughness and elegance of mind.

MARIANNE MOORE

"Senhora Helena"

My Life as a Little Girl was published in 1942—primarily to amuse family and friends and now a Brazilian classic. It continually rivals poetry; furthermore is "one of those rare stories that combines worldly success and a happy ending," its translator says; in its universal-personal insights is irresistible.

"Helena Morley" (a pseudonym) had, as ancestor, an English doctor who was for a time on the staff of a gold-mining affiliate of the São del Rey Mining Company and remained in Brazil for reasons of health, settled in Diamantina, and married a Brazilian lady. "Senhora Helena," now a favorite in Rio de Janeiro society, is the wife of Dr. Augusto Mario Caldeira Brant, President of the Bank of Brazil, at whose suggestion the Diary was published.

In Diamantina, a center for gold and diamond mining, the Diary depicts life as lived by the Morleys and their many relatives. That a translator should share the qualities of work translated, Miss Bishop exemplifies in her gift for fantasy, her use of words and hyper-precise eye. The attitude to life revealed by the Diary, Helena's apperceptiveness, and innate accuracy, seem a double portrait; the exactness of observation in the introduction being an extension, in manner, of Miss Bishop's verse and other writing, as when she differentiates between marbleized or painted window-frames to imitate stone, and stone ones painted to imitate grained wood; again, in the description of rain-pipe funnels "flaring like trumpets," sometimes with "tin petals or feathers down them and around the mouth . . . repeated in tiles set edgewise up the ridges of the roofs, dragonlike and very 'Chinese.'" And it would be hard to find a process more accurately described than this, of panning for diamonds in a stream

A Marianne Moore Reader (New York: Viking, 1961), pp. 226–28. First published in *Poetry* (July 1959).

by the road: "A small quantity of gravel in the wide round sieve is held just beneath the surface of the water, swirled around and around and lifted out" and, "with the gesture of a quick-fingered housewife turning out a cake," the panner "turned the whole thing upside down on the ground, intact. He put on his horn-rimmed glasses, lowered himself to his knees in the wet mud, and stared, passing a long wooden knife over the gravel from side to side"—"the simplest of all forms of diamond 'mining.'" "One sometimes gets the impression that the greater part of the town, black and white, 'rich' and poor, when it hasn't found a diamond lately, gets along by making sweets and pastries, brooms and cigarettes and selling to each other. . . ." "Black beans instead of the bread of other countries, seem to be equated with life itself."

The personality of Helena Morley would be hard to match. Besides an ardor synonymous with affection, she "steps in and out of superstition" as Miss Bishop says, "Reason, belief, and disbelief, without much adolescent worrying. She would never for a moment doubt that the church is a good thing." "I admire good and holy people," she says, "but I can't possibly stop being the way I am." A main part of being the way she was, was compassion. On a night during the family's summer outing, when all were kept awake by a crying baby, Helena says, "To let her cry with pain, and then to beat her. I couldn't stand it. . . . I didn't even have to stay with her half an hour"—provoking a remonstrance from Mrs. Morley: "This girl, this mania of not being able to hear a baby cry without wanting to comfort it. She'll be the death of me." In recording the incident, Helena says, "I think if this little girl had been white, mama wouldn't have minded." On any page of the Diary we encounter similar "fire"; as here: "I don't have a corner to do my lessons in. So, with the help of God, I found something simply wonderful. I went to pick mulberries and climbed the tree to the very top. What a discovery. The mulberry was so overgrown with a vine that it looked like a mattress. I'd tell grandma that I was going to study under the mulberry tree and then I'd climb up and stay on top looking at the view which is perfectly beautiful." "José Rabela spends his time weighing vultures in the scales in order to invent a flying machine. Wouldn't that be wonderful! . . . I feel envious when I see the vultures soaring up so high." Not everything was wonderful. Of visiting the dentist, Helena says, "It is more nauseating than finding a toad in one's bed. He can't say a thing without a diminutive. 'Will you do me the favor of opening your little mouth?' . . . 'little mouth, little ache, little tooth.' I almost fainted in the chair, I disliked him so much." The Diary has tone. With regard to having a post-office, Helena says, "Wouldn't it be better . . . if they put in street lamps for us so that on dark nights we wouldn't have to walk slowly for fear of falling over a cow. And water pipes. . . . Nobody's going to die without a letter, but the water has killed lots of people who might have been living today." Then of submerged problems, "All year long, mama struggles with him [papa] to go to confession." "I suffered a great deal because of grandfather and don't want to suffer now too because of papa. My grandfather was not buried in the church because he was a Protestant. 'Any ground God made is holy ground,' he said." Alert to every pretext favorable to satire, Helena says, "Joas de Assis suffers from a strange complaint, he's so sorry for everyone, no matter who," and "Everybody says father is a good husband and yet nobody says mama is a good wife." She tells how, when a *calderao* is found (a pocket of diamonds), a slave falls on his knees, exclaiming, "My Lord and Heavenly Father, if this wealth endangers my soul, let it vanish." Charmed observation and reflexive ingenuity never pall. Helena's susceptibility to personality and commensurate candor constantly leave one with a sense of originality that nothing could impair. In an agony of diffidence because of having withheld at confession the sin of having thought a priest "homely," she is told that she should confess it, and to the same priest from whom she had withheld it; then admits, "But the priest is you, Father."

Being able to observe imagination in action here is like opening a watch and studying the continuous uninterfering operation of wheels and wheels. We see, furthermore, as Miss Bishop says, "that happiness does not consist in worldly goods but in a peaceful home, in family affection,—things that fortune cannot bring and often takes away." And "it happened, that is the charm and the point of *Mina Vida de Menina.*"

ROBERT LOWELL

From an Interview

Interviewer: [Concerning] your admiration for Elizabeth Bishop's poetry. I know that you've said the qualities and the abundance of its descriptive language reminded you of the Russian novel more than anything else.

Lowell: Any number of people are guilty of writing a complicated poem that has a certain amount of symbolism in it and really difficult meaning, a wonderful poem to teach. Then you unwind it and you feel that the intelligence, the experience, whatever goes into it, is skin-deep. In Elizabeth Bishop's "Man-Moth" a whole new world is gotten out and you don't know what will come after any one line. It's exploring. And it's as original as Kafka. She's gotten a world, not just a way of writing. She seldom writes a poem that doesn't have that exploratory quality; yet it's very firm, it's not like beat poetry, it's all controlled.

Interviewer: What poets among your contemporaries do you most admire?

Lowell: The two I've been closest to are Elizabeth Bishop—I spoke about her earlier—and Jarrell, and they're different. Jarrell's a great man of letters, a very informed man, and the best critic of my generation, the best professional poet. He's written the best war poems, and those poems are a tremendous product of our culture, I feel. Elizabeth Bishop's poems, as I said, are more personal, more something she did herself, and she's not a critic but has her own tastes, which may be very idiosyncratic. I enjoy her poems more than anybody else's.

An interview with Frederick Seidel in *Writers at Work: The Paris Review Interviews,* Second series (New York: Viking, 1963), pp. 337–68. Originally published in *The Paris Review* 7 (1961).

RANDALL JARRELL

From "Fifty Years of American Poetry"

Elizabeth Bishop's *Poems* seems to me one of the best books an American poet has written, one that the future will read almost as it will read Stevens and Moore and Ransom. Her poems are quiet, truthful, sad, funny, most marvelously individual poems; they have a sound, a feel, a whole moral and physical atmosphere, different from anything else I know. They are honest, modest, minutely observant, masterly; even their most complicated or troubled or imaginative effects seem, always, personal and natural, and as unmistakable as the first few notes of a Mahler song, the first few patches of a Vuillard interior. Her best poems—poems like "The Man-Moth," "The Fish," "The Weed," "Roosters," "The Prodigal Son," "Faustina, or Rock Roses," "The Armadillo"—remind one of Vuillard or even, sometimes, of Vermeer. The poet and the poems have their limitations; all exist on a small scale, and some of the later poems, especially, are too detailedly and objectively descriptive. But the more you read her poems, the better and fresher, the more nearly perfect they seem; at least half of them are completely realized works of art.

Third Book of Criticism (New York: Farrar, Straus and Giroux, 1969), p. 325. Originally published in *Prairie Schooner* (Spring 1963), pp. 1–27.

ROBERT LOWELL

On "Skunk Hour"
How the Poem Was Written

. . . I began writing lines in a new style. No poem, however, got finished and soon I left off and tried to forget the whole headache. Suddenly, in August, I was struck by the sadness of writing nothing, and having nothing to write, of having, at least, no language. When I began writing "Skunk Hour," I felt that most of what I knew about writing was a hindrance.

The dedication is to Elizabeth Bishop, because re-reading her suggested a way of breaking through the shell of my old manner. Her rhythms, idiom, images, and stanza structure seemed to belong to a later century. "Skunk Hour" is modeled on Miss Bishop's "The Armadillo," a much better poem and one I had heard her read and had later carried around with me. Both "Skunk Hour" and "The Armadillo" use short line stanzas, start with drifting description and end with a single animal.

This was the main source.

"On 'Skunk Hour,'" *The Contemporary Poet as Artist and Critic,* ed. Anthony Ostroff (Boston: Little, Brown and Co., 1964), pp. 107–10.

JAMES MERRILL

From an Interview

Q: You mentioned Elizabeth Bishop before. A number of other poets today have singled her out. Would you say, in terms of form, that she has provided valuable examples for poets, especially in your own poetry?

A: The unpretentiousness of her form is very appealing. But I don't know if it's simply a matter of form. Rather, I like the way her whole *oeuvre* is on the scale of a human life; there is no oracular amplification, she doesn't go about on stilts to make her vision wider. She doesn't need that. She's wise and humane enough as it is. And this is rather what I feel about Stevens. For all the philosophy that intrudes in and between the lines, Stevens' poetry is a body of work that is man-sized. Whereas I wouldn't say that of Pound; he tries, I think, to write like a god. Stevens and Miss Bishop merely write like angels.

"An Interview with Donald Sheehan," *Contemporary Literature* (Winter 1968), pp. 1–14.

JOHN ASHBERY

The Complete Poems

One hopes that the title of Elizabeth Bishop's new book is an error and that there will be more poems and at least another *Complete Poems*. The present volume runs to a little more than 200 pages, and although the proportion of pure poetry in it outweighs many a chunky, collected volume from our established poets (Miss Bishop is somehow an establishment poet herself, and the establishment ought to give thanks; she is proof that it can't be all bad), it is still not enough for an addict of her work. For, like other addicting substances, this work creates a hunger for itself; the more one tastes it, the less of it there seems to be.

From the moment Miss Bishop appeared on the scene it was apparent to everybody that she was a poet of strange, even mysterious, but undeniable and great gifts. Her first volume, *North & South* (1946), was the unanimous choice of the judges in a publisher's contest to which 800 manuscripts were submitted. Her second won the Pulitzer Prize. One of her poems is enough to convince you that you are in expert hands and can relax and enjoy the ride; in the words of Marianne Moore reviewing *North & South,* "At last we have someone who knows, who is not didactic." Few contemporary poets can claim both virtues.

Her concerns at first glance seem special. The life of dreams, always regarded with suspicion as too "French" in American poetry; the little mysteries of falling asleep and the oddness of waking up in the morning; the sea, especially its edge, and the look of the creatures who live in it; then diversions and reflections on French clocks and mechanical toys that recall Marianne Moore (though the two poets couldn't be more different; Miss

New York Times Book Review (June 1, 1969), pp. 8, 25.

Moore's synthesizing, collector's approach is far from Miss Bishop's linear, exploring one).

And yet, what more natural, more universal experiences are there than sleep, dreaming and waking; waking, as she says in one of her most beautiful poems, "Anaphora," to: "the fiery event / of every day in endless / endless assent." And her preoccupation with wildlife and civilized artifacts comes through as an exemplar of the way we as subject feel about the objects, living or inert, that encircle us. We live in a quandary, but it is not a dualistic conflict between inner and outer reality, it is rather a question of deciding how much the outer reality is our reality, how far we can advance into it and still keep a toe-hold on the inner, private one, "For neither is clearer / nor a different color / than the other," as Miss Bishop says.

This strange divided singleness of our experience is a theme that is echoed and alluded to throughout Miss Bishop's work, but never more beautifully than in a short prose poem called "Rainy Season; Sub-Tropics," here collected for the first time. It consists of three monologues spoken by a giant toad, a crab and a giant snail, respectively, somewhat along the lines of Jules Renard's *Histoires Naturelles,* yet Miss Bishop's poems are actually brief, mordant essays on the nature of being. Conceivably these are thoughts that could occur to the creatures in question, yet at the same time they are types, and not metaphors, of thoughts that occur to an intellectually curious person. "I live, I breathe, by swallowing," confides the toad, who also mentions "the almost unused poison that I bear, my burden and my great responsibility." And the snail, frank but bemused, observes: "I give the impression of mysterious ease, but it is only with the greatest effort of my will that I can rise above the smallest stones and sticks."

One can smile at the way these creatures imperfectly perceive their habitat, but their dilemma is ours too, for we too confusedly feel ourselves to be part thing and part thought. And "we'd rather have the iceberg than the ship, / although it meant the end of travel." Our inert thingness pleases us, and though we would prefer not to give up "travel" or intellectual voyaging, in a showdown we would doubtless choose the iceberg, or object, because it mysteriously includes the soul: "Icebergs behoove the soul / (both being self-made from elements least visible) / to see them so: fleshed, fair, erected indivisible."

This quality which one can only call "thingness" is with her throughout, sometimes shaping a whole poem, sometimes disappearing right after the beginning, sometimes appearing only at the end to add a decisive fillip. In "Over 2000 Illustrations and a Complete Concordance," which is possibly her masterpiece, she plies continually between the steel-engraved vignettes of a gazetteer and the distressingly unclassified events of a real voyage. A nightmarish little prose tale called "The Hanging of the Mouse" concludes with a description so fantastically accurate that it shoots currents of meaning backward into the enigmatic story. "His whiskers rowed hopelessly round and round in the air a few times and his feet flew up and curled into little balls like young fern-plants."

As one who read, reread, studied and absorbed Miss Bishop's first book and waited impatiently for her second one, I felt slightly disappointed when it finally did arrive nine years later. *A Cold Spring* (1955) contained only sixteen new poems, and the publishers had seen fit to augment it by reprinting *North & South* in the same volume. Moreover, some of the new poems were not, for me, up to the perhaps impossibly high standard set by the first book. Several seemed content with picture-making: they made marvelous pictures, it is true, but not like those in *North & South* which managed to create a *trompe-l'oeil* that conquered not just the eye and the ear but the mind as well. And in several, the poet's life threatened to intrude on the poetry in a way that didn't suit it. One accepted without question the neutral "we" in earlier poems as the necessary plural of "I," but a couple of the new ones veered dangerously close to the sentimental ballad of the Millay-Teasdale-Wylie school, to one's considerable surprise, notably "Varick Street" with its refrain: "*And I shall sell you sell you / sell you of course, my dear, and you'll sell me.*"

A Cold Spring does, however, contain the marvelous "Over 2000 Illustrations" which epitomizes Miss Bishop's work at its best; it is itself "an undisturbed, unbreathing flame," which is a line of the poem. Description and meaning, text and ornament, subject and object, the visible world and the poet's consciousness fuse together to form a substance that is undescribable and a continuing joy, and one returns to it again and again, ravished and unsatisfied. After twenty years (the poem first appeared in *Partisan Review* in 1948) I am unable to exhaust the meaning and mysteries of its concluding line: "And looked and looked our infant sight away," and I suspect that its secret has very much to do with the nature of Miss Bishop's poetry. Looking, or attention, will absorb the object with its meaning. Henry James advises us to "be one of those on whom nothing is lost," without specifying how this is to be accomplished. Miss Bishop, at the end of her poem "The Monument," which describes a curious and apparently insignificant monument made of wooden boxes, is a little more specific: "Watch it closely," she tells us. The power of vision, "our infant sight," is both our torment and our salvation.

Her next book, *Questions of Travel* (1965), completely erased the doubts that *A Cold Spring* had aroused in one reader. The distance between Varick Street and Brazil may account for the difference not just in thematic material but in tone as well. We are introduced to the country in the opening poem, "Arrival at Santos," with its engagingly casual rhymes ("seen" rhymes with "Miss Breen," a fellow passenger) and rhythms; its prosy, travel-diary style, its form so perfectly adapted to its content that there isn't a bulge or a wrinkle. After telling us about the ocean voyage and the port where it has ended, she terminates as only she can with a brief statement of fact that seems momentous: "We leave Santos at once; / we are driving to the interior."

Her years in the *la-bas* of Brazil brought Miss Bishop's gifts to maturity. Both more relaxed and more ambitious, she now can do almost anything she pleases, from a rhymed passage "From Trollope's Journal" to a Walker Evansish study of a "Filling Station"; and from a funny shapshot of a bakery in Rio at night ("The gooey tarts are red and sore") to "The Burglar of Babylon," a ballad about the death of a Brazilian bandit in which emotionally charged ellipses build up a tragic grandeur as in Godard's *Pierrot le Fou*.

Perhaps some of the urgency of the *North & South* poems has gone, but this is more than compensated by the calm control she now commands. Where she sometimes seemed nervous (as anyone engaged in a task of such precision has a right to be) and (in *A Cold Spring*) even querulous, she now is easy in a way that increased knowledge and stature allow. Her mirror-image "Gentleman of Shalott" in *North & South* was perhaps echoing the poet's sentiments when he said, "Half is enough." But the classical richness of her last poems proves that frugality need not exclude totality; the resulting feast is, for once, even better than "enough."

ROBERT LOWELL

On *The Complete Poems*

I am sure no living poet is as curious and observant as Miss Bishop. What cuts so deeply is that each poem is inspired by her own tone, a tone of large, grave tenderness and sorrowing amusement. She is too sure of herself for empty mastery and breezy plagiarism, too interested for confession and musical monotony, too powerful for mismanaged fire, and too civilized for idiosyncratic incoherence. She has a humorous, commanding genius for picking up the unnoticed, now making something sprightly and right, and now a great monument. Once her poems, each shining, were too few. Now they are many. When we read her, we enter the classical serenity of a new country.

Jacket blurb to *The Complete Poems* (New York: Farrar, Straus and Giroux, 1969).

ROBERT LOWELL

For Elizabeth Bishop 4

The new painting must live on iron rations,
rushed brushstrokes, indestructible paint-mix,
fluorescent lofts instead of French *plein air.*
Albert Ryder let his crackled amber moonscapes
ripen in sunlight. His painting was repainting,
his tiniest work weighs heavy in the hand.
Who is killed if the horseman never cry halt?
Have you seen an inchworm crawl on a leaf,
cling to the very end, revolve in air,
feeling for something to reach to something? Do
you still hang your words in air, ten years
unfinished, glued to your notice board, with gaps
or empties for the unimaginable phrase—
unerring Muse who makes the casual perfect?

History (New York: Farrar, Straus and Giroux, 1973), p. 198.

RICHARD HOWARD

Comment on "In the Waiting Room" and Herbert's "Love Unknown"

A decade ago, when she chose "The Man-Moth" for an anthology, Elizabeth Bishop remarked on the misprint (for "mammoth") by which "an oracle spoke from the page of the *New York Times*. . . . One is offered such oracular statements all the time but often misses them . . . the meaning refuses to stay put." In this recent poem—published since the fortunately mistitled *Complete Poems*—the oracle is, in part, the *National Geographic,* whose "volcano, / black, and full of ashes; /. . . spilling over / in rivulets of fire," just like Herbert's "font, wherein did fall / A stream of bloud, which issued from the side / Of a great rock," functions as an instrument of tempering. Pain, war, all the horrors of the flesh, the inadequacies of mere selfhood ("Better than you know me, or (which is one) / Then I myself," Herbert chatters on, as Miss Bishop more laconically discerns: "Without thinking at all / I was my foolish aunt, / I— we—were falling")—these are the means by which we are brought home to ourselves as we must be if we are authentically alive, "new, tender, quick."

Both poems are triumphs of tonality, of patience with material event in its likelihood of revealing what is beyond the material, the image of a speaking voice beguiling us into the deeps until every word (even Bishop's innocuous title, even Herbert's "natural" slip of the tongue: "I found that some had stuff'd the bed with thoughts. I would say *thorns*") turns incandescent in the "spacious fornace" of experience, of experiment, of trial. The result is that the process I have called tempering (the word

---

Preferences (New York: Viking, 1974), p. 31.

covers the famous "temperament" of the modern poet as well as the *Temple* in which the metaphysical one lodges his entire utterance) collocates, fuses: "held us all together / or made us all just one," for to possess an identity is to acknowledge society ("I felt: you are an *I*, / you are an *Elizabeth*, / you are one of *them*."). Such participation is of course explicit in Herbert, for the Sacraments are institutionalized and available, "into my cup for good"; in Bishop, they are momentary and delusive ("the meaning refuses to stay put"), and though at the ultimate source of the word she is a religious poet—religion as a binding together, a unifying of what can never be uniform—there is no redemption for her; there is the waiting room, which like the caldron of affliction is "bright and too hot," and "then I was back in it," just as Herbert goes back to bed. "It" is the world, that "scalding pan" which affords these poets their presumption of membership as well as their "sensation of falling."

MARK STRAND

From a Conversation

. . . I'm also a great admirer of Elizabeth Bishop. There's something about the shape of her stanzas, the tone of her poems—a certain distance or neutrality she maintains without sacrificing intensity, a strong perceptual energy that works without destroying the balance and clarity of her poems. I'm also fascinated by the sudden, unexplained intrusion of dreams, or ghoulish humor, or something slightly awry that her poems manage to absorb effortlessly. There's never a false note. She's an absolutely sure craftswoman.

And I like her quatrains. This may sound ridiculous, but as I was writing quatrains I would remember her quatrains in "Love Lies Sleeping" or "A Summer's Dream" or "The Burglar of Babylon."

"A Conversation with Norman Klein," *Ploughshares* 2, no. 3 (1975), p. 100.

OCTAVIO PAZ

Elizabeth Bishop, or the Power of Reticence

Poetry in America began with the voice of a woman: Sor Juana Ines de la Cruz. Since then, with a kind of astronomical regularity, from Argentina to Canada, in all the languages of our hemisphere, certain names appear which are centers of poetic gravitation: Emily Dickinson, Marianne Moore, Gabriela Mistral, Elizabeth Bishop. Each one of them distinct, unique. To class poets by gender is no less deceptive than classifying racehorses by the color of their eyes. Gender is as important a determinant as the poet's language, the time and the society in which he lives, the family he comes from, the dreams he dreamed as a child. . . . But poetry is the art of transforming determinants in autonomous works. The poem has a life independent from the poet and from the gender of the poet. Poetry is the *other voice*. The voice that comes from *there,* a *there* that is always *here.*

What is the color, the temperature, the tone, the quality of Elizabeth Bishop's voice? Is it obscure, sharp, profound, luminous? Where does it come from? Like the voice of any authentic poet, her voice comes from there, from the other side, which can be anywhere and anyplace. The voice the poet hears she does not hear in the oracle's cave but in her own room. Yet as soon as poetry occurs, "suddenly you're in a different place / where everything seems to happen in waves," one side of the buildings glistens like a field of wheat, and in the taxi "the meter glares like a moral owl." The poetic act frees things from their habitual associations and relations; on walking along the beach we see "a track of big dog-prints," and at the end of the poem we discover that "those big, majestic paw-prints" were but those of the "lion

Translated and printed in *World Literature Today* (Winter 1977), pp. 15–16. First published in *Plural* 5, no. 1 (October 1975), pp. 6–7.

sun, a sun who'd walked the beach the last low tide. . . ." In the poetry of Elizabeth Bishop things waver between being what they are and being something distinct from what they are. This uncertainty is manifested at times as humor and at other times as metaphor. In both cases it is resolved, invariably, in a leap that is a paradox: things become other things without ceasing to be the things they are. This leap has two names: one is imagination, the other is freedom. They are synonymous. Imagination describes the poetic act as a gratuitous game; freedom defines it as moral choice. The poetry of Elizabeth Bishop has the lightness of a game and the gravity of a decision.

Fresh, clear, potable: these adjectives that are usually applied to water and that have both physical and moral meanings suit perfectly the poetry of Elizabeth Bishop. Like water, her voice issues from dark and deep places; like water, it satisfies a double thirst: thirst for reality and thirst for marvels. Water lets us see things that repose in its depths yet are subjected to a continual metamorphosis: they change with the merest changes of light, they undulate, they are shaken, they live a ghostly life, a sudden blast of wind scatters them. Poetry that is heard as water is heard: murmur of syllables among stones and grass, verbal waves, huge zones of silence and transparency.

Water but also air: poetry in order to see, visual poetry. Words limpid as a perfect day. The poem is a powerful lens that plays with distances and presences. The juxtaposition of spaces and perspectives makes the poem a theatre where the oldest and most quotidian of mysteries is represented: reality and its riddles. Poetry in order to travel with eyes open or closed: The Seven Wonders of the World, a bit "tired" now, or the childhood scene transfixed—"the iron kettle" sings on top of the "Marvel Stove" and, hovering like a bird, the almanac says: "time to plant tears"; the mountain *fazenda,* hung with waterfalls in the rainy season, or the mist's "white mutations" on Cape Breton; voyages within the self or outside the self, to the past or to the present, to the secret cities of memory or along the circular corridors of desire.

Poetry as if water spoke, as if air thought. . . . These poor comparisons are but ways of alluding to perfection. Not the perfection of the triangle, the sphere or the pyramid, but the irregular perfection, the imperfect perfection of the plant and of the insect. Poems perfect as a cat or a rose, not as a theorem. Living objects: muscles, skin, eyes, ears, color, temperature. Poems that change, breathe, feel, weep (with discretion), smile (with intelligence). Objects made of words that speak but, above all, objects that know how to keep silent. From political discourse to ideological sermon, from surrealistic "ceaseless murmur" to public confession, twentieth-century poetry has become garrulous. We are drowning not in a sea but in a swamp of words. We have forgotten that poetry is not in what words say but in what is said between them, that which appears fleetingly in pauses and silences. In the poetry workshops of universities there should be a required course for young poets: learning to be silent. The enormous power of reticence—that is the great lesson of the poetry of Elizabeth Bishop. But I am wrong to speak of lessons. Her poetry teaches us nothing. To hear it is not to hear a lesson; it is a pleasure, verbal and mental, as great as a spiritual experience. Let's listen to Elizabeth Bishop, hear what her words say to us and what, through them, her silence tells us.

FRANK BIDART

On Elizabeth Bishop

I want to begin by quoting Randall Jarrell: "The more you read [Elizabeth Bishop's] poems, the better and fresher, the more nearly perfect they seem." I think that this is true; but I want to emphasize the pain and tremendous struggle beneath this "perfection." For I'm scared to imagine *observing* as much as Miss Bishop does: a phrase in E. M. Cioran comes to mind, "the calvary of nuance." The poems often, of course, assert that the world is, despite so much evidence, livable; in "Roosters," Saint Peter's "dreadful rooster come[s] to mean forgiveness." But I think of Miss Bishop's "Giant Toad," who says: "My eyes bulge and hurt. They are my one great beauty, even so. They see too much, above, below, and yet there is not much to see." Her "Giant Snail" says: "I give the impression of mysterious ease, but it is only with the greatest effort of my will that I can rise above the smallest stones and sticks." The world in Miss Bishop's work seems almost to *demand* that someone observe, describe, bear it; the great triumph in her descriptions, I think, is the drama of perception lying beneath them and enacted by them, her sense of the cost as well as pleasures of such observing.

"In the Waiting Room" and "Crusoe in England" are about journeys—journeys which threaten to diminish or destroy the self, but which also leave one with a sense of the tyranny and constriction of the ordinary world, the world one left. Crusoe says:

> The knife there on the shelf—
> it reeked of meaning, like a crucifix.
> It lived. How many years did I
> beg it, implore it, not to break?
> . . .
> Now it won't look at me at all.

The little girl of "In the Waiting Room" suddenly feels that she is falling off the "round, turning world / into cold, blue-black space." She saves herself by clinging to the objects of the world—her name, "trousers and skirts and boots / and different pairs of hands / lying under the lamps." Or is the fact that she has suddenly realized that she is *like* that world, the reason that she began to fall off?

> How had I come to be here,
> like them, and overhear
> a cry of pain that could have
> got loud and worse but hadn't?

I feel here something like a tragic dilemma: it is terrible and painful to be "my aunt, / or me, or anyone"; but the alternative is coldness, blank darkness, mere space.

I think that Miss Bishop is a great poet, and that we are very lucky to have her.

The preceding paragraphs were written as an introduction to a reading Elizabeth Bishop gave at Wellesley College in 1976. I wanted to emphasize Elizabeth's "dark side"—too often she had been considered "cool" and "perfect," and not the profound, even tragic artist she is.

Her favorite poet, I think, was Herbert; like Herbert her own poems have an astonishingly unvarnished force, the intimacy of a unique self speaking. "There is," as Eliot says in *Four Quartets,* "no competition." If the future is smart, surely her poems will continue to be read. Great poems don't replace one another; each does something nothing else does. The pathos and intimacy in her work deepened until the very end of her life. On October 6, 1979, we ran out of luck.

1981

WILLIAM MEREDITH

Invitation to Miss Elizabeth Bishop

With an Epigraph and Invocation and Fourteen Maxims

The Epigraph

I chose her because she's my favorite living poet.
> John Ashbery, nominating Miss Bishop
> for the Books Abroad—Neustadt
> International Prize for Literature

The Invocation

From 437 Lewis Wharf, by Amtrak's uncertain rails
    trailing your zip-code one four two two six,
come dawdling down from Boston this late December day
    crossing the Harlem River thin as Styx
to where Session 565 lovingly travails,
    claiming your vast geographies for MLA.
Come dawdling anyway.

The Maxims

1. We speak of certain artists as great, others as important, still others, grudgingly, as original. When we say, *I choose her because she's my favorite poet,* we praise a one-to-one relationship with a writer who alters our lives a little for the better.

2. The scholars of literature and the makers of it are said to exist in a symbiotic relationship. But at best the relationship is more comradely than that: we have both bet our sweet lives on the efficacy of literature to alter human lives a little for the better.

Written for and delivered during Session 565, Modern Language Association Convention, December 28, 1976, New York City.

(That famous elegy which tells us that poetry makes nothing happen, ends, you will recall, by asking the dead poet to alter our lives vastly for the better.)

3. When Elizabeth Bishop published her *Complete Poems*—85 of them, counting five translations she laid especial claim to—we realized that we had grown sadly accustomed to *incomplete* ones.

4. The *oeuvre* is small, like Piero della Francesca's and Sappho's, but here elimination has been achieved by a more deliberate process than time and accidental loss.

5. One wonders whether, if poet X had published only Miss Bishop's now total of 95 poems instead of his 17 books, 2 *Selecteds* and one medium-sized and one mammoth *Collected Poems,* a silky confection of sows ears might have resulted. One thinks that unlikely. The stuff is different.

6. A sign of major vision: the artist is as careful to bring the small insight to perfection as the large. "Late Air" is no less a Bishop poem, no more a Bishop poem than "Visits to St Elizabeths."

7. Foolish critics "judge a problem by its awkwardness," in Auden's phrase, measure a poem by its pretension, as if David had never picked up a slingshot or Emily Dickinson a robin.

8. Foolish critics reproached Frost and Auden—very early on, it now appears—for little poems, small themes, taking these for trivia, signs of decline in powers. Miss Bishop was too quick for them. From the first, she has cut small jewels along with the large.

9. The appropriateness of form in these poems constitutes a lucid, enduring maxim which only a very unwise person would try to paraphrase. I would paraphrase it, *total attention*.

10. We are accustomed to a certain technical sloppiness in revolutionary artists. We used to speak tolerantly of the nursemaid

who "threw out the baby with the bath water," although nobody really approved of that. What are we to say of the nurseries today, with the window wide open, dirty bath water steaming in the basin, and no baby to be found?

11. If you want to see perfection of organic form, look at "Visits to St. Elizabeths (a round), "Sandpiper" (quatrains), the "Sestina" ("September rain falls on the house. . . ."), "One Art" (a villanelle) and "Roosters" (triplets). Clean babies.

12. She will yet civilize and beguile us from our silly schools. The Olsons will lie down with the Wilburs and the Diane Wakoskis dance quadrilles with the J. V. Cunninghams and the Tooth Mother will suckle the rhymed skunk kittens of Lowell.

13. The two kinds of poetry are, Excellent and Other (as with scholarship). They cannot lie down together because somebody always get squashed.

14. Elizabeth Bishop, so far as we know, writes only the one kind. Most other poets show off, in print, their greater versatility.

SYBIL P. ESTESS

Description and Imagination in Elizabeth Bishop's "The Map"

The filmmaker Michelangelo Antonioni maintains that he attempts in his movies to focus on details in order to emphasize his ways of perceiving. He writes, "I am obliged to linger ad infinitum on the details, on the repetition of the most futile gestures, in order that what I show may assume a form and a sense."[1] Joseph Conrad's statement in the preface to The Nigger of the "Narcissus" is now a classic one: "—My task which I am trying to achieve is, by the power of the written word, to make you hear, to make you feel—it is, before all, to make you see. That—and no more, and it is everything." Randall Jarrell commented on Elizabeth Bishop's first book, "All her poems have written underneath I have seen it."[2] Indeed the inclination of modern and postmodern literature has long been to communicate individual vision rather than abstract truth. Bishop, like Conrad, like Antonioni, like most modern and contemporary artists, takes as her task enabling us to see as she sees. She makes description the most salient characteristic of her poetry and prose. Poems such as "The Map," "The Fish," and "The Bight," though at first glance realistic descriptions of ordinary entities, are actually much more: they are guides to her own vision of those realities. Many Bishop poems evolve toward what James Joyce thought of as an epiphanic vision.

Elizabeth Bishop seldom violates objects by imposing on them preconceived definitions, a priori interpretations, or sentimental descriptions. But even though she may seem to look at things with the exactitude and tenacity of a naturalist, Bishop

---

Parts of this essay appeared, in a different form, in Southern Review 13 (October 1977), pp. 705–27.

necessarily creates art out of her personal life experiences, and ultimately out of her synthesized vision of whatever she chooses to describe; her "empiricism" is not as unalloyed as it may first appear.

In the poem "The Map," Bishop offers a significant hint to her sense of how an "objective" work of art may embody the artist's subjective experience of a given reality. "The Map" embodies a way of understanding her work, for she placed it first in both *North & South* (1946) and in *The Complete Poems* (1969). On one level, the poem objectively describes an actual map: "Land lies in water; it is shadowed green." But beginning as early as the second line of the poem, Bishop's subjective kind of seeing becomes apparent. She starts to question what seem to her the various nuances of the map's configurations.

> Shadows, or are they shallows, at its edges
> showing the line of long sea-weeded ledges
> where weeds hang to the simple blue from green.

On her first look at the map, she seems to see water as surrounding and supporting land. In the following lines, however, we see the possibility that sea and land form an alliance so complementary that it is difficult to determine the exact nature of their interdependence:

> Or does the land lean down to lift the sea from under,
> drawing it unperturbed around itself?
> Along the fine tan sandy shelf
> is the land tugging at the sea from under?

Bishop's map enables us to imagine myriad kinds of connections between land and sea. The land's peninsulas may seem to "take the water between thumb and finger / like women feeling for the smoothness of yard-goods." A configuration such as Norway's may appear a "hare" which "runs south in agitation." Bishop suggests in these lines that what one sees depends upon how one looks.

Is it not, then, our perspectives on the real which determine its very nature? The initial stanza of "The Map" seems to suggest that the essence of reality may be determined by our manner of seeing. Do "sea-weeded ledges . . . / hang to the simple blue from green"? "Or does the land lean down to lift the sea from under"? It all depends, Bishop first seems to say, on our chosen vantage point.

Yet reality is not merely relative to how we see it. As the poem progresses, we find that the imagination cannot create nor can it alter things as they are. A map's images can never be arbitrarily presented. As Wallace Stevens writes in what he calls an *opusculum paedagogum:* "The pears are not seen / as the observer wills" ("Study of Two Pears"). On maps, the poet's interlocutor asks of her, are countries colored "what suits the character or the native waters best"? Must reality, then, always be scrupulously and unerringly presented?

The issue at stake is that the images on maps are by definition constructions of the mind, as the mind attempts to plot the landscape in order to find its way. Though such artifacts must be "accurate," must be faithful to things as we know them, they may still be imaginatively constructed or arranged. Bishop's kind of navigational description is an invention derived not only from her empirical eye but also from her mind, as it becomes the agent which charts the various depths of the waters of her personal imagination. Such compositions are, as A. D. Hope writes, "held between the intellectual eye and the landscape."[3] Bishop seems to make a judgment in "The Map" concerning the efficacy of all "maps," of all invented, artistic images. Though the shadows of their new-found-lands may (like those of Newfoundland) appear to lie "flat and still" in comparison to real sea or land, their waters too have a strategic function: they lend the land "their waves' own conformation." No aesthetic images, even Bishop's verisimilar kind of description, should be taken as exhaustive of reality. The maps to experience which her art provides are the result of the constant intrusion of things-as-they-are upon her particular power to come to terms with them. Bishop attempts in descriptive poems to make form and imaginative sense of what she sees. It is through her personalized, imaginative perspective that she allows us, as Stevens would have it, to "see the earth again."

As in most Bishop poems, the meaning of "The Map" extends far beyond a mere realistic description of a literal object. This poem delineates the nature of a relationship between objective reality and one's subjective and imaginative assimilation of such "facts." Bishop suggests in "The Map" that an art work may be seen as a map to an artist's particular sense of things. The analogy, of course, can be drawn further: her works—cumulations of realistic details shaped into an imaginative form—are maps to and of her own sensibility.

"Mapped waters are more quiet than the land is," the poem says. It concludes, however, "More delicate than the historians' are the map-makers' colors." Here Bishop adds to the correlation between the task of the poet and the task of the historian an even subtler dimension than did Aristotle when he claimed that "poetry is higher than history." She implies that, like the historian, the map-maker should not distort "truth"; yet she seems to know too that it is impossible to be completely objective. For just as the individual sensibility of the historian informs what he records, the artist's particular vision (with all its peculiar slants) shapes what he or she creates. Thus any poet's images are the delicate result of the imagination lending its conformation to manifestations of the real. A fragile, perhaps, yet keen and subtle sense of discrimination—"the map-makers' colors"—comprises an artist's way of seeing.

NOTES

1. Michel Mardore, "Antonioni, je suis an incurable optimiste," *Les lettres française,* No. 924 (Sept. 6, 1962), p. 6; cited and translated by Ted Perry in "A Contextual Study of M. Antonioni's Film *L'Eclisse,*" *Speech Monographs* 37, no. 2 (June 1970), p. 92.

2. *Poetry and the Age* (1953; reprint ed., New York: Farrar, Straus and Giroux/Noonday, 1972), p. 5.

3. "The Esthetic Theory of James Joyce," in *Joyce's Portrait: Criticisms and Critiques,* ed. Thomas E. Connolly (New York: Appleton-Century-Crofts Press, 1962), p. 200.

ASHLEY BROWN

Elizabeth Bishop in Brazil

Future biographers will probably make a great deal of Elizabeth
Bishop's twenty years in Brazil. This was the country of her
middle age and her full maturity as a poet, and it continues to
provide a background for her years in Boston. As I stood re-
cently on her balcony looking at the water-life on Boston Har-
bor, I thought back easily to the first time I met her in an
apartment high above Guanabara Bay at Rio de Janeiro, and then
I thought: She always has the most spectacular views! I hope she
doesn't mind my stating in print that she is farsighted; I rather
envy her that. When I, quite myopic, could barely see a freighter
steaming across the bay, Elizabeth was already describing the
activity on deck. Brazil is a good place for the keen observer. It
is teeming with particularities, and when I first lived there I (a
former philosophy major) thought that the easy way out was to
become a complete nominalist; one had to keep one's head. But
Elizabeth seemed perfectly in harmony with this barrage of
sights, sounds, and smells that awaited one at every hand. She
was staying then in a section called Leme, and over the telephone
she explained, before I went there the first time, that the way to
remember it was to recite "Now I lay me down to sleep" in the
taxi.

The time was 1964. I had with me a letter of introduction
from Flannery O'Connor, an old friend, who had written: "I'm
up here in the hospital else I would send you some peafowl
feathers to take her from me. She sent me an altar in a bottle."
This was Flannery's last letter to me; I did not realize then how
close to death she was, but later that summer I read about it in

Southern Review 13 (October 1977), pp. 688–704.

the *Jornal do Brasil*. Flannery and Elizabeth had never met; they had spoken only once by long-distance telephone, but they had corresponded for some years and formed a friendship based on a wonderful sense of humor as well as a mutual respect for each other's literary worth. The altar in the bottle I had admired on Flannery's bookshelves in the parlor at Andalusia Farm. Actually it was a wooden cross with bits of paper and tinfoil and a rooster at the top (reminiscent of Elizabeth's poem "Roosters"?). It probably came from the Northeastern state of Bahĭa, which is especially rich in folklore. I always thought it was a kind of emblem of some artistic trait that these two writers shared—perhaps their unusual unsentimental love of the beauty to be found in common life.

Much of the time in those days Elizabeth lived with a friend, Lota de Macedo Soares, in a really handsome modern house in the mountains above Petrópolis. Another spectacular view. Petrópolis, a couple of hours' drive from Rio, is the old imperial summer capital, and Rio society still repairs there during the hot season. The house was called "Samambaia," after a fern with rather coarse leaves that grows in many parts of Brazil. It was long and low but went off in several directions from a room, open much of the time, where people breakfasted or dined. Indeed, most of the house could be open, and I remember with delight the hummingbirds that darted through. Elizabeth, an amateur ornithologist, said that there were two hundred species in Brazil. Was that possible? But she lived in the house week in and week out, and in a lovely poem called "Song for the Rainy Season" (1960) she gives us the scene that the casual visitor might overlook;

> House, open house
> to the white dew
> and the milk-white sunrise
> kind to the eyes,
> to membership
> of silverfish, mouse,
> bookworms,
> big moths; with a wall

for the mildew's
ignorant map;

darkened and tarnished
by the warm touch
of the warm breath,
maculate, cherished,
rejoice!

"Samambaia" is the setting for several other poems: "Electrical Storm," which immortalizes Tobias the cat; "The Armadillo"; and the somewhat later "Rainy Season; Sub-Tropics." "The Armadillo" takes place during a festive season that is celebrated in June—the feast of São João, which comes at the winter solstice there. The fire balloons in the poem are illegal with good reason:

With a wind,
they flare and falter, wobble and toss;
but if it's still they steer between
the kite sticks of the Southern Cross,

receding, dwindling, solemnly
and steadily forsaking us,
or, in the downdraft from a peak,
suddenly turning dangerous.

This poem, one of the finest, is absolutely sensitive to every nuance of movement. Although it is contained within a pictorial setting (all can be visualized), Miss Bishop's rhythmic control largely accounts for the *pretty, dreamlike mimicry* that prepares the way for the final moral statement.

"Rainy Season; Sub-Tropics" (1967) might be regarded as a companion piece to "Song for the Rainy Season" if you shifted your attention to the animal life outside the house. It turns on the theme of self-pity that Elizabeth Bishop has often dealt with in various subtle forms. I suspect that it is the human quality she most dislikes, though she sometimes presents it in a good-natured way, as in "Crusoe in England," where she has her hero reminisce:

> I told myself
> "Pity should begin at home." So the more
> pity I felt, the more I felt at home.

"Rainy Season" is a triptych of prose-poems with these speakers: a giant toad, a strayed crab, and a giant snail (the lesser orders of nature come very large in Brazil). They are all displaced; they all embody human feelings (vanity, aggression, envy, fear, longing for repose, and so on) in a disconcerting way; and their reactions to each other in the three monologues compose a scenario. The brilliance of the description cannot be conveyed in a brief quotation. About the time that I first read this I saw Beckett's *Play* (1964), with its three characters in urns up to their necks, each lit in turn by a spotlight as he blames the others for his plight. (The situation that is being recollected in a kind of purgatory is a tawdry adultery.) I thought: How interesting that Elizabeth's characters with their density of concrete life and Beckett's with their babble of clichés should come so close together in one's mind. "Pity me," says the toad in his first line. "Pity me," says the snail near the end. "Pity them," says Beckett's Man halfway through, and his sad trio run the same gamut of feelings as the poor rain-creatures.

At "Samambaia" you could go forward onto a great stone terrace that overlooked the valley towards Petrópolis. This, however, could be dangerous for the acrophobic, and I gathered that Aldous Huxley, a visitor a few years earlier, had almost pitched over the edge. If you walked up from the house you came to Elizabeth's study, a small cottage. This was situated above a waterfall that rushed down the mountainside. (Her snail says, "The waterfall below will vibrate through my shell and body all night long. In that steady pulsing I can rest.") Elizabeth had the splendid idea of having the cascade dammed, just momentarily, to make a tiny swimming pool, and you could descend there from the study through a clump of bamboos. The study itself was comfortable and clearly the working-place for a serious writer and reader with a large eclectic taste; nothing formal about it. Photographs of Baudelaire and Marianne Moore and Lowell were tacked to the wall. Here and in the main house were superb artistic objects from various parts of Brazil, where by this time Elizabeth had travelled extensively. She has always liked simple things that most people would reject. I remember a dishpan made of colorful flattened-out cans that had contained soybean oil or peas or perhaps cheese; they had been soldered together. (This brief phase of industrial folk-art is over in the 1970s, and now housewives along the Amazon use plastic dishpans like everyone else's.) I mention these details, trivial as they may seem, because they suggest the human scale of Elizabeth's poetry. A poem like "Jerónimo's House" is composed almost entirely of such details, and in its quiet way it bears out a "rage for order" as much as any poem by Stevens.

Elizabeth landed in Brazil somewhat by accident in late November, 1951. She had actually intended to land there, but only to stop during a voyage round South America. This incident is amusingly recalled in "Arrival at Santos," done from the tourist's point of view. Miss Breen, Elizabeth's fellow passenger, the retired police lieutenant, really existed, and she rather liked being put in the poem. One curious textual matter: in the original version the author was taking Scotch through the customs; when the poem was reprinted in *Questions of Travel* it became bourbon. Which *was* it? Then Elizabeth ate some item of fruit (a *cajú*, I believe) that disagreed horribly with her; she was laid up for an extended recovery; and her ship sailed on without her. But she had friends in Brazil whom she had known in New York during an earlier period; she liked the country, and she stayed.

The poems in *Questions of Travel* are the chief literary legacy of Elizabeth Bishop's Brazilian years, but as a professional writer she occasionally turned her hand to other things, and eventually she became an important translator and an intermediary between Brazilian and American culture. The Brazilian government awarded her the Order of Rio Branco in 1971. In a conversation piece published some years ago in *Shenandoah* (Winter 1966)* I asked her whether she had been able to get anything from the

*See pp. 289–302.—EDS.

country except its appearances, and she replied:

> Living in the way I have happened to live here, knowing Brazilians, has made a great difference. The general life I have known here has of course had an impact on me. I think I've learned a great deal. Most New York intellectuals' ideas about "underdeveloped countries" are partly mistaken, and living among people of a completely different culture has changed a lot of my old stereotyped ideas.

Elizabeth managed to put some of her knowledge into an illustrated book commissioned by Time Incorporated in 1962. Her text was no doubt "edited" to some extent in New York, but I can detect scarcely a trace of *Time*-style, and in fact, the book is still the best introduction to the subject. This is because the author is very close to the rich popular life around her; unlike so many of her compatriots, she is not blinkered by statistics and theories about economic "take-off." Much that she observed only twenty years ago is already passing into oblivion as the Brazilian population moves into the big cities. Not many North Americans could have written this:

> In the field of popular culture, however, undoubtedly the greatest achievement is the creation of the figureheads used on boats on the Rio São Francisco. Called *carrancas,* the figureheads depict animals, women and characters from Afro-Brazilian folklore, but one of the favorites is always the "Great Worm," the most dreadful of the spirits that live in the river. Some of these figureheads are very fine, towering several feet above the bow of the boat and carved in a strong and simple style reminiscent of Romanesque sculpture. Unfortunately, *carrancas* are being used less and less today, and the art of carving them is dying out.

One evening in Rio we were invited to the house of a rich man who had collected a number of *carrancas* and placed them round his garden and swimming pool; they *were* impressive looming out of the dark, almost theatrical in this setting with its expensive lighting effects. What would they have looked like on the river? Very few people in Brazil could have seen them. Elizabeth, an indefatigable traveller, finally went down the Rio São Francisco on an endless trip in 1967. But it was a mixed experience; her immediate reaction came on a postcard:

> . . . in retrospect I'm glad I did it + some of the worst will no doubt seem funny as time goes on—but never never the hideous poverty. The boat a very quaint stern-wheeler made in the U S A 70 years ago—everyone nice and polite, but each and every one asked if I had a "family" and when I said no, they all commiserated with me, but also, I felt, rather avoided me as being not quite all there.

This, I think, records her *un*sentimental love of common life.

Elizabeth, who already had Spanish (from a period in Mexico during the 1940s) and French (from an even earlier period in Paris), learned Portuguese soon enough during her first years in Rio. In any case, nearly all of her friends were Brazilians. About this time she was introduced to an elderly lady, Sra. Alice Brant, who had grown up in Diamantina, a somewhat remote town in the state of Minas Gerais (General Mines). Alice Brant was half-English by descent; her grandfather had gone out as a doctor with a mining company and remained; but she was brought up as a Brazilian. As a young girl in the 1890s she wrote a diary that she later called *Minha Vida de Menina* (*My Life as a Little Girl*). It was not till 1942, when she was living in Rio, that she had any idea of publishing it; her husband, the president of the Bank of Brazil, made the suggestion. She used the pseudonym "Helena Morley." Although the Diary was only intended to amuse her family and friends, it was recommended to the public by the French novelist Georges Bernanos, who was in wartime exile in Brazil, and it has had a kind of classic status ever since; one can often find a copy in the stationery shops.

Elizabeth proposed to translate the Diary and immersed herself in the subject. It was a good excuse for another journey, this time to Diamantina, which was not easy to reach twenty-five years ago. Nowadays the town, with its fine old houses, is rather famous among connoisseurs of architecture, and one can drive there on an excellent road. The Diary is, among other things, an authentic record of provincial life at a moment when Brazil was moving into another epoch of its history. (Slavery had been abolished in 1888 and the Empire succeeded by the first Republic the following year.) But its main interest lies in its loving but candid account of a family, a theme to which Elizabeth would return. Her introduction to the translation is one of her best pieces of prose, and, as Marianne Moore said in a review (*Poetry*, July 1959)* "The attitude of life revealed by the Diary, Helena's apperceptiveness, and innate accuracy, seem a double portrait; the exactness of observation in the introduction being an extension, in manner, of Miss Bishop's verse and other writing. . . ." The Diary in fact occupies an important place in Elizabeth Bishop's canon.

The Brazilian poems in *Questions of Travel* are not arranged according to their date of composition, but they do compose a set of related responses to a scene. All of them were retained by the author in the Chatto and Windus *Selected Poems* of 1967. Needless to say, they exemplify a wide range of style; Miss Bishop, as her readers know, has large resources of poetic "attack." "Arrival at Santos," which originally came near the end of *A Cold Spring,* looks just right when it is reprinted as the opening poem in *Questions of Travel.* Then comes "Brazil, January 1, 1502," which was first printed in the *New Yorker*'s number for the New Year in 1960, after the poet had lived in Brazil for eight years and assimilated a great deal of its history as well as its landscape. New Year's Day of 1502 was the date on which the Portuguese caravels arrived at Guanabara Bay, which they mistakenly thought was the mouth of a great river—hence Rio de Janeiro (January). This is a poem of wonder, however; the poet assumes the vision of the Portuguese discoverers, and the texture of the verse could not be more different from that of "Arrival at Santos." Indeed, the word *texture* is appropriate here, because this is a verbal tapestry, and we move in and out of the setting as though we still had the allegorical sense of the sixteenth century ("Still in the foreground there is Sin: / five sooty dragons near some massy rocks.") The historical theme shouldn't be overlooked. In her text for the *Time* book Miss

*See pp. 194–96.—Eds.

230

Bishop observes that "the Portuguese lacked the bloodthirsty missionary zeal of the Spaniards," but the Christians of her poem are "hard as nails"; and at least a century of Brazil's early history comes out in this passage:

> Directly after Mass, humming perhaps
> L'Homme armé or some such tune,
> they ripped away into the hanging fabric,
> each out to catch an Indian for himself—
> those maddening little women who kept calling,
> calling to each other (or had the birds waked up?)
> and retreating, always retreating, behind it.

For a decade or so I have thought this poem fascinating as an act of perception: that is, on what terms does the mind approach a scene, and with what preconceptions? And how can one recover the sense of any earlier period? The author briefly quotes Kenneth Clark's *Landscape into Art* as an epigraph. I would suggest E. H. Gombrich's *Art and Illusion* as being even more useful for speculating on this theme.

The title poem, "Questions of Travel," was first published in 1956, about four years after Elizabeth had taken up residence in Brazil. The tourist has now become the passionate observer and, in a sense, has lost her innocence. The poem is a wonderful mosaic of things that one can see and hear along a Brazilian highway—say, along the road to Petrópolis. (Some of these phenomena are, I fear, doomed as highway culture in Brazil resembles ours more and more.) The mechanic's wooden clogs "carelessly clacking" over the floor of the filling-station, the bird in its fancy bamboo cage above the broken gasoline pump—what a pity, says the poet, to have missed these things in all their particularity. And what random historical causes lay behind them? The poem builds up in a seemingly (but only seemingly) casual way to the two formal stanzas in italics at the end, where the traveller asks herself:

> *Continent, city, country, society:*
> *the choice is never wide and never free.*
> *And here, or there . . . No. Should we have stayed at home,*
> *wherever that may be?*

But she has already answered her question in the poem, where, for me at any rate, a whole phase of lost experience has been transmuted into something permanent. The English poet Charles Tomlinson took her to task in his review of *Questions of Travel* (*Shenandoah*, Winter 1966), in which he said, "For the fact of the matter is, Miss Bishop travels because she likes it, not because she is homeless in the way that Lawrence or Schoenberg were." But is it really necessary to insist on this kind of "radical homelessness"? It seems to me perfectly obvious that Elizabeth Bishop has followed Henry James, Katherine Anne Porter, and certain other Americans who have gone out into the world, and these are the names to mention. She knows very well who she is. Again, speaking for myself, I have often wondered about the accidents of history that have made my Brazilian friends different from me—they come from a country as old and large and diverse as ours, they had slavery twenty-five years after we did, they too are apt to make exaggerated claims. Elizabeth's poems have more of the "feel" of life in Brazil than anything else written by a North American because they undercut the large generalizations that we all have when we approach a subject on this scale.

The remaining poems in *Questions of Travel* are about poor people in various parts of Brazil, and I think that Mr. Tomlinson misses the point again when he says that "the better-off have always preferred their poor processed by style." I suppose one could turn that remark against Wordsworth in "Resolution and Independence," but surely his old leech-gatherer is *dignified* by being put into *rime royale*. One could hardly think that Wordsworth knew his poor more intimately than Miss Bishop, and he is the master of this kind of experience in English poetry. Miss Bishop in fact has often chosen to write about the humble for reasons of her own—and poems like "Jerónimo's House," "Songs for a Colored Singer," "At the Fishhouses," and "Faustina, or Rock Roses" are among her most assured successes. I don't think she would have done better with intellectuals or diplomats' wives as subjects.

"Manuelzinho" and "Squatter's Children," which were written around the same time as "Questions of Travel," are about people who might be found on the hillside leading to "Samambaia." (A group of three "Samambaia" poems that I have already mentioned comes next in the collection.) Flannery O'Connor would have regarded them with the same steady humorous gaze (though she would have put them in more drastic situations), and I could easily imagine Manuelzinho with a change of name at Andalusia Farm. His poem is one of Elizabeth Bishop's most developed works of portraiture—an elusive maddening figure seen in the round, at different seasons, in different lights. Quotation hardly does it justice; the effect is unusually cumulative, and much lies behind this wry conclusion:

> You helpless, foolish man,
> I love you all I can,
> I think. Or do I?
> I take off my hat, unpainted
> and figurative, to you.
> Again I promise to try.

The remaining poems take us to different parts of Brazil where Elizabeth lived or travelled. "Twelfth Morning; or What You Will" is set at Cabo Frio (Cold Cape), which is east along the coast from Rio. This is another poem that radiates a "sense of glory" (I borrow the phrase from Herbert Read). The black boy Balthazár, coming out of the mist, over the "shopworn" dunes and debris and the rusted wire, is like a young prince, the four-gallon can on his head notwithstanding:

> You can hear the water now,
> inside, slap-slapping. Balthazár is singing.
> "Today's my Anniversary," he sings,
> "the Day of Kings."

And here at the end of the poem the rhymes finally emerge, the sense of glory is complete. One of Elizabeth Bishop's favorite poets is George Herbert; perhaps the naturalness of tone and the craftsmanship owe something to him. Placed between two longer, more ambitious poems, her own celebration of Epiphany (called "The Day of Kings" in Brazil) is modest but a delight.

"The Riverman" is so long that one could easily devote an

essay to it. But perhaps this is unnecessary. It is partly worked up from *Amazon Town,* a book by the anthropologist Charles Wagley, as Miss Bishop acknowledges in her headnote. The book was published in 1958; she was writing her poem the next year. *Amazon Town* is admired in professional circles as a work of scholarship, and I should say that it is a work of considerable literary merit as well. There is no need to trace the prose passages that Miss Bishop has used; the important thing is the transmutation into poetry, and here James Merrill has made the right comment: "Wonderful, fluid, pulsing lines—you hardly feel the meter at all." (*Shenandoah,* Summer 1968). This poem of the river runs through 158 lines based on three stresses in each line: a constant undercurrent, as it were, for the action. (For comparison one might turn to Eliot's adaptation of the first paragraphs of *The Heart of Darkness* in *The Waste Land,* III.) An even more important matter is this: For the poet, the experience of reading Charles Wagley's book meshes with her own experience along the Amazon. It is like the case of Wordsworth's "Solitary Reaper"; we know he took the poem out of someone's travel-book, but he could not have brought it off without his excursions through the Lake District.

"The Burglar of Babylon" returns us to Rio and the apartment in Leme, which lies below the hill of Babylon. The *favelas,* or hillside slums, are now almost gone in this section, but fifteen years ago they were very much in evidence. This is Elizabeth Bishop's longest narrative. The subject was at hand; it was reported at length in the newspapers; and from the terrace of the apartment she could see the soldiers hunting down the young criminal Micuçú. How was this to be presented, given the possibilities? Elizabeth instinctively used the modern ballad, which for some readers means Auden's poems in this form, the ones about Miss Gee and Victor. (The latter, I should think, is more successful in its tragicomic treatment of a stereotyped subject.) "The Burglar of Babylon" also owes something to cinematic technique in its camera angles, its "cutting" from one shot to another. But its perspectives are finally verbal. Not only the echoes of the old ballad idiom, but the conversation of the people in the bar, Micuçú's auntie, the soldiers, Micuçú himself—all of this goes perfectly into traditional quatrains. The poem was first published in *The New Yorker* in November, 1964; simultaneously a remarkable translation by Flávio Macedo Soares appeared in the literary review *Cadernos Brasileiros* in Rio. The translation in fact testifies to the success of the original, as though the English and the Portuguese were descended from the same source:

> Nos morros verdes do Rio
> uma mancha temível cresce:
> os pobres que vêm para o Rio
> e não têm como regresse.

All things considered, this is the best as well as the most humane of modern ballads.

Two more poems from Leme are included in the last section of *The Complete Poems:* "House Guest" and "Going to the Bakery." These are slighter than the Brazilian pieces in *Questions of Travel.* The details are sharply etched, especially in the latter poem (Flaubert himself would be impressed by the *progression d'effet*), but the sense of wonder, always one of Elizabeth Bishop's strong points, has diminished. The last of *The Complete Poems* (but far from the last of Elizabeth's poems, I'm glad to say) is "Under the Window: Ouro Preto." This is an affectionate tribute to a town in the mountains of Minas Gerais that has survived from the eighteenth century. Ouro Preto (Black Gold) was the capital of the state till about 1900, then abandoned and difficult to reach, then rediscovered during the last generation. It is a splendid repository of late-Portuguese baroque built during a period of wealth, much of it designed and executed by the legendary Aleijadinho, a poor crippled mulatto who became his country's greatest artist. Elizabeth, who had often visited Ouro Preto, even when the going was rough, finally succumbed to its charms in 1965 and bought an old house, which she proceeded to restore. It dated from about 1730. When the work began, she discovered that the *pau-a-pique,* the thick wall of wattle and mud, was actually tied together with rawhide in some places, and a bit of this architectural oddity was preserved under glass when the restoration was finished. And as usual a balcony, in this case overlooking the whole range of Ouro Preto on its steep hills. Although the trucks from the bauxite mines hurtled alarmingly close to the front door, a certain order prevailed inside. "Under the Window" is a low-keyed, amusing rendition of Brazilian life, so much of which is spent out-of-doors, and another demonstration of how a poem can be made out of the most unlikely materials.

After 1960 Elizabeth Bishop turned increasingly to the art of translation, and she will have to be included in any future edition of George Steiner's anthology (*The Penguin Book of Modern Verse Translation*, 1966). In 1963 she brought out three of the eighteen sections of João Cabral de Melo Neto's *Morte e Vida Severina*, which had been composed in 1954–55. *The Death and Life of a Severino*, as she calls it, is a Pernambuco Christmas play by a most sophisticated poet-diplomat from the Northeast, and it is intended for performance. The story is simple but moving and partakes of the folklore of the Northeast: The "Severino" is a typical, almost anonymous poor man whose pilgrimage takes him through the dry backlands; there is a birth, a sense of the miraculous; presents are brought. The subject must have been very sympathetic to Elizabeth; she is unusually sensitive to the special qualities of the verse and easily manages a line in English that resembles the original:

> Somos muitos Severinos
> iguais em tudo e na sina:
> a de abrandar estas pedras
> suando-se muito em cima,
> a de tentar despertar
> terra sempre mais extinta,
> a de querer arrancar
> algum roçado da cinza.

> We are many Severinos
> and our destiny's the same:
> to soften up these stones
> by sweating over them,
> to try to bring to life
> a dead and deader land,
> to try to wrest a farm
> out of burnt-over land.

The play, incidentally, has had a considerable success. The verse lends itself to music, and some years ago it was set by the young composer Chico Buarque de Hollanda, now very famous in Brazil. After being performed by the student dramatic group of the Catholic University of São Paulo, it was taken to France, where it was awarded first prize at the International Festival of Theater at Nancy.

Elizabeth Bishop's translations from Brazilian poetry are not extensive, but they have set the standard for the rest of us who have attempted this. Pre-Bishop translations are mostly lumps of words that have no rhythmic life in English, and part of her superiority certainly comes from her verve and control of the meter. As an admirer of Marianne Moore she always uses the most natural order of words in an English sentence. And she knows how to suppress words in one place and add them in another. Here is the first line of the "Sonnet of Intimacy" by Vinícius de Moraes, followed by her rendition:

> Nas tardes da fazenda há muito azul demais.

> Farm afternoons, there's much too much blue air.

The opening phrase is reduced from seven syllables to four and two contractions (prepositions plus articles) are dropped, but it seems just as long in English, where the sense of languor is increased by the comma, a clear gain. And then the translator adds *air,* which isn't present in the Portuguese, but it echoes *there's* and carries out the idea nicely. A splendid iambic pentameter line comes out of Vinícius' alexandrine. Vinícius de Moraes is an immensely popular poet in Brazil; he has long made a success of the colloquial manner and turned it to account in lyrics for *bossa nova,* but I don't think he could be as *gracefully* colloquial as Elizabeth is in the last lines of the sonnet. Vinícius says of himself and the cows:

> Nós todos, animais, sem comoção nenhuma
> Mijamos em comum numa festa de espuma.

Literally rendered:

> We all, animals, without any commotion
> Urinate together in a festival of spray.

This isn't exactly graceful. Elizabeth Bishop has it:

> All of us, animals, unemotionally
> Partake together of a pleasant piss.

In the last line she has had to abandon Vinícius' internal rhyming (*comum, numa, espuma*), but the alliteration that she substitutes (more common in English) is very deft. A small triumph of poetic discretion, I call it.

The poet who has most deeply engaged Elizabeth's imagination, Carlos Drummond de Andrade, comes from Minas Gerais, and in fact his native village, Itabirito, is on the highway to Ouro Preto. Nearby is Itabira, a large mountain of iron ore that has been extensively mined. As one can see, just by driving through the countryside, life could be austere. Although Carlos Drummond has lived in Rio for many years (he is a former civil servant), he often writes about the place where he grew up, and I should think that it has contributed much to his strength as a writer. Elizabeth has translated seven of his poems. In 1965 she brought out two of the early pieces in a light mood, "Seven-Sided Poem" and "Don't Kill Yourself," in *Shenandoah*. That same season she published "Travelling in the Family" in *Poetry*. I think that from the beginning this was recognized as one of those cases where a distinguished poem in one language becomes something more than a "translation" in another. It was soon included in the Penguin anthology, *Latin American Writing Today* (1967), and Robert Penn Warren used lines from it as the epigraph to his poem-sequence, *Audubon: A Vision*. Now one can read it in the Brooks–Lewis–Warren anthology of American literature, and in a sense it has been naturalized.

In the poem the shade of Carlos Drummond's father is his guide, but his dream of the past is hesitant:

> In the desert of Itabira
> the shadow of my father
> took me by the hand.

So much time lost.
But he didn't say anything.
It was neither day nor night.
A sigh? A passing bird?
But he didn't say anything.

The movement of the poem is a painful re-creation of a family
and its failures of love, but something has endured that the poet
yearns to possess. Through eight stanzas that refrain, "But he
didn't say anything," draws out the painful disclosures. The
poem is three quarters over before the poet can say *you:*

Only now do we know each other!
Eye-glasses, memories, portraits
flow in the river of blood.
Now the waters won't let me
make out your distant face,
distant by seventy years . . .

And the reconciliation at the end is just as hesitant as the be-
ginning:

I felt that he pardoned me
but he didn't say anything.
The waters cover his moustache,
the family, Itabira, all.

The longish companion poem, "The Table," confronts the
subject more directly. Here the family ruled by the patriarch
assemble in the poet's imagination again; now the tone is vari-
ously humorous, defiant, loving; the dining table itself is the
symbol of the family's existence:

And now the table, replete,
is bigger than the house.
We talk with our mouths full,
we call each other names,
we laugh, we split our sides,
we forget the terrible
inhibiting respect . . .

This poem moves through 353 lines without any stanzaic break, as though the obsessive quality of the subject could never permit the speaker to pause. As an occasional guest at *mineiro* family dinners, I have been astonished by the huge amounts of food, the good-natured intensity of the arguments, the endless hours that people could spend at the table. I think that Elizabeth has lived through this experience many times; her translation is deeply felt. More recently she has filled out the picture, as it were, with three shorter poems from Carlos Drummond in the anthology of Brazilian poetry that she edited with Emanuel Brasil in 1972, and taken together, her versions of this poet's work are a considerable achievement.

This brief account of Elizabeth Bishop at a certain period of her career of course omits a great deal. For instance, she wrote several of her Nova Scotia poems during these years, and this is a locale to which she has returned imaginatively if not actually many times. The world of her poetry is large. Although it differs from that of Wallace Stevens in some ways, I think that she, more than anyone else today, has the same humanist vision of north and south, the seasonal round, the imagination creating its order sometimes in most discouraging circumstances.

JAMES MERRILL

Her Craft

Elizabeth Bishop—swan boat or
Amazon steamer? Neither: a Dream Boat.
Among topheavy wrecks, she stays afloat.
Mine's this white hanky waving from the shore
—In lieu of the requested "essay." (Faute
De pire, if I may say so. Less is more.)

29.vii.77

MARK STRAND

Elizabeth Bishop Introduction

I met Elizabeth Bishop twelve years ago when I was teaching English at the University of Brasil in Rio de Janeiro. We met in her apartment in Leme. I recall seeing copies of *Encounter* and the *Hudson Review* on the coffee table in the room where we were having tea. It was a pleasant but odd meeting, for we were two Americans in Brasil, talking about Nova Scotia and then about what American poets we liked to read. I recall we agreed on Robert Lowell right away. A few years later in San Francisco we again spent some time together. We talked about Brasil. She was in the midst of working on her masterful translation of Carlos Drummond de Andrade's poem, "A Mesa" (The Table). Since then we have met in Boston, in New York, and in Mexico.

I do not wish to suggest that one has to have travelled to the same places Elizabeth Bishop has to appreciate her poems. Certainly this has not been the sole source of my admiration for her work, but it has been, I admit, an enjoyable coincidence that has never stood in the way.

The presence of geographical and topographical concerns in Elizabeth Bishop's poetry forms the background against which our knowledge of the world is gained. For in her poems travel is a metaphor for our finding out in what relation to the world we exist. Our knowledge "is historical, flowing, and flown," she tells us in the poem, "At The Fishhouses." But, as we discover again and again, and especially in recent poems like "Crusoe in England" and "Poem," time and space, for Elizabeth Bishop, become interchangeable. It is the traveller's destiny to suffer loss in order to keep going, and he keeps going even though the object of his quest is illusory—"another inscrutable house," "a proto-dream house" or "home, wherever that may be." In the poem, "One Art," she tells us that the art of losing "isn't hard to master" and suggests that the practice of losing is the practice of living. In fact, because the poem's speaker *has* mastered the art of losing, she is giving a lesson in it; happily, it is a lesson only survivors can give. This is a central and subtle irony in the poem, one underlined by the fact that it is a villanelle, unquestionably the most recuperative of forms with its constant rhymes and interlocking refrains. It is a form which allows nothing to be lost, not even the articulation of loss.

But beyond (or is it behind) such characterizations of difficulties most of us have experienced is a saving lack of sentimentality. There is absolutely no self-pity in Elizabeth Bishop's writing. Instead, there is an unusual amount of common-sense, a kind of realism in which the poem is always responsible to the observable, factual world. And complementing this is her fancifulness—what some have called her "quirkiness"—which is always apparent. What is amazing is that these elements coexist so easily in her work, without destroying the integrity of an established tone or texture, the music of a line, or the clear argument of a stanza.

At a recent reading in New York, James Merrill alluded to Elizabeth Bishop as our greatest national treasure. I think she is. It gives me great pleasure to introduce Elizabeth Bishop.

Guggenheim Museum
November 29, 1977

243

JOHN HOLLANDER

Elizabeth Bishop's Mappings of Life

Geography III is a magnificent book of ten poems whose power
and beauty would make it seem gross to ask for more of them.
Its epigraph is a catechistic geography lesson quoted from a
nineteenth-century textbook, claimed for parable in that seam-
less way of allowing picture to run into image that the poet has
made her own, in this instance, by her own added italicized
questions about mapped bodies—of land, of water—and about
direction, following the epigraph in its own language but now
become fully figurative. The opening poem of Miss Bishop's
first volume, *North & South,* is called "The Map"; in all the
work that has followed it, the poet has been concerned with
mappings of the possible world. More generally, she had pur-
sued the ways in which pictures, models, representations of all
sorts, begin to take on lives of their own under the generative
force of that analogue of loves between persons which moves
between nature and consciousness. We might, somewhat
lamely, call it passionate attention. Its caresses, extended by
awareness that pulses with imagination, are not only those of the
eye and ear at moments of privileged experience, but rather at
the times of composition, of representing anew. The map-
makers' colors, "more delicate than the historians'," are as much
part of a larger, general Nature as are the raw particulars of
unrepresented sea and sky, tree and hill, street and storefront,
roof and watertank. Much of the praise given Miss Bishop's
work has directed itself to her command of observation, the
focus of her vision, the unmannered quality of her rhetoric—
almost as if she were a novelist, and almost as if love of life
could only be manifested in the accuracy and interestingness of

Parnassus (Fall 1977), pp. 359–66.

one's accounts of the shapes which human activity casts on nature.

But the passionate attention does not reveal itself in reportage. Love remains one of its principal tropes, just as the reading, interpreting and reconstituting of nature in one's poems remains a model of what love may be and do. The representations—the charts, pictures, structures, dreams and fables of memory—that one makes are themselves the Geographies which, in our later sense of the word, they map and annotate. The radical invention of a figurative geography in *North & South,* the mapping of personal history implicit there, are perhaps Miss Bishop's *Geography I;* after the Nova Scotian scenes and urban landscapes to the south of them in *A Cold Spring,* lit and shaded by love and loss, the grouped Brazilian poems and memories, rediscoveries even, of childhood yet further to the north, asked questions of travel. A literal geographic distinction, a north and south of then and now, gained new mythopoetic force; all that intensely and chastely observed material could only have become more than very, very good writing when it got poetically compounded with the figurative geography books of her earlier poems. *Questions of Travel* is thus, perhaps, her *Geography II.*

This new book is a third, by title, by design and, by its mode of recapitulation, a review of the previous two courses as well as an advanced text. Like all major poetry, it both demands prerequisites and invites the new student, and each of these to far greater degrees than most of the casual verse we still call poetry can ever do. The important poems here seem to me to derive their immense power both from the energies of the poet's creative present and from the richness and steadfastness of her created past ("A yesterday I find almost impossible to lift," she allows in the last line of the last poem in the book). Yes, if yesterdays are to be carried as burdens, one would agree; but even yesteryears can themselves, if one is imaginatively fortunate, become monuments to be climbed, to be looked about and even ahead from, to be questioned and pondered themselves.

And so here with the monuments of the earlier Bishop poetry: the reader keeps seeing them in these later poems—in the background or in pictures hung as it were on their walls. Rhe-

torically, a villanelle echoes the formal concerns of the earlier
sestinas and, at a smaller level, the characteristic use of repeated
terminal words in adjacent lines, whether in a rhymed or un-
rhymed poem, continues to be almost synecdochic, in these
poems, of the imperceptible slip from letter into spirit of mean-
ing. The magnificent earlier "The Monument," echoed in this
volume in part of "The End of March" (of which more later)
resounds even through Miss Bishop's wonderful translation of
an Octavio Paz homage to Joseph Cornell—a string of boxed
tercets. "12 O'Clock News" recapitulates a whole cycle of em-
blematic poems in her previous work, this strange prose poem
being a kind of Lilliputian itinerary of the poet's own desk, a
microcosmography of the world of work. The piece called brief-
ly—but hardly simply—"Poem" is something of a meditation
upon the earlier poem "Large Bad Picture" as well as, man-
ifestly, upon the small good one which presents a view, a spot of
time, in Nova Scotia, a moment in the past which is recollected
from its fragments in the attempt to puzzle out an ambiguous
sign, a representation of a *something* that may or may not be part
of one's own life. (. . . *Well, of somebody's,* we are tempted to go
on in one of Miss Bishop's characteristic tones—there is no lack
of human significance in the pictures of life in the world about
which she broods, and the problem with them is rather one of
mapping the directions in which they urge the viewer to turn.)
The scene in this little painting has assembled itself out of con-
templation, rather than commerce; the artist turns out to have
been a great-uncle "quite famous, an R.A." The poet goes on:

> I never knew him. We both knew this place,
> apparently, this literal small backwater,
> looked at it long enough to memorize it,
> our years apart. How strange. And it's still loved,
> or its memory is (it must have changed a lot).
> Our visions coincided—"visions" is
> too serious a word—our looks, two looks:
> art "copying from life" and life itself,
> life and the memory of it so compressed
> they've turned into each other. Which is which?

But "vision" is, of course, not too serious a word (as, I suppose, "serious" is too unvisionary a one). A major rhetorical device in American poetry of the past century and more has been a mode of evasion of the consequences of visionary seriousness; it can take the form of a pretending, for example, whether in Hawthorne or Frost, that anecdote is merely that and not myth showing a momentary face, a defense of whimsy or skepticism. Stevens' way was to pretend to a theory of just that sort of pretending, to discuss the ground-rules by which experiences and names for them play with each other. Elizabeth Bishop is not obviously Stevensian, even when she makes figures of figures (as in that wrenching early epigram, "Casabianca"); and in her celebrated and profoundly original diction there are few echoes of the whole of harmonium (save perhaps for the trace of "Disillusionment of Ten O'Clock" in her "Anaphora" from *North & South,* where day "sinks through the drift of classes / to evening, to the beggar in the park / who, weary, without lamp or book / prepares stupendous studies"). Her personal mode of rhetorical questioning, of demands for truth directed toward the mute objects she has herself invented, is certainly an analogue of Stevensian turnings in the wind of the leaves of imagery itself. These questionings ("Are they assigned, or can the countries pick their colors?") occur in her earliest poems, and continue to quicken all her fictions, giving the breath of life—as do Stevens' "qualifications"—to her molded figures and scenes. Miss Bishop's characteristic mythopoetic mode is one in which description, casually and apparently only heuristically figurative, bends around into the parabolic. What happens in the latter part of "At the Fishhouses" is possibly the *locus classicus* of this movement in her work: the almost painted scene offers up its wisdom not with the abrupt label of a moralization, but gradually, as images of place begin to be understood—almost to understand themselves—as images of the condition of consciousness itself.

It is that poem which seems to lie in the background of the powerful "The Moose" in the new book. Although its anecdotal frame might suggest "The Fish" as a prototype, the nonviolent encounter with the animal presence here is very different and far more profound: a bus ride southward from maritime provinces of the past is halted at the end of the poem as a she-moose emerges "out of / the impenetrable wood / and stands there, looms, rather, / in the middle of the road." Underscored by a deceptively disarming cadence of lightly-rhymed stanzas of six trimeter lines, the account of the bus-ride becomes parabolic with its ability to contain the past rather than merely to observe traces of it through the windows; a sort of Sarah Orne Jewett dialogue between two ancestral voices emerges from the back seats of the bus and the poet's mind as they move toward Boston, and the great creature appearing out of the woods, at a kind of border between the possibility of one sort of life and that of another, comes into the poem as a great living trope of the structures which get wrecked in crossing such borders—"high as a church, / homely as a house / (or, safe as houses)." The appearance of the creature is a phenomenon at once unique and paradigmatic, an "embodiment" in momentary dramaturgy of Something in nature analogous (the antlerless form?) which came of the poet's crying out to life for "original response" ("As a great buck it powerfully appeared"). The moose's powerful appearance is too important a manifestation, as always in Bishop's poetic world, to occasion the squandering of poetic diction. Even the gently ironic homeliness of the chorus of other travellers ("'Sure are big creatures.' / 'It's awful plain.' / 'Look! It's a she!'") echoes point by point the narrator's admittedly guarded mythologizing ("high," "homely," "safe"), and with the effect of domesticating even more the awe and the pressure of significance. We are tempted to think of her language at the most sublime moments of her travel talks as "cold" or "casual," but it is neither of these. Her great originality has always washed other kinds of voice away, and notwithstanding her "Invitation to Miss Marianne Moore," in *A Cold Spring,* to descend as a tutelary muse upon her, Miss Elizabeth Bishop's work seems as self-begotten as any in our time. What seems cold in her language is warmed by the breath of its own life.

Of the two major masterpieces in *Geography III,* the astonishing longish poem called "Crusoe in England" engages some of the larger meditative consequences of this self-sufficiency. It is a great dramatic monologue of the famous Solitary returned to a world of memory and discourse, the larger isle of England,

"another island, / that doesn't seem like one, but who decides?"
It is as if the narrator had come from an island of myth (the fable
of what one was? what one made, and made of one's life?) to our
overhearing and growing suspicion that he had been as responsi-
ble for the lay of the land upon which he had been cast up as for
his own survival in it. As usual, a tone of detached gazetteering
(again, suggesting the distanced detailings of "The Monument"
and, even more, the narrative cadences of "The Riverman")
colors a stanza of frighteningly powerful vision:

> The sun set in the sea; the same odd sun
> rose from the sea,
> and there was one of it and one of me.
> The island had one kind of everything:
> one tree snail, a bright violet-blue
> with a thin shell, crept over everything,
> over the one variety of tree,
> a sooty, scrub affair.
> Snail shells lay under these in drifts
> and, at a distance,
> you'd swear that they were beds of irises
> There was one kind of berry, a dark red.
> I tried it, one by one, and hours apart.
> Sub-acid, and not bad, no ill effects;
> and so I made home-brew. I'd drink
> the awful, fizzy, stinging stuff
> that went straight to my head
> and play my home-made flute
> (I think it had the weirdest scale on earth)
> and, dizzy, whoop and dance among the goats.
> Home-made, home-made! But aren't we all?
> I felt a deep affection for
> the smallest of my island industries.
> No, not exactly, since the smallest was
> a miserable philosophy.

The very island is an exemplar, a representation; it is a place
which stands for the life lived on it as much as it supports that
life. Its unique species are emblems of the selfhood that the

whole region distills and enforces, and on it, life and work and art are one, and the home-made Dionysus *is* (rather than blesses from without or within) his votary. "Solitude" itself is a forgotten word in this place of isolation. Terrors of madness assaulted, even as they necessitated, the retreat into poetry of the Crusoes and Castaways of William Cowper, solitaries to whom the very tameness of the animals was frightening as a mark of wildness that had never known the human, nor ever learned to fear and be fearsome, solitaries who would "start at the sound" of their own voices. But for Bishop's Crusoe, madness is not the problem, particularly the eighteenth-century madness kept at bay by faith. The one mount of speculation on his island is named "*Mont d'Espoir* or *Mount Despair*" indifferently (for Defoe's Crusoe, "Despair" only), and he is rescued from one insulation to another in a different, colder sea enisled, "surrounded by uninteresting lumber."

But one cannot begin to do this splendid piece justice in a brief essay: it is the centerpiece of the book's geographies, and a poem of the first importance. So, too, is "The End of March," a beach-poem in which, again, "vision" is not too serious a word, a strange, late domestication of the poet's earlier Nova Scotia sea-scapes. But this time it is not a meditation on a scene so much as a movement against a scene, a classic journey out and back, toward a treasured image of imagined fulfillment, along a stretch of beach that yields up none of the comforts of place ("Everything was withdrawn as far as possible, / indrawn: the tide far out, the ocean shrunken"), past objects from which meaning itself has withdrawn. The goal is never reached, and the walk back presents glimpses of an almost infernal particularity:

> On the way back our faces froze on the other side.
> The sun came out for just a minute.
> For just a minute, set in their bezels of sand,
> the drab, damp, scattered stones
> were multi-colored,
> and all those high enough threw out long shadows,
> individual shadows, then pulled them in again.
> They could have been teasing the lion sun,
> except that now he was behind them . . .

This moment is itself, in its replacement of a wrecked hope, a splendid monument to a poetry that has always remained measured, powerful in imagination and utterly clear—radiantly and distinctly—in its language. If it seems to manifest rhetorical or eschatological withdrawals, these are never movements away from truth, or even from the struggle for it. Miss Bishop's poems draw themselves in when they do, like wise and politic snails, from the rhetorics of self-expression, the figures of jealousy and pity, the boring industry of innovation. Withdrawn or not, so many of her poems have moved themselves into the few unoccupied corners of perfection that seem to remain, that we can only end as readers where philosophy is said to begin, in wonder.

LLOYD SCHWARTZ

Elizabeth Bishop, 1911–1979

Elizabeth Bishop's sudden death, last week, meant a profound loss to the local and international literary community. But her wonderful poems, stories, and translations, her impressive catalogue of awards, honors, and reviews never made her famous outside those walls. I think her lack of celebrity was connected both to the kind of person she was and, in a way, to the very nature of her artistic achievement, as well as to the way we demand over-abundance and self-promotion from our artists in this country. Elizabeth Bishop was among the most private of contemporary literary figures, living her life as much out of the public eye as her poems refused to indulge in intimate revelations. She was at times painfully shy in front of an audience (only recently seeming to overcome her dread of readings), nervous about teaching, uncomfortable at interviews, even disturbed by photographs of herself. Her ambition (if it could be called that) was not to be recognized or mobbed by fans and followers, but to be left alone enough to write the best poetry she could—which for her was slow, relentlessly painstaking work. She published only 101 original poems.

She was occasionally rueful about her relative lack of notoriety, her "dull life," and was surprised when someone she didn't know knew who she was. Recently, recovering from a minor illness, she told with great amusement and self-irony how an intern, noticing her name plate during some standard but embarrassing hospital procedure, asked her if she was a well-known poet and requested her autograph.

At first, the reticence in her poetry gave the illusion of aloofness. To some critics, her poems seemed merely "perfect," min-

Boston Phoenix (October 16, 1979), p. 12.

iaturist and precious. Significantly, her greatest and most perceptive admirers seem mainly to have been other poets—beginning with Marianne Moore, Randall Jarrell, and Robert Lowell, reviewing her first book, in the mid-'40s. John Ashbery, nominating her for the Neustadt International Prize in 1976 (which she was the first woman and the first American to receive), called her a "writer's writer's writer."

It's no coincidence. Who ought to be better prepared to appreciate the music of an intelligent, "speaking" voice or the subtleties of inflection and moral distinction than others facing the same problems in their own way? She was proud that she was "not a part of any school"—the least-imitated of poets because she had the most delicate ear and the fewest mannerisms. Gradually, each new poem shed more light on the depths of feeling present even in the most seemingly detached of its predecessors. They were becoming more open, too, more directly personal, even autobiographical. And within the past six or seven years, her readings—sometimes, out of nerves and shyness, almost numbingly flat—took on the real, though still restrained, warmth of the poems, their humor, animation, and untheatrical yet forthright emotion.

Rereading the poems this week, I've been astonished again by their range and intensity of feeling and experience. In their unique way, they combine some of the best qualities of her favorite writers—Chekhov's tolerance and understatement, George Herbert's honesty and stunning clarity of detail, Darwin's "endless, heroic observations," Gerard Manley Hopkins's "timing," his sense of "the mind in action." She liked to say her poems were "just description."

Her own range of experience was enormous. Her early uprootedness, with the death of her father and the mental collapse of her mother, made her by necessity, and later by avocation (or habit), a traveller. She lived in Poughkeepsie and Paris, Seattle and Key West, Nova Scotia and Brazil. (The titles of her books include *North & South, Questions of Travel* and *Geography III*.) And she read widely, and idiosyncratically (diaries; ornithology and architecture; philosophy and mystery stories; science and history and art). She was shocked at how students seemed to read so little, and loved to repeat the story about the undergraduate she had hired to organize her library who shelved *To the Finland Station* among the geography books.

Though she never quite got over her resentment of having to teach, she was very fond of her students (and extremely loyal to several of them). It was a sign of particular affection for one of her Harvard classes to have invited them to an informal poetry session at her extraordinary apartment (virtually a museum of Brazilian art and artifacts). But then, she was never predictable, and never academic. She loved to make things—collages, nettle-baskets, marmalade. Her musical taste included Mozart (*not* Beethoven), Cole Porter, and "Fats" Waller. Billie Holiday was a friend ("Songs for a Colored Singer" were written for her). Her favorite example of "perfect" iambic pentameter was: "I hate to see that evenin' sun go down."

"There are some people," she wrote, "whom we envy not because they are rich or handsome or successful, although they may be any or all of these, but because everything they are and do seems to be all of a piece, so that even if they wanted to they could not be or do otherwise." Her friend Robert Lowell once compared her originality to Kafka's: "You don't know what will come after any one line. It's exploring. . . . She's gotten a world, not just a way of writing." That's why so much of what is most treasurable about her remains in her work. It's one of the things great art is supposed to do.

ROBERT PINSKY

Elizabeth Bishop, 1911–1979

In Elizabeth Bishop's bizarre, sly, deceptively plainspoken late poem "Crusoe in England," the famous solitary looks back on his life near its end, recalling his isolation and rescue in ways deeper and more unsettling than Defoe could have dreamed. After painting the hallucinatory, vivid island, with hissing volcanoes and hissing giant turtles—an unforgettable terrain—Bishop's Crusoe muses on the dried-out, wan relics of a life. It's tempting, after Elizabeth Bishop's sudden death a few weeks ago, to understand that passage as a master-artist's commentary on the mere furniture of personality and biography—the facts, the manuscripts, the ups and downs of public reputation:

> The local museum's asked me to
> leave everything to them:
> the flute, the knife, the shrivelled shoes,
> my shedding goatskin trousers
> (moths have got in the fur),
> the parasol that took me such a time
> remembering the way the ribs should go.
> It still will work but, folded up,
> looks like a plucked and skinny fowl.
> How can anyone want such things?
> —And Friday, my dear Friday, died of measles
> seventeen years ago come March.

In the perspective of loss, and actual feeling, artifacts and art can seem withered remnants. In their modesty of outward manner, and their immensely proud awareness of their own power,

---

New Republic (November 10, 1979), pp. 32–33.

Bishop's poems always show us, and never tell us, that they are the exception: in her poems, isolation is suspended, as the artifact rises from the dust to unfold its living soul.

She could afford her indifference toward celebrity, and her cool amusement at the literary museum of biography and criticism, because her work was unequaled in its particular intensity. Rereading Bishop's *Complete Poems,* and the more recent *Geography III* (1976), I find the emotional force and penetration of her work amazing. In a way, she had to write *Geography III,* and especially its first two poems ("In the Waiting Room" and "Crusoe in England") in order to teach us readers the full extent to which her poems were not merely what critics and fellow-poets had always called them—"perfect," "crafted," "readable," "exquisite"—but profoundly ambitious as well.

The critical cliché for years was to praise Bishop for her "eye"—a convention she mischievously, perhaps a bit contemptuously, abetted by remarking that her poems were "just description." The purpose of the "eye" and of the description (as "In the Waiting Room" makes explicit) is for Bishop an act of fierce self-definition: she saw the world with such preternatural clarity in order to distinguish herself from it. "You are an *I,*" the child in the waiting room realizes, "You are an *Elizabeth,* / you are one of *them.* / *Why* should you be one, too?" And later, "The War was on" does not refer only to the First World War. Crusoe on his island has "nightmares of other islands," a vision of

> islands spawning islands,
> like frogs' eggs turning into polliwogs
> of islands, knowing that I had to live
> on each and every one, eventually,
> for ages, registering their flora,
> their fauna, their geography.

She wrote so well about people and places because she had a powerful motive, embattled; that motive, in nearly all the poems, is to define oneself away from two opposing nightmares: the pain of isolation, and the loss of identity in the mass of the visible world.

In other words, "description" in Bishop is not the notation of pretty or quaint details, but the surest form of knowledge; and knowledge is the geography of survival. Her poems are "just description"—in the same sense that the ocean at the conclusion of her great poem "At the Fishhouses" is just the ocean:

> I have seen it over and over, the same sea, the same,
> slightly, indifferently swinging above the stones,
> icily free above the stones,
> above the stones and then the world.
> If you should dip your hand in,
> your wrist would ache immediately,
> your bones would begin to ache and your hand would burn
> as if the water were a transmutation of fire
> that feeds on stones and burns with a dark gray flame.
> If you tasted it, it would first taste bitter,
> then briny, then surely burn your tongue.
> It is like what we imagine knowledge to be:
> dark, salt, clear, moving, utterly free,
> drawn from the cold hard mouth
> of the world, derived from rocky breasts
> forever, flowing and drawn, and since
> our knowledge is historical, flowing, and flown.

The grandeur of this vision of knowledge, and the tragic sense of knowledge's limitations, are folded up carefully into the strict discipline of description like the ribs of Crusoe's umbrella. I'll stop for a moment over just one detail: the wit—the *sublime* wit, though it sounds too fancy to say so—of "flowing, and flown" at the end. In a lesser writer, the brilliant stroke that makes two distinct verbs seem like two forms of one verb would be a notable ornament; but in Bishop's line, the wit is made to bear up triumphantly under the pressure of a large intellectual construct—the way wit operates in Shakespeare. It is this kind of thing that led John Ashbery to call Bishop "a writer's writer's writer."

The obituaries for Elizabeth Bishop were not loud or hyperbolic; they were immensely respectful, and perhaps slightly uncomprehending, just like the "local museum" that she drily invented to accept for vague public use the loner Crusoe's chattels. The year 1979 may be remembered for her loss, long after many of the clowns, heroes, and villains of our headlines fade from memory.

JAMES MERRILL

Elizabeth Bishop, 1911–1979

She disliked being photographed and usually hated the result.
The whitening hair grew thick above a face each year somehow
rounder and softer, like a bemused, blue-lidded planet, a touch
too large, in any case, for a body that seemed never quite to have
reached maturity. In early life the proportions would have been
just right. A 1941 snapshot (printed in last winter's Vassar Bul-
letin) shows her at Key West, with bicycle, in black French
beach togs, beaming straight at the camera: a living doll.

The bicycle may have been the same one she pedaled to the
local electric company with her monthly bill *and* Charles
Olson's, who one season rented her house but felt that "a Poet
mustn't be asked to do prosaic things like pay bills." The story
was told not at the Poet's expense but rather as fingers are
crossed for luck—another of her own instinctive, modest, life-
long impersonations of an ordinary woman, someone who dur-
ing the day did errands, went to the beach, would perhaps that
evening jot a phrase or two inside the nightclub matchbook
before returning to the dance floor.

Thus the later glimpses of her playing was it poker? with
Neruda in a Mexican hotel, or pingpong with Octavio Paz in
Cambridge, or getting Robert Duncan high on grass—"for the
first time!"—in San Francisco, or teaching Frank Bidart the
wildflowers in Maine. Why talk *letters* with one's gifted col-
leagues? They too would want, surely, to put aside work in
favor of a new baby to examine, a dinner to shop for and cook,
sambas, vignettes: Here's what I heard this afternoon (or saw
twenty years ago)—imagine! Poetry was a life both shaped by
and distinct from the lived one, like that sleet storm's second tree
"of glassy veins" in "Five Flights Up." She was never unwilling

The New York Review of Books (December 6, 1979), p. 6.

to talk about hers, but managed to make it sound agreeably beside the point. As in her "A Miracle for Breakfast" she tended to identify not with the magician on his dawn balcony but with the onlookers huddled and skeptical in the bread-line below.

This need for relief from what must have been an at times painful singularity was coupled with "the gift to be simple" under whatever circumstances. Once, after days of chilly drizzle in Ouro Preto, the sun came out and Elizabeth proposed a jaunt to the next town. There would be a handsome church and, better yet, a jail opposite, whose murderers and wife-beaters wove the prettiest little bracelets and boxes out of empty cigarette packages, which they sold through the grille. Next a taxi was jouncing through sparkling red-and-green country, downhill, uphill, then, suddenly, *under* a rainbow! Elizabeth said some words in Portuguese, the driver began to shake with laughter. "In the north of Brazil," she explained, "they have this superstition, if you pass underneath a rainbow you change sex." (We were to pass more than once under this one.) On our arrival the prisoners had nothing to show us. They were mourning a comrade dead that week—six or eight men in their cavernous half-basement a narrow trench of water flowed through. They talked with Elizabeth quietly, like an old friend who would understand. It brought to mind that early prose piece where she imagines, with anything but distaste, being confined for life to a small stone cell. Leaving, she gave them a few coins; she had touched another secret base.

In Ouro Preto literary visitors were often a matter of poets from other parts of Brazil—weren't there 15,000 in Belem alone? These would arrive, two or three a week during the "season," to present her with their pamphlets, receiving in turn an inscribed *Complete Poems* from a stack on the floor beside her. The transaction, including coffee, took perhaps a quarter of an hour, at whose end we were once more by ourselves. The room was large, irregular in shape, the high beams painted. Instead of a picture or mirror one white wall framed a neat rectangular excavation: the plaster removed to show timbers lashed together by thongs. This style of construction dated the house before

1740. Across the room burned the cast-iron stove, American, the only one in town. More echoes, this time from "Sestina."

I was her first compatriot to visit in several months. She found it uncanny to be speaking English again. Her other guest, a young Brazilian painter, in town for the summer arts festival and worn out by long teaching hours, merely slept in the house. Late one evening, over Old-Fashioneds by the stove, a too recent sorrow had come to the surface; Elizabeth, uninsistent and articulate, was in tears. The young painter, returning, called out, entered—and stopped short on the threshold. His hostess almost blithely made him at home. Switching to Portuguese, "Don't be upset, José Alberto," I understood her to say, "I'm only crying in English."

The next year, before leaving Brazil for good, she went on a two-week excursion up the Rio Negro. One day the rattletrap white river-steamer was accosted by a wooden melon-rind barely afloat, containing a man, a child of perhaps six, and a battered but ornate armchair which they were hoping to sell. Nothing doing. However, a "famous eye" among the passengers was caught by the boatman's paddle—a splendidly sanded and varnished affair painted with the flags of Brazil and the United States; it would hang on her wall in Boston. When the riverman understood that the eccentric foreign Senhora was offering, for this implement on which his poor livelihood depended, more money ($6, if memory serves) than he could dream of refusing, his perplexity knew no bounds. Then the little boy spoke up: "Sell it Papá, we still have *my* paddle!"—waving one no bigger than a toy. Which in the event, the bargain struck, would slowly, comically, precariously ply them and their unsold throne back across the treacherous water.

Will it serve as momentary emblem of her charm as a woman and her wisdom as a poet? The adult, in charge of the craft, keeping it balanced, richer for a loss; the child coming up with means that, however slow, quirky, humble, would nevertheless—

Nevertheless, with or without emblems, and hard as it is to accept that there will be no more of them, her poems remain. One has to blush, faced with poems some of us feel to be more wryly radiant, more touching, more unaffectedly intelligent than any written in our lifetime, to come up with such few blurred snapshots of their maker. It is not her writings—even to those magically chatty letters—whose loss is my subject here. Those miracles outlast their performer; but for her the sun has set, and for us the balcony is dark.

RICHARD WILBUR

Elizabeth Bishop

A memorial tribute read at the American
Academy of Arts & Letters, 7 December 1979

My wife and I first met Elizabeth Bishop at the Eberharts' apart-
ment in Cambridge, more than thirty years ago. She had just
recently published her first book, *North & South,* which the
reviewers had admired but which had also had the rarer fate of
being instantly precious to many of her fellow poets, who right-
ly saw it as something new, distinguished, and inexhaustibly
fresh. The woman we met that evening was not a literary figure,
and was clearly not embarked on anything so pompous and
public as a career. She was quiet, comely, friendly, amusing, and
amusable; she spoke in a modest and somewhat murmuring
way, often asking questions as if she expected us Cantabrigians
to have the answers. But in matters of importance to her she
turned out to have quite definite answers of her own. For exam-
ple, she told me that Poe's best poem, for her taste, was a little-
known piece called "Fairy-Land." Years of re-reading that
poem have brought me close to her opinion, and have led me to
see that her fondness for it was based on a true affinity. "Fairy-
Land" is a charming dream-vision, written in a transparent style
unusual for Poe; at the same time, its weeping trees and multi-
tudinous moons are repeatedly and humorously challenged by
the voice of common sense; out of which conflict the poem
somehow modulates, at the close, into a poignant yearning for
transcendence. All of the voices of that poem have their counter-
parts in Elizabeth's own work.

Reticent as she was, Elizabeth Bishop wrote several auto-
biographical pieces in which she testified to a lifelong sense of
dislocation. That is, she missed from the beginning what some

---

Ploughshares 6, no. 2 (1980), pp. 10–14.

enjoy, an unthinking conviction that things ought to be as they are; that one ought to exist, bearing a certain name; that the schoolbus driver should have a fox terrier; that there should be a red hydrant down at the corner; that it all makes sense. Her short prose masterpiece, "In the Village," is quite simply an account of how, in childhood, her confidence in the world's plausibility and point was shaken. Behind the story lies her father's death in the first year of her life; hanging over the story, in the Nova Scotian sky, is the scream of her mother, who was forever lost to the child through an emotional breakdown. Here are two resonant sentences from the story, having to do with the sending of family packages to her mother. "The address of the sanitarium is in my grandmother's handwriting, in purple indelible pencil, on smoothed-out wrapping paper. It will never come off."

If the world is a strange place, then it readily shades into dream. So many of Elizabeth's poems take place at the edge of sleep, or on the threshold of waking, lucidly fusing two orders of consciousness. Some of them are written out of remembered dreams. And then there are superb poems like "The Man-Moth," in which a tragic sensibility is portrayed *under the form* of dream. In a later poem, "The Riverman," her capacity for navigating the irrational enabled her to enter the mind of a witch-doctor, and visit the water-spirits of the Amazon. All this has little to do with the influence of French surrealism, I think; as her Robinson Crusoe says of his artifacts in *Geography III,* Elizabeth Bishop's poems are "home-made."

In another kind of poem, she sets some part of the world before her and studies it with a describing eye, an interrogating mind, and a personality eager for coherence. This is the kind of poem, written in a style at once natural and lapidary, in which her stunning accuracies of perception and comparison make us think of her friend and early encourager, Marianne Moore. A sandy beach "hisses like fat"; she sees on a wall "the mildew's ignorant map"; on a gusty day in Washington she notes how "Unceasingly, the little flags / Feed their limp stripes into the air." One could go on quoting such felicities forever, and it is such things which have led the critics to use the words *wit, delight, precision, elegance* and *fastidiousness;* at the same time, her descriptive genius has led some to say that her poetry is a poetry of surfaces. At moments she seems to have felt this herself, as when, at the close of her poem "The Armadillo," she grows suddenly impatient of the prettiness of poetry and speaks in italics of fear and pain. But in fact her poems, for all their objectivity, are much involved in what they see: though she seldom protests, or specifies her emotions, her work is full of an implicit compassion, and her friend Robert Lowell justly ascribed to her a tone "of large, grave tenderness and sorrowing amusement."

That expression "sorrowing amusement" is wonderfully exact, and of course it would be quite wrong to overstress the sorrow part of it. If she was afflicted by the absurdity of things, she also took delight in everything curious, incongruous, or crazy; that's one reason why she was the best of company. Almost all of my mental pictures of her belong somewhere on a scale between amiability and hilarity; and we have one real picture—a snapshot—in which, with the fiercest of expressions, she is about to use my head as a croquet-ball.

When she looked in her poetry for ultimate answers, she generally expressed the search in the key of geography, of travel. And she always reported that such answers were undiscoverable. In the poem "Cape Breton" she says, "Whatever the landscape had of meaning appears to have been abandoned." In "Arrival at Santos," she mocks the tourist with his "immodest demands for a different world, / and a better life, and complete comprehension / of both at last," and concludes with the intensely ironic line, "We are driving to the interior." In another poem about travel, she regrets that so many sights in Rome or Mexico or Marrakesh have failed to make a pattern, that everything has been "only connected by 'and' and 'and'." She wishes that some revelation, some Nativity scene, might have brought all into focus. In and out of her poetry, she lamented her want of a comprehensive philosophy; yet I cannot be sorry that so honest a nature as hers refused to force itself into a system, and I question whether system is the only way to go deep into things.

Though she had no orthodox convictions, and wondered at such certainties in others, Elizabeth Bishop had religious concerns and habits of feeling. I think of her poem about St. Peter; I think of the "pure and angelic note" of the blacksmith's hammer in her story "In the Village," and the way that story ends with the cry, "O, beautiful sound, strike again!" I think of the fact that when she was asked to make a selection of someone's poems for a poetry newsletter, she came up with an anthology of hymns. (Her favorite hymn, by the way, was the Easter one which begins, "Come ye faithful, raise the strain / Of triumphant gladness.") Above all, I think of her poem called "Twelfth Morning": it is a poem about Epiphany, the day when things are manifested, and its opening lines say:

> Like a first coat of whitewash when it's wet,
> the thin grey mist lets everything show through . . .

One thing that comes through the mist is a sound from the shore, the sound of "the sandpipers' / heart-broken cries," and that I take for a sign that grief is a radical presence in the world. But there is also another phenomenon, a black boy named Balthazár who bears the name of one of the Magi, and on whose head is a four-gallon can which "keeps flashing that the world's a pearl." The vision of Balthazár and his four-gallon pearl is qualified by amusement; nevertheless it is a vision. It seems to me that Elizabeth Bishop's poetry perceives beauty as well as absurdity, exemplifies the mind's power to make beauty, and embodies compassion; though her world is ultimately mysterious, one of its constants is sorrow, and another is some purity or splendor which, though forever defiled, is also, as her poem "Anaphora" says, perpetually renewed.

This appreciation has been too literary, with too little of the personal in it. Elizabeth herself would not have been guilty of such disproportion. She attended to her art, but she also attended to other people and to the things of every day. James Merrill put this happily, in a recent reminiscence, when he spoke of her "lifelong impersonation of an ordinary woman." Well, she was an incomparable poet and a delectable person; we loved her very much.

MARY McCARTHY

Symposium
I Would Like to Have Written . . .

Elizabeth Bishop. I envy the mind hiding in her words, like an "I" counting up to a hundred waiting to be found. We were a class apart at Vassar, a hemisphere apart during her crucial years in Brazil, and somewhat remote, I guess, in general outlook, but when I think of the writers I like, starting with Chaucer, there is no one but her that I can truly wish to have been. Not that I want to have written her works but that I would like to have had her quiddity, her way of seeing that was like a big pocket magnifying glass. *Of course* it would have hurt to have to use it for ordinary looking: that would have been the forfeit.

New York Times Book Review (December 6, 1981), p. 68.

PART THREE   *In Her Own Words*

From "Time's Andromedas"

One afternoon last fall I was studying very hard, bending over my book with my back to the light of the high double windows. Concentration was so difficult that I had dug myself a sort of little black cave into the subject I was reading, and there I burrowed and scratched, like the Count of Monte Cristo, expecting Heaven knows what sudden revelation. My own thoughts, conflicting with those of the book, were making such a wordy racket that I heard and saw nothing—until the page before my eyes blushed pink. I was startled, then realized that there must be a sunset at my back, and waited a minute trying to guess the color of it from the color of the little reflection. As I waited I heard a multitude of small sounds, and knew simultaneously that I had been hearing them all along,—sounds high in the air, of a faintly rhythmic irregularity, yet resembling the retreat of innumerable small waves, lake-waves, rustling on sand.

Of course it was the birds going South. They were very high up, a fairly large sort of bird, I couldn't tell what, but almost speck-like, paying no attention to even the highest trees or steeples. They spread across a wide swath of sky, each rather alone, and at first their wings seemed all to be beating perfectly together. But by watching one bird, then another, I saw that some flew a little slower than others, some were trying to get ahead and some flew at an individual rubato; each seemed a variation, and yet altogether my eyes were deceived into thinking them perfectly precise and regular. I watched closely the spaces between the birds. It was as if there were an invisible thread joining all the outside birds and within this fragile net-work they possessed the sky; it was down among them, of a paler color, moving with them. The interspaces moved in pulsation too, catching

Vassar Journal of Undergraduate Studies (May 1933), pp. 102–20.

up and continuing the motion of the wings in wakes, carrying it on, as the rest in music does—not a blankness but a space as musical as all the sound.

The birds came in groups, each taking four or five minutes to fly over; then a pause of two or three minutes and the next group appeared. I must have watched them for almost an hour before I realized that the same relationships of birds and spaces I had noticed in the small groups were true of the whole migration at once. The next morning when I got up and went to the window they were still going over, and all that day and part of the next whenever I remembered to listen or look up they were still there.

It came to me that the flying birds were setting up, far over my head, a sort of time-pattern, or rather patterns, all closely related, all minutely varied, and yet all together forming the *migration,* which probably in the date of its flight and its actual flying time was as mathematically regular as the planets. There was the individual rate of each bird, its rate in relation to all the other birds, the speed of the various groups, and then that mysterious swath they made through the sky, leaving it somehow emptied and stilled, slowly assuming its usual coloring and faraway look. Yet all this motion with its effect of precision, of *passing* the time along, as the clock passes it along from minute to minute, was to result in the end in a thing so inevitable, so absolute, as to mean nothing connected with the passage of time at all—a static fact of the world, the birds here or there, always; a fact that may hurry the seasons along for us, but as far as bird migration goes, stands still and infinite.

From "Gerard Manley Hopkins
Notes on Timing in His Poetry"

It is perhaps fanciful to apply the expression *timing* to poetry—
race horses, runners, are timed: there is such a thing as the
timing of a crew of oarsmen, or a single tennis stroke—it may be
a term only suited to physical motions. But as poetry considered
in a very simple way is motion too: the releasing, checking,
timing, and repeating of the movement of the mind according to
ordered systems, it seems fair enough to admit that in some way
its discipline involves a method of timing, even comparable to
that used for literal actions. For me at least, an idea of *timing* in
poetry helps to explain many of those aspects of poetry which
are so inadequately expressed by most critics: why poets differ
so from each other; why using exactly the same meters and
approximate vocabularies two poets produce such different ef-
fects; why some poetry seems at rest and other poetry in action.
Particularly in referring to Father Hopkins, the most intricate of
poets technically and most taxing emotionally, does some such
simplified method of approach seem necessary.

The most general meaning of *timing* as applied to any particu-
lar physical activity is co-ordination: the correct manipulation of
the time, the little duration each phase of the action must take in
order that the whole may be perfect. And the time taken for each
part of an action is decided both by the time of the whole, and of
the parts before and after. (This sounds involved, but can be
made quite clear, I think, by picturing for a minute a crew of
men rowing a shell, and considering the enormous number of
tiny individual motions going to each stroke, to each man, and
the whole shell.) The whole series together sets up a *rhythm,*

Vassar Review (February 1934), pp. 5–7.

which in turn enables the series to occur over and over again—possibly with variations once it is established.

Just so in poetry: the syllables, the words, in their actual duration and their duration according to sense-value, set up among themselves a rhythm, which continues to flow over them. And if we find all these things harmonious, if they amalgamate in some strange manner, then the *timing* has been right. This does not mean that a monotonous, regularly beating meter means good timing—duration of sense and sound each play a part, I believe, nearly equal, and *sense* is the quality which permits mechanical irregularities while preserving the unique feeling of timeliness in the poem. . . .

II

So far I have meant by *timing* some quality within the poem itself; now I wish to take the same expression and use it in a different way, for a different thing. A man stands in a shooting gallery with a gun at his shoulder aiming at a clay pigeon which moves across the backdrop at the end of the gallery. In order to hit it he must shoot not at it directly but a certain distance in front of it. Between his point of aim and the pigeon he must allow the necessary small fraction of space which the pigeon will cross in exactly the same amount of time as it will take the bullet to travel the length of the shooting gallery. If he does this accurately the clay pigeon falls, and his *timing* has been correct. In the same way the poet is set on bringing down onto the paper his poem, which occurs to him not as a sudden fixed apparition of a poem, but as a moving, changing idea or series of ideas. The poet must decide at what point in its movement he can best stop it, possibly at what point he can manage to stop it; i.e., it is another matter of timing. Perhaps, however, the image of the man in the shooting gallery is incorrect, since the mind of the poet does not stand still and aim his shifting idea. The cleavage implied in the comparison is quite true, I think—anyone who has even tried to write a single poem because he felt he had one somewhere in his head will recognize its truth. The poem, unique and perfect seems to be separate from the conscious mind, deliberately avoiding it, while the conscious mind takes difficult steps toward it. The process resembles somewhat the more familiar one of puzzling over a momentarily forgotten name or word which seems to be taking on an elusive brain-life of its own as we try to grasp it. Granted that the poet is capable of grasping his idea, the shooting image must be more complicated; the target is a moving target and the marksman is also moving. His own movement goes on; the target must be stopped at an unknown critical point, whenever his sense of timing dictates. I have heard that dropping shells from an airplane onto a speeding battleship below, in an uncertain sea, demands the most perfect and delicate sense of timing imaginable. . . .

From Two Letters to Marianne Moore about "A Miracle for Breakfast"

. . . the sestina is just a sort of stunt.

September 15, 1936

You are no comfort to me, at all, Miss Moore, the way you inevitably light on just those things I knew I shouldn't have let go—I must be unusually insensitive to be able to bear being brought face to face with my conscience this way over and over. I mean in A MIRACLE FOR BREAKFAST. I knew I should not have let the "bitterly" and "very hot" in the second stanza go. It is as yet unsolved. The boisterousness of "gallons of coffee" I want to overlook because I like "gallons" being near "galleries." And the "crumb" and "sun" is of course its greatest fault. It seems to me that there are two ways possible for a sestina—one is to use unusual words as terminations, in which case they would have to be used differently as often as possible—as you say, "change of scale." That would make a very highly seasoned kind of poem. And the other way is to use as colorless words as possible—like Sydney, so that it becomes less of a trick and more of a natural theme and variations. I guess I have tried to do both at once. It is probably just an excuse, but sometimes I think about certain things that without one particular fault they would be without the means of existence. I feel a little that way about "sun" and "crumb!"—but I know at the same time it is only justified about someone else's work.

January 5, 1937

Candace W. MacMahon, *Elizabeth Bishop: A Bibliography 1927–1979* (Charlottesville: University Press of Virginia, 1980), pp. 143–44.

From "Gregorio Valdes, 1879–1939"

There are some people whom we envy not because they are rich or handsome or successful, although they may be any or all of these, but because everything they are and do seems to be all of a piece, so that even if they wanted to they could not be or do otherwise. A particular feature of their characters may stand out as more praiseworthy in itself than others—that is almost beside the point. Ancient heroes often have to do penance for and expiate crimes they have committed all unwittingly, and in the same way it seems that some people receive certain "gifts" merely by remaining unwittingly in an undemocratic state of grace. It is a supposition that leaves paintings like Gregorio's a partial mystery. But surely anything that is impossible for others to achieve by effort, that is dangerous to imitate, and yet, like natural virtue, must be both admired and imitated, always remains mysterious.

Partisan Review (Summer 1939), pp. 91–96.

From "As We Like It"

These things make even our greatest poet, when he attempts something like them, appear full of preconceived notions and over-sentimental. A wounded deer has been abandoned by his "velvet friends." And Shakespeare is supposed to have been familiar with deer.

> The wretched animal heav'd forth such groans
> That their discharge did stretch his leathern coat
> Almost to bursting, and the big round tears
> Cours'd one another down his innocent nose
> In piteous chase . . .
>
> *As You Like It*

I do not understand the nature of the satisfaction a completely accurate description or imitation of anything at all can give, but apparently in order to produce it the description or imitation must be brief, or compact, and have at least the effect of being spontaneous. Even the best *trompe-l'oeil* paintings lack it, but I have experienced it in listening to the noise made by a four-year-old child who could imitate exactly the sound of water running out of his bath. Long, fine, thorough passages of descriptive prose fail to produce it, but sometimes animal or bird masks at the Museum of Natural History give one (as the dances that once went with them might have been able to do) the same immediacy of identification one feels on reading about Miss Moore's

> Small dog, going over the lawn, nipping the linen and saying
> that you have a badger

Quarterly Review of Literature (Marianne Moore Issue 1948), pp. 129–35.

or the butterfly that

> flies off
> diminishing like wreckage on the sea,
> rising and falling easily.

Does it come simply from her gift of being able to give herself up entirely to the object under contemplation, to feel in all sincerity how it is to be *it?* From whatever this pleasure may be derived, it is certainly one of the greatest the work of Miss Moore gives us.

Sometimes in her poetry such instances "go on" so that there seems almost to be a compulsion to this kind of imitation. The poems seem to say, "These things exist to be loved and honored and we *must*," perhaps the sense of duty shows through a little too plainly.

> Did he not moralize this spectacle?
> O yes, into a thousand similes.
>> *As You Like It*

And although the tone is frequently light or ironic the total effect is of such ritualistic solemnity that I feel in reading her one should constantly bear in mind the secondary and frequently sombre meaning of the title of her first book: *Observations.*

Review of *XAIPE: Seventy-one Poems* by E. E. Cummings

The famous man of little-letters, e. e. cummings, presents here his first book of poems since 1×1 appeared in 1944. It is appropriate that the book should appear in the spring, since spring is Mr. Cummings' favorite season, speaking to him of flowers, rain, new moons, love and joy. Most of the seventy-one poems take up these themes, but there is the usual scattering of involuted and sometimes rather unpleasant epigrams, and this time a few sympathetic and touching portraits as well. Often Mr. Cummings' approach to poetry reminds one of a smart-alec Greenwich Village child saying to his friends: "Look! I've just made up a new game. Let's all write poems. There! I've won!" And in front of the wood-and-coal man's basement shop, on the wall of the Chinese laundry, along the curbs of the dingy but flourishing park, appear poems and ideograph poems in hyacinth-colored chalks. The obscene and epigrammatic ones have most of this happy hooligan quality; in others he is still playing his game and winning it, but it has been refined into a game resembling a one-man Japanese poetry competition, using the same symbols over and over again, formally, but delicately, freshly and firmly, as no one else can.

In this collection there is a poem in memory of the critic Peter Monroe Jack, a particularly fine one in memory of Ford Madox Ford, one on a wood-and-coal man, and one on "chas sing," a laundryman. One can still enjoy Cummings' inexhaustible pleasure in double o's, parentheses, and question marks, but when *honi soit qui mal y pense* becomes "honey swo R ky mollypants" one feels that something should be done about it. Yet at his best he remains one of our greatest lyricists.

The United States Quarterly Book Review (June 1950), pp. 160–61.

It All Depends [In Response to a Questionnaire]

To all but two of the questions raised here my answer is *it all depends*. It all depends on the particular poem one happens to be trying to write, and the range of possibilities is, one trusts, infinite. After all, the poet's concern is not consistency.

I do not understand the question about the function of overtone, and to the question on subject matter (any predilections? any restrictions?) I shall reply that there are no restrictions. There *are,* of course, but they are not consciously restrictions.

Physique, temperament, religion, politics, and immediate circumstances all play their parts in formulating one's theories on verse. And then they play them again and differently when one is writing it. No matter what theories one may have, I doubt very much that they are in one's mind at the moment of writing a poem or that there is even a physical possibility that they could be. Theories can only be based on interpretations of other poet's poems, or one's own in retrospect, or wishful thinking.

The analysis of poetry is growing more and more pretentious and deadly. After a session with a few of the highbrow magazines one doesn't want to look at a poem for weeks, much less start writing one. The situation is reminiscent of those places along the coast where warnings are posted telling one not to walk too near the edge of the cliffs because they have been undermined by the sea and may collapse at any minute.

This does not mean that I am opposed to all close analysis and criticism. But I am opposed to making poetry monstrous or boring and proceeding to talk the very life out of it.

Mid-Century American Poets, ed. John Ciardi (New York: Twayne, 1950), p. 267.

From "What the Young Man Said to the Psalmist"

Tremont Temple and its Baptist sermons, Symphony Hall, the Harvard Glee Club, the Museum of Fine Arts—all these were part of my own childhood background, and as I read his book I could not help making comparisons between Mr. Fowlie's early impressions and my own. My own first ride on a swan boat occurred at the age of three and is chiefly memorable for the fact that one of the live swans paddling around us bit my mother's finger when she offered it a peanut. I remember the hole in the black kid glove and a drop of blood. I do not want to set myself up as a model of facing the sterner realities of swan boat rides in order to discredit Mr. Fowlie's idealization,—but there is re- markably little of blood, sweat, or tears in Mr. Fowlie's book.

Review of Wallace Fowlie's *Pantomime, A Journal of Rehearsals*, in *Poetry* (January 1952), pp. 212–14.

From "The Manipulation of Mirrors"

. . . By now everyone knows how to review a book of translated poetry. First, one says it's impossible. Second, one implies that the translator is an ignoramus, or if that's going too far, that he has missed the play on words; and then one carps about the inevitable mistakes. The first objection is still true: it is impossible to translate poetry, or perhaps only one aspect can be translated at a time, and each poem needs several translations. But Mr. Smith has made an exceptionally good try and I think his faithfulness to the French will impress most reviewers. But the quickness, the surprise, the new sub-acid flavor, have disappeared. Mr. Smith is too intelligent not to know this; he says:

> Translating poetry is like converging on a flame with a series of mirrors, mirrors of technique and understanding, until the flame is reflected in upon itself in a wholly new and foreign element. Such an operation is rarely, if ever, successful: the manipulation of the mirrors depends to such an extent on the sensibility and skill of the translator.

Besides being a pretty image, this is a true one, as anyone who has ever tried translating poetry will know. But surely, besides sensibility and skill, it depends (about 50 percent, I'd say) on luck: the possibilities of the second language's vocabulary. Without luck the worst happens, the flame goes out, and we shouldn't blame Mr. Smith when it does. But if anyone thinks he could do better he should sit down and try.

Review of *Selected Writings of Jules Laforgue,* edited and translated by William Jay Smith, *New Republic* (November 19, 1956), pp. 23–24.

From Introduction to *The Diary of "Helena Morley"*

In one of his letters to Robert Bridges, Hopkins says that he has bought some books, among them Dana's *Two Years Before the Mast,* "a thoroughly good one and all true, but bristling with technicality—seamanship—which I most carefully go over and even enjoy but cannot understand; there are other things, though, as a flogging, which is terrible and instructive *and it happened*—ah, that is the charm and the main point." And that, I think, is "the charm and the main point" of *Minha Vida de Menina.* Its "technicalities," diamond digging, say, scarcely "bristle," and its three years in Diamantina are relatively tame and unfocussed, although there are incidents of comparable but casual small-town cruelty. But—*it really happened;* everything did take place, day by day, minute by minute, once and only once, just the way Helena says it did.

The Diary of "Helena Morley," translated, edited, and with an introduction by Elizabeth Bishop (New York: Farrar, Straus and Cudahy, 1957).

On *Life Studies* by Robert Lowell

As a child, I used to look at my grandfather's Bible under a powerful reading-glass. The letters assembled beneath the lens were suddenly like a Lowell poem, as big as life and as alive, and rainbow-edged. It seemed to illuminate as it magnified; it could also be used as a burning-glass.

This new book begins on Robert Lowell's now-familiar trumpet-notes (see "Inauguration Day"), then with the autobiographical group the tone changes. In these poems, heartbreaking, shocking, grotesque and gentle, the unhesitant attack, the imagery and construction, are as brilliant as ever, but the mood is nostalgic and the meter is refined. A poem like "My Last Afternoon with Uncle Devereux Winslow," or "Skunk Hour," can tell us as much about the state of society as a volume of Henry James at his best.

Whenever I read a poem by Robert Lowell I have a chilling sensation of here-and-now, of exact contemporaneity: more aware of those "ironies of American History," grimmer about them, and yet hopeful. If more people read poetry, if it were more exportable and translatable, surely his poems would go far towards changing, or at least unsettling, minds made up against us. Somehow or other, by fair means or foul, and in the middle of our worst century so far, we have produced a magnificent poet.

Jacket blurb for Robert Lowell's *Life Studies* (New York: Farrar, Straus and Cudahy, 1959).

On "The Man-Moth"

This poem was written in 1935 when I first lived in New York City.

I've forgotten what it was that was supposed to be "mammoth." But the misprint seemed meant for me. An oracle spoke from the page of the *New York Times,* kindly explaining New York City to me, at least for a moment.

One is offered such oracular statements all the time, but often misses them, gets lazy about writing them out in detail, or the meaning refuses to stay put. This poem seems to me to have stayed put fairly well—but as Fats Waller used to say, "One never knows, do one?"

Poet's Choice, ed. Paul Engle and Joseph Langland (New York: The Dial Press, 1962), p. 103.

On Flannery O'Connor

. . . Something about her intimidated me a bit; perhaps natural awe before her toughness and courage; perhaps, although death is certain for all, hers seemed a little more certain than usual. She made no show of *not* living in a metropolis, or of being a believer,—she lived with Christian stoicism and wonderful wit and humor that put most of us to shame.

I am very glad to hear that another collection of her stories is to be published soon. I am sure her few books will live on and on in American literature. They are narrow, possibly, but they are clear, hard, vivid, and full of bits of description, phrases, and odd insights that contain more real poetry than a dozen books of poems. Critics who accuse her of exaggeration are quite wrong, I think. I lived in Florida for several years next to a flourishing "Church of God" (both white and black congregation), where every Wednesday night Sister Mary and her husband "spoke in tongues." After those Wednesday nights, nothing Flannery O'Connor ever wrote could seem at all exaggerated to me.

From "Flannery O'Connor, 1925–1964," *The New York Review of Books* (October 8, 1964), p. 21.

The "Darwin" Letter

There is no "split" [between the role of consciousness and sub-consciousness in art]. Dreams, works of art (some) glimpses of the always-more-successful surrealism of everyday life, unexpected moments of empathy (is it?), catch a peripheral vision of whatever it is one can never really see full-face but that seems enormously important. I can't believe we are wholly irrational—and I do admire Darwin—But reading Darwin one admires the beautiful solid case being built up out of his endless, heroic observations, almost unconscious or automatic—and then comes a sudden relaxation, a forgetful phrase, and one feels that strangeness of his undertaking, sees the lonely young man, his eyes fixed on facts and minute details, sinking or sliding giddily off into the unknown. What one seems to want in art, in experiencing it, is the same thing that is necessary for its creation, a self-forgetful, perfectly useless concentration.

Letter to Anne Stevenson, *Elizabeth Bishop* (New York: Twayne, 1966), p. 66.

ASHLEY BROWN

An Interview with Elizabeth Bishop

Brazil: Elizabeth Bishop's study is a small house which lies up the hill from her home in the mountains near Petrópolis, the old imperial summer capital. The study is perched above a waterfall. One looks through the windows at a clump of bamboos which descend to a tiny swimming-pool, momentary repose in the course of the cascading water. The room is filled with books, comfortable armchairs, piles of old literary quarterlies. An exquisite oratório *from Minas Gerais and other small miscellaneous objects stand on the bookcases. A literary visitor will notice photographs of Baudelaire, Marianne Moore, and Robert Lowell near the poet's work-table. Tobias, an elderly cat, and Suzuki, his younger Siamese companion, reluctantly move from the vicinity of the typewriter.*

Interviewer: I think you have one of the handsomest settings in the world. What poet could ask for more? Do you find that a dazzling landscape like this is an incentive to write, or do you prefer to shut yourself off from visual distractions when you are working?

Miss Bishop: You will notice that the study turns its back on the view of the mountains—that's too distracting! But I have the intimate view to look at; the bamboo leaves are very close. Everybody who comes here asks about the view: is it inspiring? I think I'll put a little sign saying "Inspiration" on those bamboos! Ideally, I suppose any writer prefers a hotel room completely shut away from distractions.

Interviewer: You have been living in Brazil since about 1952, haven't you?

Shenandoah 17, no. 2 (Winter 1966), pp. 3–19.

Miss Bishop:　Yes, it was the end of November, 1951, when I came here; you remember my poem, "Arrival at Santos."

Interviewer:　As far as your poetry goes, have you been able to get anything from Brazil except its appearances? I mean, can you draw on the social and literary traditions here?

Miss Bishop:　Living in the way I have happened to live here, knowing Brazilians, has made a great difference. The general life I have known here has of course had an impact on me. I think I've learned a great deal. Most New York intellectuals' ideas about "underdeveloped countries" are partly mistaken, and living among people of a completely different culture has changed a lot of my old stereotyped ideas.

As for the literary milieu in Brazil, it is so remote from ours. In Rio for example, the French influence is still powerful. I find the poetry very interesting, but it hasn't much to do with contemporary poetry in English. Our poetry went off in a different direction much earlier.

Interviewer:　When you say our poetry went off in a different direction, what do you mean?

Miss Bishop:　What happened with Eliot and Pound as early as 1910—modernism. The Brazilians' poetry is still more formal than ours—it's farther from the demotic. It is true, of course, that they had a *modernismo* movement in 1922, led by Mario de Andrade and others. But they still don't write the way they speak. And I suppose they have still never quite escaped from romanticism. It's an interesting fact that there is no word in Portuguese for "understatement." Marianne Moore's poetry is nearly all understatement. How can they understand us? So much of the English-American tradition consists of this. They have irony, but not understatement.

By the way, I lived in Mexico for a time twenty years ago and I knew Pablo Neruda there. I think I was influenced to some extent by him (as in my "Invitation to Miss Marianne Moore"), but he is still a rather "advanced" poet, compared with other South American poets.

To summarize: I just happened to come here, and I am influenced by Brazil certainly, but I am a completely American poet, nevertheless.

Interviewer: What about the Portuguese language? Do you find that reading it and speaking it (and being surrounded by it) have increased your awareness of English?

Miss Bishop: I don't read it habitually—just newspapers and some books. After all these years, I'm like a dog: I understand everything that's said to me, but I don't speak it very well. I don't really think that my awareness of English has been increased. I felt much the same when I lived in France before the war. What I really like best is silence! Up here in Petrópolis, in the mountains, it is very quiet.

Interviewer: How would you describe Portuguese as a poetic language?

Miss Bishop: From *our* point of view, it seems cumbersome— you just can't use colloquial speech in that way. Grammatically, it is a very difficult language. Even well-educated Brazilians worry about writing their own language; they don't speak their grammar, as it were. I imagine it's easier to write free verse in Portuguese—because it gets you away from the problem. They did take to free verse very quickly here.

Interviewer: Now, if I may, I'd like to recall you to North America and your childhood. You actually spent your earliest years in Nova Scotia, didn't you? Did you live in the kind of house where people encouraged the children to read? Or did your literary interests come later?

Miss Bishop: I didn't spend all of my childhood in Nova Scotia. I lived there from 1914 to 1917 during the first World War. After that I spent long summers there till I was thirteen. Since then I've made only occasional visits. My relatives were not literary in any way. But in my aunt's house we had quite a few books, and I drew heavily on them. In some ways the little village in Canada where I lived was more cultured than the suburbs of Boston where I lived later. As for the books in our house, we had Emerson, Carlyle, all the old poets. I learned to read very early, and later I used to spend all of my allowance on books. They were all I ever wanted to buy.

Interviewer: What were some of your favorite books? Were you ever deeply impressed by something you read in those days?

Miss Bishop: I was crazy about fairy tales—Anderson, Grimm, and so on. Like Jean-Paul Sartre (as he explains it in *Les Mots*), I also read all kind of things I didn't really understand. I tried almost anything. When I was thirteen, I discovered Whitman, and that was important to me at the time. About that time I started going to summer camp and met some more sophisticated girls who already knew Emily Dickinson and H. D. and Conrad and Henry James. One of them gave me Harriet Monroe's anthology of modern poets. That was an important experience. (I had actually started reading poetry when I was eight.) I remember coming across Harriet Monroe's quotations from Hopkins, "God's Grandeur" for one. I quickly memorized these, and I thought, "I must get this man's work." In 1927 I saw the first edition of Hopkins. I also went through a Shelley phase, a Browning phase, and a brief Swinburne phase. But I missed a lot of school and my reading was sporadic.

Interviewer: Did you write anything much before you went to Vassar? I remember your saying you had some exceptionally good teachers at Walnut Hill School in Natick.

Miss Bishop: I wrote a good deal, starting at the age of eight. When I was twelve I won an American Legion prize (a five dollar gold piece) for an essay on "Americanism." This was the beginning of my career. I can't imagine what I said on *this* subject! I was on the staff of the literary magazine at school and published some poems there. I had a good Latin teacher and a good English teacher at Walnut Hill. The teaching was of a very high quality. I only studied Latin then. I didn't take up Greek till I went to Vassar. I now wish I'd studied nothing but Latin and Greek in college. In fact I consider myself badly educated. Writing Latin prose and verse is still probably the best possible exercise for a poet.

Interviewer: You were in what turned out to be a brilliant literary generation at Vassar—Mary McCarthy, Eleanor Clark, Muriel Rukeyser, besides yourself. Did your friends set a high standard of criticism even in those days?

Miss Bishop: Actually I was a close friend only with Mary. Eleanor and I were friends, too, but she left for two years, and

Muriel was there for just a year. Yes, they, we, were all terribly critical then. One big event for us was a little magazine we started. Mary has recently talked about this. This is the way I remember it: The regular literary magazine was dull and old-fashioned. Mary and Eleanor and I and several others decided to start one in competition. It was to be anonymous. We used to meet in a speakeasy and drink dreadful red wine and get slightly high. (Afterwards the college physician analyzed the wine and found it contained fifty per cent alcohol, she said, but I can't believe that.) We called the magazine *Con Spirito*. We got out only three numbers, I think, but we prevailed. I published several poems and stories in *Con Spirito*. T. S. Eliot came to Vassar about this time. I was elected to interview him and I was absolutely terrified. But he was very gentle, and later he flattered us by saying he liked some of the things in our magazine.

Interviewer: In those days did you think about becoming a poet or a novelist?

Miss Bishop: I never *thought* much about it, but I believe I was only interested in being a poet.

Interviewer: You grew up in the Marxist '30s. Do you think this radical political experience was valuable for writers? Or did it blunt people's perceptions to be thinking in such exclusively political terms?

Miss Bishop: I was always opposed to political thinking as such for writers. What good writing came out of that period, really? Perhaps a few good poems; Kenneth Fearing wrote some. A great deal of it seemed to me very false. Politically I considered myself a socialist, but I disliked "social conscious" writing. I stood up for T. S. Eliot when everybody else was talking about James T. Farrell. The atmosphere in Vassar was left-wing; it was the popular thing. People were always asking me to be on a picket-line, or later to read poems to a John Reed Club. I felt that most of the college girls didn't know much about social conditions.

I was very aware of the Depression—some of my family were much affected by it. After all, anybody who went to New York and rode the Elevated could see that things were wrong. But I had lived with poor people and knew something of poverty at firsthand. About this time I took a walking-trip in Newfoundland and I saw much worse poverty there. I was all for being a socialist till I heard Norman Thomas speak; but he was *so* dull. Then I tried anarchism, briefly. I'm much more interested in social problems and politics now than I was in the '30s.

Interviewer: What poets did you meet when you started moving around in the world? I believe you have known Marianne Moore for many years.

Miss Bishop: I met Marianne Moore in 1934, the last year I was in college, through Fanny Borden, the college librarian, an old friend of the Moore family. (I had read a few of her poems in anthologies.) I asked Miss Borden why she didn't have *Observations* in the college library, and she said, "Are you interested in Marianne Moore? I've known her since she was a child!" And she introduced me to her shortly afterwards.

When I was a junior, *Hound and Horn* had a contest for students. I sent in a story and a poem and got honorable mention for both. I also had a story and a poem in a magazine called *The Magazine,* run by Howard Baker and his wife. Baker's friend Yvor Winters wrote me; I think he wanted to take me under his wing. But nothing came of that. He introduced me to a former student of his, Don Stanford, who was then at Harvard.

Interviewer: Were you in any way affected by Auden during the '30s?

Miss Bishop: Oh, yes! I started reading him in college. I bought all his books as they came out and read them a great deal. But he didn't affect my poetic practice. I think that Wallace Stevens was the contemporary who most affected my writing then. But I got more from Hopkins and the Metaphysical poets than I did from Stevens or Hart Crane. I've always admired Herbert.

Interviewer: What do you like especially about Herbert?

Miss Bishop: To begin with, I like the absolute naturalness of tone. Coleridge has some good remarks on this, you remember. And some of Herbert's poems strike me as almost surrealistic, "Love Unknown" for instance. (I was much interested in surrealism in the '30s.) I also like Donne, of course, the love poems particularly, and Crashaw. But I find myself re-reading Herbert a great deal.

Interviewer: Do you owe any of your poems to Herbert?

Miss Bishop: Yes, I think so. "The Weed" is modelled somewhat on "Love Unknown." There are probably others.

Interviewer: Do you have any comments on the religious poetry of the '40s? I am referring especially to the long poems by Eliot and Auden, also to such books as Tate's *The Winter Sea* and Lowell's *Lord Weary's Castle*. In those days we seemed to be moving into something rather unexpected, a brilliant period of Christian poetry. But this has scarcely continued, has it?

Miss Bishop: As far as Eliot and Auden are concerned, I find Eliot much easier to understand. He led up to the *Four Quartets* by a long process. Eliot is not very dogmatic, not in his poetry (the prose is another matter). Auden's later poetry is sometimes spoiled for me by his didacticism. I don't like modern religiosity in general; it always seems to lead to a tone of moral superiority. Of course I have the greatest admiration for Auden as a poet. As for religious poetry and this general subject, well, times have changed since Herbert's day. I'm not religious, but I read Herbert and Hopkins with the greatest pleasure.

Interviewer: Do you think it is necessary for a poet to have a "myth"—Christian or otherwise—to sustain his work?

Miss Bishop: It all depends—some poets do, some don't. You must have something to sustain you, but perhaps you needn't be conscious of it. Look at Robert Lowell: he's written just as good poetry since he left the Church. Look at Paul Klee: he had 16 paintings going at once; *he* didn't have a formulated myth to look to, apparently, and his accomplishment was very considerable. The question, I must admit, doesn't interest me a great deal. I'm not interested in big-scale work as such. Something needn't be large to be good.

Interviewer: But some poets and critics have been terribly concerned about this, haven't they?

Miss Bishop: Some people crave organization more than others—the desire to get everything in its place. Auden really thinks this way, I suppose. Marianne Moore, on the other hand, has no particular "myth," but a remarkable set of beliefs appears over and over again, a sort of backbone of faith.

Interviewer: I know you have a lively interest in the other arts—music and painting especially. Have your poems been much affected by these things?

Miss Bishop: I think I'm more visual than most poets. Many years ago, around 1942 or 1943, somebody mentioned to me something that Meyer Shapiro, the art critic, said about me: "She writes poems with a painter's eye." I was very flattered. All my life I've been interested in painting. Some of my relatives painted. As a child I was dragged round the Boston Museum of Fine Arts and Mrs. Gardner's museum and the Fogg. I'd love to be a painter.

Interviewer: What about "Songs for a Colored Singer"? You didn't compose those to tunes, as it were?

Miss Bishop: I was hoping somebody would compose the tunes for *them.* I think I had Billie Holiday in mind. I put in a couple of big words just because she sang big words well—"*conspiring* root" for instance. As for music in general: I'd love to be a composer! I studied counterpoint and the piano for years, and I suppose I'm still "musical." But I wanted to be a doctor, too, and I got myself enrolled at Cornell Medical School. I think Marianne Moore discouraged me from going on with that.

Interviewer: I wonder if you sometimes "feel" your way into a poem with a sense of its rhythms even before the subject has declared itself—you know, the way in which "Le cimetière marin" was composed?

Miss Bishop: Yes. A group of words, a phrase, may find its way into my head like something floating in the sea, and presently it attracts other things to it. I do tend to "feel" my way into a poem, as you suggest. One's mind works in unexpected ways. When I was writing "Roosters," I got hopelessly stuck; it just refused to get written. Then one day I was playing a record of Ralph Kirkpatrick performing Scarlatti: the rhythms of the sonata imposed themselves on me and I got the thing started again.

Interviewer: In composing a poem like this, do you start from a kind of pleasure in the stanzaic arrangement as such, or do you let the experience dictate the form?

Miss Bishop: In this case I couldn't say which came first. Sometimes the form, sometimes the subject, dominates the mind. All other poets I've ever talked to say pretty much the same thing. On this subject I rather like Housman's essay, *The Name and Nature of Poetry*. That's only one side of the question, but it's very well stated.

Interviewer: I wonder if you could reveal the *donnée* for your sestina called "A Miracle for Breakfast." It has an attractive surrealist quality about it, but I'm curious about the kind of experience which brought the poem into being.

Miss Bishop: Oh, that's my Depression poem. It was written shortly after the time of souplines and men selling apples, around 1936 or so. It was my "social conscious" poem, a poem about hunger.

Interviewer: That was the heyday of surrealism, too, wasn't it?

Miss Bishop: Yes, and I had just come back from my first year in France, where I had read a lot of surrealist poetry and prose.

Interviewer: When I read the poem here in Brazil, my students keep asking, "Was she waiting for the ferry?" You remember that early in the poem you have one crossing the river.

To move on to something else: "At the Fishhouses" is my favorite in your second book. This seems to me a kind of Wordsworthian poem, something like "Resolution and Independence." But your poem is mostly in the present tense and is more immediate and "existentialist." Wordsworth really seems to mean "emotion recollected in tranquillity" and puts his poem mostly in the past tense. Do you have any comment on this comparison?

Miss Bishop: I think it's a question of how poetry is written. There has been a great change in the knowledge of, or at any rate the attitude towards, poetic psychology. One of the great innovators here is Hopkins. When I was in college I wrote a piece on him. While I was preparing it, I came across an essay on seventeenth century baroque prose. The author—I've forgotten who—tried to show that baroque sermons (Donne's for instance) attempted to dramatize the mind in action rather than in repose. Applying this to Hopkins in the paper I was writing, I used a phrase which impressed me in "The Wreck of the Deutschland," where he says, "Fancy, come faster." He breaks off and addresses himself. It's a baroque poem. Browning does something like this, but not so strikingly. In other words, the use of the present tense helps to convey this sense of the mind in action. Cummings does this in some poems. Of course poets in other languages (French especially) use the "historical present" more than we do. But that isn't really the same device. But switching tenses always gives effects of depth, space, foreground, background, and so on.

Interviewer: Perhaps something like switching keys in music.

Miss Bishop: Yes, indeed, very much so.

Interviewer: What do you think about the dramatic monologue as a form—you know, when the poet assumes a rôle? This "poetry of experience" has been very attractive to a lot of poets. I believe you have done this two or three times—for instance in "Songs for a Colored Singer" and "Jerónimo's House."

Miss Bishop: I haven't given it much thought. Robert Lowell and others have done brilliant things in this form. I suppose it should act as a sort of release. You can say all kinds of things you couldn't in a lyric. If you have scenery and costumes, you can get away with a lot. I'm writing one right now.

Interviewer: I've just been reading a poem of yours called "A Summer's Dream." It's a wonderful miniature, an evocation of a dying seaside town. Every detail counts. Did you reduce this from something longer?

Miss Bishop: I went for the summer once to Cape Breton. This little village was very small indeed. I think in the poem I said the population contained a number of freaks. Actually there were a few more people. But some exceptional giants came from this region, and I think in the poem I conveyed some idea of what the people were like. No, I didn't compress the poem.

Interviewer: Do you find yourself revising a poem like this?

Miss Bishop: No. After a poem is published, I just change a word occasionally. Some poets like to rewrite, but I don't.

Interviewer: How did you happen to go to Key West, where you wrote some beautiful things? Did you find it a good place for writing?

Miss Bishop: In 1938, I believe, I was on the West Coast of Florida to fish. I went to Key West just for a couple of days to see what the fishing was like there. I liked the town and decided to go back there in 1939, after another eight months or so in Europe. Eventually I acquired a modest but beautiful old house. I can't say Key West offered any special advantages for a writer. But I liked living there. The light and blaze of colors made a good impression on me, and I loved the swimming. The town was absolutely broke then. Everybody lived on the W.P.A. I seemed to have a taste for impoverished places in those days. But my Key West period dwindled away. I went back for winters till 1949, but after the war it wasn't the same.

Interviewer: While I'm mentioning Key West, would you say something about John Dewey, whom you knew so well there? I think you'd agree that his prose style, even in his book on aesthetics, can be rather clumsy and does his reputation no good. But he was a very sensitive man, wasn't he?

Miss Bishop: Yes, very. I found him an adorable man. He could work under any conditions. Even at the age of eighty-five he missed no detail. He and Marianne Moore are the only people I have ever known who would talk to everyone, on all social levels, without the slightest change in their manner of speaking. I think this shows something important about Dewey and Marianne Moore—they have the kind of instinctive respect for other people which we all wish we could have but can only aspire to. No matter how foolish your question, he would always give you a complete and tactful answer. He loved little things, small plants and weeds and animals, and of course he was very generous in dealing with people. I remember when "Roosters" came out in *The New Republic;* he read it and said, "Well, Elizabeth, you've got these rhymes in threes very well. I wish I'd learned more about writing when *I* was young."

Interviewer: Some people might be surprised to know that Flannery O'Connor admired Dewey. The last time I saw her, in 1963, she was reading two of his books.

Miss Bishop: Well, I'm sure she knew more about his philosophy than I do!

Interviewer: You've been a literary associate of Robert Lowell's for quite a few years, haven't you?

Miss Bishop: I think, and I hope, we have been very good friends for twenty years. Both his life and his work have been of great importance to me. He is one of the few poets whose name in a table of contents or on the cover of a magazine gives me a sense of hopefulness and excitement even before I've read the poem.

Interviewer: What do you think of the turn his poetry has taken in the last few years—beginning with *Life Studies?*

Miss Bishop: One does miss the old trumpet blast of *Lord Weary's Castle,* but poets have to change, and possibly the more subdued magnificence of his later tone is more humane.

Interviewer: I think I have you about up to 1950 now. This would be the period when you had the appointment at the Library of Congress. You were there shortly after the Bollingen Prize fiasco, weren't you?

Miss Bishop: Léonie Adams was my predecessor, and she got the worst of that affair. MacLeish had a good idea about the job, and some of the poets fitted in rather well. I didn't really earn my keep—I didn't give lectures and readings, in fact never do. But for the only time in my life I saw bureaucracy functioning, and it certainly contributed to my education.

Interviewer: Like many literary people, you visited Pound during the '50s. Do you have any prose comment, as it were, to make about him? You've already put yourself on record in verse in "Visits to St. Elizabeths."

Miss Bishop: I think I've said all I want to in that poem. I admired his courage enormously; he proved his devotion to literature during those thirteen years.

Interviewer: By the way, I'm rather interested in the formal scheme of that poem. How did you hit on it?

Miss Bishop: It's the old nursery rhyme, "This was the house that Jack built." I've always liked nursery rhymes, and this one seemed to work here.

Interviewer: Here in Brazil poets like Vinícius de Moraes have been writing lyrics for *bossa nova*. Have you ever wanted to do something like this in English?

Miss Bishop: I've always wanted to write popular songs, and I've tried several times but never succeeded. I like some popular song lyrics very much, "Mean to Me" for instance.

Interviewer: I think quite a few people have already seen and admired your new poem, the ballad called "The Burglar of Babylon." It's a knockout. Did you have any trouble in finding a suitable medium for this poem? It's really worked up from some journalistic material, isn't it?

Miss Bishop: No, I sat down and wrote it almost straight off, with a few additions and changes. Most of it was written in one day. It naturally seemed to present itself as a ballad. It's a true story, taken from the newspaper accounts; I made only two minor changes in the facts.

Interviewer: Did you actually see Micuçú being hunted down on the *morro* of Babylon in Rio?

Miss Bishop: No, but I saw the soldiers. We could watch them through binoculars from the terrace of the apartment house.

Interviewer: With your new book of poems, *Questions of Travel,* about to come out, what are your immediate literary plans?

Miss Bishop: Well, they are always the same, to write poems when I can. I'm also planning a book of prose about Brazil. It is tentatively called *Black Beans and Diamonds*. It's to be a combination of a travel book, a memoir, and a picture book. I am quite interested in photography. I'd like to make Brazil seem less remote and less an object of picturesque fancy. It's not really so far from New York. I think that since the great naturalists (Darwin, Wallace, Bruce, and so on) there hasn't been much close observation (at least by foreigners) of Brazil. Except perhaps for Lévi-Strauss.

Interviewer: What do you think about the state of American poetry right now?

Miss Bishop: Very good. We have lots of fine poets. Perhaps I'd better not mention any names, but I really admire and read with pleasure at least seven of my contemporaries. As far as poetry goes, although I am afraid that is not very far, this is a period that I enjoy.

On "Confessional Poetry"

. . . really something new in the world. There have been diaries that were frank—and generally intended to be read after the poet's death. Now the idea is that we live in a horrible and terrifying world, and the worst moments of horrible and terrifying lives are an allegory of the world. . . . The tendency is to overdo the morbidity. You just wish they'd keep some of these things to themselves.

"Poets," *Time* (June 2, 1967), pp. 35–42.

An Inadequate Tribute

Randall Jarrell was difficult, touchy, and oversensitive to criticism. He was also a marvelous conversationalist, brilliantly funny, a fine poet, and the best and most generous critic of poetry I have known. I am proud to remember that, although we could rarely meet, we remained friends for twenty years. Sometimes we quarreled, silently, in infrequent letters, but each time we met we would tell each other that it had meant nothing at all; we really were in agreement about everything that mattered.

He always seemed more alive than other people, as if constantly tuned up to the concert pitch that most people, including poets, can maintain only for short and fortunate stretches.

I like to think of him as I saw him once after we had gone swimming together on Cape Cod; wearing only bathing trunks and a very queer straw cap with a big visor, seated on the crest of a high sand dune, writing in a notebook. It was a bright and dazzling day. Randall looked small and rather delicate, but bright and dazzling, too. I felt quite sure that whatever he was writing would be bound to share the characteristics of the day and of the small man writing away so busily in the middle of it all.

Randall Jarrell 1914–1965, ed. Robert Lowell, Peter Taylor, and Robert Penn Warren (New York: Farrar, Straus and Giroux, 1967), pp. 20–21.

On "The Burglar of Babylon"

The story of Micuçú* is true. It happened in Rio de Janeiro a few years ago. I have changed only one or two minor details, and, of course, translated the names of the slums. I think that actually the hill of Kerosene had been torn down shortly before Micuçú's death, but I liked the word, so put it in.

I was one of those who watched the pursuit through binoculars, although really we could see very little of it: just a few of the soldiers silhouetted against the skyline of the hill of Babylon. The rest of the story is taken, often word for word, from the daily papers, filled out by what I know of the place and the people.

At the time, people said that the name Micuçú was short for *Mico Sujo*, or *"Dirty Marmoset,"* but finally it was decided that this was wrong and that it is the colloquial name for a deadly snake, in the north of Brazil. A young man trying to be a real gangster, like in the films, would certainly prefer to be called by the name of a deadly snake. Also, the poor people who live in the slums of Rio have usually come from the north or northeast of Brazil and their nicknames are apt to be Indian words, or the common names (frequently derived from the Indian) used for things or creatures in those far-off regions.

"Introduction," *The Ballad of the Burglar of Babylon* (New York: Farrar, Straus and Giroux, 1968).
*Pronounced *mē-coo-soo*.

Lines Written in a Copy of *Fannie Farmer's Boston Cooking School Cookbook,* Given to Frank Bidart

You won't become a *gourmet** cook
By studying our Fannie's book—
Her thoughts on Food & Keeping House
Are scarcely those of Levi-Strauss.
Nevertheless, you'll find, Frank dear,
The *basic elements*** are here.
And if a problem should arise:
The Soufleé fall before your eyes,
Or strange things happen to the Rice
—You know I *love* to give advice.

Elizabeth

*forbidden word
** 	" " phrase

Christmas, 1971

P.S. Fannie should not be underated;
     She has become sophisticated.
     She's picked up many *gourmet** tricks
     Since the edition of '96.

On *Golden State* by Frank Bidart

Just possibly, Frank Bidart has achieved, in his first book, exactly what all young poets would like to: he has discovered and brought together a set of images, emotionally disturbing, apparently disparate, but in combination having the uncanny power of illuminating the poet's personal history and History itself, literary life and plain Life, at the same time.

Jacket blurb for Frank Bidart's *Golden State* (New York: Braziller, 1973).

From "A Brief Reminiscence and a Brief Tribute"

I met Auden only a few times, and although I wanted to, I was a little afraid of talking to him. I regret this now very much. I find it sad that the young students and poets I have met in the past four years usually seem to know only a few of his anthology pieces, rarely read him at all, and apparently never for pleasure. One reason for this may be that Auden, the most brilliant of imitators himself, has been, or was, so much imitated that his style, his details and vocabulary, the whole atmosphere of his poetry, seems over-familiar, old hat. But when I was in college, and all through the thirties and forties, I and all my friends who were interested in poetry, read him constantly. We hurried to see his latest poem or book, and either wrote as much like him as possible, or tried hard not to. His then leftist politics, his ominous landscape, his intimations of betrayed loves, war on its way, disasters and death, matched exactly the mood of our late-depression and post-depression youth. We admired his apparent toughness, his sexual courage—actually more honest than Ginsberg's, say, is now, while still giving expression to technically dazzling poetry. Even the most hermetic early poems gave us the feeling that here was someone who *knew*—about psychology, geology, birds, love, the evils of capitalism—what have you? They colored our air and made us feel tough, ready, and in the know, too.

I almost always agree with Auden critically, except when he gets bogged down in his categories (and except that I haven't yet been able to read Tolkien), and I admire almost all of his poems except the later preachy ones. . . .

Harvard Advocate (Auden Issue 1975), pp. 47–48.

From Book-of-the-Month Club
Interview

On poetry "groups":

I've gone up and down the East Coast, living everywhere from Nova Scotia to Key West, but I've never seemed to live long enough in one place to become a member of a poetry "group," and when I was in Brazil there weren't any groups handy. I've been a friend of Marianne Moore's and Robert Lowell's but not a part of any school.

On "The Moose":

It is one of the few poems my Canadian relatives have liked. It was written in bits and pieces over a number of years and, finally, it all came together. After I read it in public for the first time, at Harvard, one of the students said, "For a poem, it wasn't bad."

On "One Art": I lost my mother's watch. And look! my last, or
next-to-last, of three loved houses went.
The art of losing isn't hard to master.

Yes, one in Key West, one in Petrópolis, just west of Rio Bay, and one in Ouro Prêto, also in Brazil. The Ouro Prêto

Interview with David W. McCullough, *Book-of-the-Month Club News* (May 1977). Reprinted in his *People, Books and Book People* (New York: Harmony Books, 1981), pp. 20–24.

house was built in 1690, and from it you can see seven baroque churches. I called it Casa Mariana, after Marianne Moore and also because it is on the road to a town called Mariana. When I left I took the name plaque off the door. There are so many places I'll never go back to. I change, the places change. I was afraid to go back to Nova Scotia, but I went not long ago, and it hadn't changed very much . . .

Statement for the English Memorial Service for Robert Lowell

Robert Lowell's first poems made such a tremendous impression on me that I was very nervous about meeting him for the first time. However, we did meet, through his friend Randall Jarrell; we took to each other immediately and were good friends for over thirty years. Beside the example he set us all by his total dedication to his work, I know that he used his influence to be helpful to me personally in more than one difficult period in my life—acts of kindness I learned of only later and by chance.

Our friendship, often kept alive through years of separation only by letters, remained constant and affectionate, and I shall always be deeply grateful for it.

October 12, 1977.

GEORGE STARBUCK

"The Work!"

A Conversation with Elizabeth Bishop

A gray late afternoon in winter. Elizabeth Bishop, dressed casually in a Harvard jersey, welcomes the interviewer and answers his polite questions about a gorgeous gilt mirror on her living-room wall. Yes, it is Venetian, those little blackamoors are Venetian, but it was picked up at an auction in Rio de Janeiro. The interviewer, sure in advance this is nothing to have asked one of his favorite poets to do, squares away with his cassette recorder on the coffee table and pops a prepared question. A wonderful expanse of books fills the wall behind the sofa. Before long there is laughter. A good memory, the thought of a quirk or extravagance in someone she knows and likes, sets Miss Bishop off. The laughter is quick, sharp, deep. No way to transcribe it.

GS: I did some research. I got out the travel book you wrote on commission for Time-Life Books. There's geography, too. You tell such wonderful bright clear stories from the history of Brazil.

EB: I can't remember too much of that book; rather, I choose not to. It was edited by Time-Life Books and they changed a lot of it. I wanted to use different, and more, pictures. There's one—the one of Dom Pedro [the last Emperor] and his official party taken in front of Niagara Falls? Well, there were more of that trip. But that one, I think, is really ironic. He travelled quite a bit in this country. And yet in Brazil he had never been to the Falls of Iguassu, which are—how much—ten times bigger than Niagara Falls . . . This was in 1876 and he went to the Phila-

Ploughshares 3, nos. 3 & 4 (1977), pp. 11–29. Cut and occasionally corrected by E. B.

delphia Centennial. Alexander Bell was there, with his telephone—a very young man, whose invention hadn't been used at all then. And Dom Pedro ordered telephones for his summer Palace, in Petropolis. He also thought that the ladies of his court didn't have enough to do, so he took each of them back a Singer sewing machine—which they didn't like very much. Did you read in that Brazil book how Longfellow gave a dinner party for him, in Cambridge?

GS: Yes, and that Dom Pedro was fond of Whittier and translated some of his poems into Portuguese.

EB: I looked up those translations. I thought they would be Whittier's abolitionist poems, because Dom Pedro was very much against slavery. [Slavery existed in Brazil until 1888.] But they weren't those poems at all. They were poems about birds, nature poems.

Whittier was very shy and at the Longfellow dinner party Dom Pedro, who was over six feet tall, strong and handsome, tried to give him the Brazilian *abraco,* twice—and poor Whittier was frightened to death.

GS: You take a set task, like that Time-Life book, and make it wholly your own. [EB: Not wholly; say two-thirds.] It always seemed that you were bursting to tell those stories. You're that way with translations. I discovered something. I went into *Geography III* without stopping off at the Table of Contents, and so I went into the Joseph Cornell poem without realizing it was a translation from Octavio Paz.

EB: It's a wonderful poem in Spanish.

GS: And in English! That's what I thought: I was reading *your* poem about Cornell. Paul Carroll has a beautiful poem about Cornell's "Medici Slot Machine." And here I'm thinking, "Elizabeth Bishop has done an even better poem about Cornell," and I turn the last page and see it's a translation.

EB: Well, I thought, of course, I should put Octavio Paz's name at the beginning, and I had it that way at first, but it didn't look right. There was the title, and then the dedication line, and the author's name seemed like too many things under the title, so I decided to put it at the end.

GS: Well, you do good poems about paintings and such. The one in *Geography III* about noticing a little painting that has been looked at but not noticed much before . . .

EB: In my first book there is a poem called "Large Bad Picture"; that picture was by the same great-uncle, painted when he was about 14 years old. They were a very poor family in Nova Scotia, and he went to sea as a cabin boy. Then he painted three or four big paintings, memories of the far North, Belle Isle, etc. I loved them. They're not very good as painting. An aunt owned several of them. I tried to get her to sell them to me, but she never would. Then Great-Uncle George went to England, and he did become a fairly well-known "traditional" painter. In 1905, I think it was, he went back to Nova Scotia for the summer to visit his sister, my grandmother. He made a lot of sketches and held "art classes" for my aunts and my mother and others. I eventually fell heir to this little sketch ("About the size of an old-style dollar bill"), the one I describe. Helen Vendler has written a wonderful paper in which she talks about this poem. Do you use this tape machine to record music, readings, things like that?

GS: This is only the second time I've used it for anything.

EB: I tried doing a lot of letters in Brazil on tape, but I gave up.

GS: I've even heard of people trying to write on them. Richard Howard trained himself to translate using a tape recorder. He was doing DeGaulle's memoirs and all those *nouveaux romans*. Book after book, for a living. He says he disciplined himself to do the whole job in two, or at most three, headlong runs through, reading the French and talking the English into the tape, having a typist transcribe it, running through again.

EB: I didn't know that was the way he did it. What was it, a hundred and twenty-seven novels? I translated *one* fairly long Brazilian book, a young girl's diary. It's probably full of mistakes, because it was one of the very first things I did. I had just started reading, trying to learn Portuguese. Someone suggested it, and I began. It was painful. I began writing in a big notebook, but a third of the way through I finally caught on to the child's style or thought I did. Then I began to translate directly on the typewriter, the rest of it. It took me about three years, as it was. Some people can write poetry right off on a typewriter, I think. Dr. Williams did, I'm told.

GS: Some poets write it out so easily it scares you. We have a neighbor who was a very young nurse working in Boston, at Mass. General Hospital, maybe forty years ago. She told me the story one time, asking me if I'd ever heard of this strange person she worked for. A weird doctor there used to give her poems that he had scribbled on the back of prescription forms, toilet paper, anything, and ask her to type them up. She'd have to go sit on the stool in a small toilet off the hall, the only place she could be out of the way, and with the typewriter on her knees she'd type the things.

EB: Was it—?

GS: Yep, it was Merrill Moore. And he also used to dictate sonnets into a dictaphone while he was driving. I mean he had a hundred thousand sonnets to get written. Wasn't that the total finally?

EB: Did she like the poems, the sonnets, when she got them?

GS: She didn't know. She didn't presume.
    I don't know how you could rush onto tape in translating poems. There's one in which you seem to have discovered something Brazilian that comes out perfectly in early English ballad style. The "Brothers of Souls! Brothers of Souls!" poem.

EB: Oh, yes. That "Severino" poem is only a few parts of a very long Christmas play. I saw it given. I've never done very much translation, and I've almost never done any to order, but every once in a while something seems to go into English. There's one poem in that book, "Travelling in the Family" (Carlos Drummond de Andrade) that came out very well, I think. The meter is almost exactly the same. Nothing had to be changed. Even the word order. Of course word order will naturally have to come out different, but this one happened to come out well. I wrote and asked Dr. Drummond if I could repeat one word instead of writing the line the way he had it, and he wrote back yes that would be fine. Portuguese has a very different metrical system, very like the French. But every once in a while a poem does go into English.

GS: I'm curious about one of your own that seems to go so easily. "The Moose."

EB: I started that, I hate to say how many years ago, probably twenty. I had the beginning, the incident with the moose, it really happened; and the very end; and the poem just sat around.

GS: Did that partial version of it have the other major movement or topic in it: the dreamy conversation, leading you back to the pillow-talk of grandparents?

EB: Yes. Yes, I'd always had that. I had written it down in notes about the trip. I'm sure it's happened to you, in planes or trains or busses. You know, you're very tired, half-asleep, half-awake. I think probably in this case it was because they were all speaking in Nova Scotian accents, strange but still familiar, although I couldn't quite make out much of what anyone was saying. But the Moose: that happens. A friend wrote me about an encounter like that, with a buck deer. He did exactly the same thing, sniffed the car all over. But in that case, instead of disappearing the way the moose did, he chased the car for about a mile.

GS: You obviously do like to know and use exact geographer's knowledge about things. You've got the language down pat, and the knowledge of particular things, but let me embarass you: I admire the philosophy of the poems, the morals.

EB: I didn't know there were any . . .

GS: OK, OK. But the aubade that ends the book—"Five Flights Up." The way the "ponderousness" of a morning becomes, lightly, our ancient uninnocence: the depression of having a past and the knowledge of what's recurring: "Yesterday brought to today so lightly! / (A yesterday I find almost impossible to lift.)"

EB: Yes, quite a few people seemed to like that poem . . .

GS: I'm a sucker for that.

EB: It must be an experience that everybody's had. You know, about my first book one fairly admiring friend wound up by saying, "But you have no philosophy whatever." And people who are really city people are sometimes bothered by all the "nature" in my poems.

GS: I suppose Crusoe was a city kid. It's such fun, the accuracy with which you borrow flora and fauna for his little island. ("Crusoe in England," in *Geography III*).

EB: It's a mixture of several islands.

GS: And the deliberate anachronisms too—like the Wordsworth reference.

EB: The *New Yorker* sent the proof back and beside that line was the word "anachronism," and also at another place in the poem, I think. But I told them it was on purpose. But the snail shells, the blue snail shells, are true.

GS: Are there snails like that on—what was his island—Juan Fernandez?

EB: Perhaps—but the ones I've seen were in the Ten Thousand islands in Florida. Years ago I went on a canoe trip there and saw the blue snails. They were tree snails, and I still may have some. They were very frail and broke easily and they were all over everything. Fantastic.

GS: He's an Adam there and you have this wonderful little penny-ante Eden with "one kind of everything: / one tree snail . . . one variety of tree . . . one kind of berry."

EB: The waterspouts came from Florida. We used to see them. You know, I am inaccurate, though. And I get caught. The poem about being almost seven, in the dentist's office, reading the *National Geographic?*

GS: "You are an *I*, / you are an *Elizabeth*, / you are one of *them*."

EB: Yes, that one. Something's wrong about that poem and I thought perhaps that no one would ever know. But of course they find out everything. My memory had confused two 1918 issues of the *Geographic.* Not having seen them since then, I checked it out in the New York Public Library. In the February issue there was an article, "The Valley of 10,000 Smokes," about Alaska that I'd remembered, too. But the African things, it turned out, were in the *next* issue, in March. When I sent the poem to the *New Yorker* I wrote Howard Moss and said I must confess that this is a little wrong. The magazine was nice about it and said it would be all right. But, since then, two people have discovered that it isn't right. They went and looked it up! I should have had a footnote.

GS: Well, all the critics are poets and all the poets are critics, but if there's a difference I believe in, it's that, as personalities, critics tend to be more focused on mere literature. And so compendious Richard Ellmann can do that big fat anthology, loaded with literary information but when he has to footnote a place name, he puts the Galapagos Islands in the Caribbean.

EB: He did it to me. I say "entering the Narrows of St. Johns" and he has a footnote saying that's an island in the Caribbean, when it's St. John's, Newfoundland.

GS: Poets are really seriously interested in places, in travels, in discoveries about the world . . . I've been rereading Lowes and there's nothing at all stupid about that book, but he pretends Coleridge had utterly unaccountable, just out-and-out screwball taste in light reading. Travel tales! One of Lowes' tropes is to astonish the reader with what Coleridge got from this obviously frivolous miscellaneous grubbing around in things that nobody in his right mind would read.

EB: Yes.

GS: It serves his point, but here was an age when actual marvels were being discovered. Coleridge went after those books for the best possible reasons.

EB: And how do they know? It takes probably hundreds of things coming together at the right moment to make a poem and no one can ever really separate them out and say this did this, that did that.

GS: What got the Crusoe poem started?

EB: I don't know. I reread the book and discovered how really awful *Robinson Crusoe* was, which I hadn't realized. I hadn't read it in a long time. And then I was remembering a visit to Aruba—long before it was a developed "resort." I took a trip across the island and it's true that there are small volcanoes all over the place.

GS: I forget the end of *Robinson Crusoe*. Does the poem converge on the book?

EB: No. I've forgotten the facts, there, exactly. I reread it all one night. And I had forgotten it was so moral. All that Christianity. So I think I wanted to re-see it with all that left out.

GS: When you were very young, which were the poets you started with?

EB: When I went to summer camp when I was twelve, someone gave me an anthology—one of the first Harriet Monroe anthologies. That made a great impression. I'd never read any of those poets before. I had read Emily Dickinson, but an early edition, and I didn't like it much. And my aunt had books like Browning, Mrs. Browning, Tennyson, Ingoldsby's Legends . . .

GS: But later, when did you begin looking around and say to yourself "Who, among the poets in the generation ahead of me, are poets I'm going to have to come to terms with?"

EB: I don't think I ever thought of it that way, but perhaps that was Auden. All through my college years, Auden was publishing his early books, and I and my friends, a few of us, were very much interested in him. His first books made a tremendous impression on me.

GS: I don't see Auden rife in your earlier poems. In fact it struck me that the closest I had seen you come to an early Auden manner or materials was a recent poem, in the new book: "12 O'Clock News."

EB: Yes, that's recent. I think I tried not to write like him then, because everybody did.

GS: It's as if, all of a sudden, decades later, there's "On the Frontier"—something you could use in it.

EB: Actually that poem, "12 O'Clock News," was another that had begun years earlier. In a different version. With rhymes, I think. Yes, I got stuck with it and finally gave up. It had nothing to do with Viet Nam or any particular war when I first wrote it, it was just fantasy. This is the way things catch up with you. I have an early poem, a long poem, written a long time ago. The Second World War was going on, and it's about that, more or less. "Roosters," I wrote it in Florida, most of it. Some friends asked me to read it a year or so ago, and I suddenly realized it sounded like a feminist tract, which it wasn't meant to sound like at all to begin with. So you never know how things are going to get changed around for you by the times.

GS: But that makes some sense. Let's see, if I can find it in the book—Sure:

> where in the blue blur
> their rustling wives admire,
> the roosters brace their cruel feet and glare
>
> with stupid eyes
> while from their beaks there rise
> the uncontrolled, traditional cries.

I'm afraid it's their banner now. You'll never get it away from them. By the way, I've heard your "Filling Station" poem used as a feminist tract.

EB: Really?

GS: In a nice apt way, by Mona Van Duyn. She read, at Bread Loaf, in lieu of a lecture, one poem each by about eight American women, with a few words in between the poems. There were a couple of poems which she seemed to want to demonstrate were too tract-y to be of any use. A Robin Morgan poem . . .

EB: Oh heavens, yes.

GS: In that context, yours did seem a nice wry study of the "woman's touch."

EB: But no woman appears in it at all.

GS: But the pot, the flowers, the . . .

EB: Crocheted doily, yes.

GS: The woman who is "not there," she's certainly an essential subject of the poem.

EB: I never saw the woman, actually. We knew the men there . . .

GS: But the evidence is . . .

EB: I never . . . Isn't it strange? I certainly didn't feel sorry for whoever crocheted that thing! Isn't that strange?

GS: Well, which are your feminist tracts?

EB: I don't think there are any. The first part of "Roosters," now, I suppose. But I hadn't thought of it that way. Tract poetry . . .

GB: What about back in college . . .

EB: I was in college in the days—it was the Depression, the end of the Depression—when a great many people were communist, or would-be communist. But I'm just naturally perverse, so I stood up for T. S. Eliot then. I never gave feminism much thought, until . . .

GS: You started to name poets important to you with a man, Auden. Did . . .

EB: When I was given that anthology when I was twelve or thirteen, in the introduction to it, Harriet Monroe, I suppose it was, talked about Hopkins, and quoted an incomplete fragment of a poem—"tattered-tasseled-tangled," and so on. I was immensely struck by those lines, and then when I went to school, in 1927 or 1928, the second Bridges edition of Hopkins came out and a friend gave me that. I wrote some very bad imitation Hopkins for a time, all later destroyed—or so I hope.

GS: Did it seem important to notice what women poets were doing?

EB: No, I never made any distinction; I never make any distinction. However, one thing I should make clear. When I was in college and started publishing, even then, and in the following few years, there were women's anthologies, and all-women issues of magazines, but I always refused to be in them. I didn't think about it very seriously, but I felt it was a lot of nonsense, separating the sexes. I suppose this feeling came from feminist principles, perhaps stronger than I was aware of.

GS: I had seen the sexist thing going on when I was a teacher in a poetry class where there happened to be some good young women poets who were, yes, exploring, systematically, trying to find positions for themselves or placements for themselves as women poets. Adrienne Rich said she had gotten to the point where she just didn't want to waste the time, in amenities and dues-paying and awkwardness, that it took, she felt, in a mixed class of male and female students . . .

EB: Really?

GS: Yes. To allow the women, of whom she obviously felt protective, to begin to talk openly and be fully and aggressively participating.

EB: I've never felt any sexual warfare in classes. Almost never. Only once or twice, perhaps, and with one boy. Maybe I'm blind. Or maybe my classes are too formal. The students are almost always polite, even gentle, with each other; they seem to treat each other as friends and equals . . . they don't argue much. The past two terms I've had outstandingly good classes. I had a "party" for one class here the night before last and I think we all had a good time. I've never visited other people's workshops. Perhaps I should go and see what they're like.

GS: Do you approve of all the creative writing classes . . .

EB: No. I try to discourage them! I tell students they'd be better off studying Latin. Latin or Greek. They are useful for verse writing. I have a feeling that if there is a great poet at Boston University or Harvard now, he or she may be hiding somewhere, writing poetry and not going to writing classes at all. However, I have had some students who have done very well (two or three "geniuses" I think and several very talented). I think the best one hopes for is that after students graduate they'll continue to read poetry for the rest of their lives. What can you teach, really teach? I'm a fussbudget, probably a fiend. I give assignments. I find it hard not to rewrite poems or prose. I try hard not to say "This is what you should do," but sometimes I can't resist.

GS: What happens then?

EB: Well, sometimes they agree with me—often they meekly agree with me!

GS: Why does that seem so dangerous and almost forbidden to do? I know it does and I agree with you. But look at painters. I was shocked the first time I went to an art class and saw the professor walking around picking up a brush, a palette knife.

EB: Just to change lines?

GS: Yes. There was this stuff on the student's easels and he changed it.

EB: One student some years ago wanted badly to write. He was very bright, but didn't show too much talent. I gave assignments, very strict. When we read the results out loud, trying to be kind, I said "Well, after all I don't expect you to do brilliantly on this; it's just a rather impossible assignment." He grew angry and said "You shouldn't say that! Any assignment isn't just an assignment, it's a poem!" Well, now I think he was right and I was wrong.

Again, about "feminism" or Women's Lib. I think my friends, my generation, were at women's colleges mostly (and we weren't all writers). One gets so used, very young, to being "put down" that if you have normal intelligence and have any sense of humor you very early develop a tough, ironic attitude. You just try to get so you don't even notice being "put down."

Most of my writing life I've been lucky about reviews. But at the very end they often say "The best poetry by a woman in this decade, or year, or month." Well, what's that worth? You know? But you get used to it, even expect it, and are amused by it. One thing I do think is that there are undoubtedly going to be more good woman poets. I've been reading Virginia Woolf's letters. Have you read them?

GS: No. I've been reading a collection of Marianne Moore letters.

EB: Oh?

GS: Published by the University of Rochester Libraries.

EB: Oh, I have that. Anthony Hecht sent it to me. But those aren't such good letters. I mean, of course, they're fascinating. The woman she wrote them to, Hildegarde Watson, who died recently, was probably her best friend. But most of them have to do with clothes, and chitchat like that. I have quite a few of her letters, and some of them, especially the gossipy, personal, literary ones, are wonderful. Telling stories, quoting things, describing. It's very interesting, that little book, but I'm sure she wrote better letters than these.

GS: And you've been reading Woolf's?

EB: I'm reading Volume Two. And this is much more interesting. The first volume I thought was rather boring, but this is where she and Woolf start the Hogarth Press. And you see how she ran into prejudice. She doesn't complain about it much, but you sense it. When she wrote *Three Guineas,* her first "feminist" book, she was rather badly treated.

Many times she'll say how unhappy she is about reviews, . . . You know she could get very cross. Have you ever read *Three Guineas?* A wonderful little book. I think I have it here. (I need a librarian.) This section down here should be Geography and Travel, and . . . Oh here's Woolf. But not *Three Guineas.*

I haven't had one of these things for years. [Christmas candy canes on the coffee table.] Peppermint sticks. You know what we used to do, with peppermint sticks? You stick it in half a lemon, and you suck the lemon juice through it.

I think I've been, oh, half-asleep all my life. I started out to study music, to be a music major. And somehow, I got into trouble with that. I liked it; I gave it up; I wasted a great deal of time; I studied Greek for a while; well I wasn't very good at that; then, when I got out of college, I thought I'd study medicine. At that time, I would have had to take an extra year of chemistry and study German. I'd already given up on German once. I actually applied to Cornell Medical College. But I'd already published a few things, and friends—partly Marianne Moore—discouraged me. Not just discouraged me.

GS: Had you submitted things to *The Dial,* or . . .

EB: *The Dial* had ceased to exist. There were other magazines . . .

GS: Well, how had Miss Moore found out about you in order to discourage you from going into medicine?

EB: Oh. Well, I knew her. I've written a piece about this that I hope to finish soon: how I happened to meet her through the librarian in college. I had just read her poems in magazines and a few pieces in anthologies. The mother of a friend of mine had first told me about her, I think. But *Observations* wasn't in the Vassar Library.

I asked the librarian why she didn't have *Observations* in the library. She said "Are you interested in her poetry?" (She spoke so softly you could barely hear her.) And I said "Yes, very much." And she said, "I've known her since she was a small child. Would you like to meet her?" Imagine! It was the only time in my life that I've ever attempted to meet someone I admired. The librarian had her own copy of *Observations,* and lent it to me, but she obviously didn't think much of it, because she'd never ordered a copy for the Vassar Library. There were a lot of clippings—mostly unfavorable reviews—tucked into it. And then I went to New York and met Miss Moore, and discovered later that there had been other Vassar girls sent down over the years, and that Miss Moore didn't look forward to this a bit. But somehow we got along. She met me on the right-hand bench outside the Reading Room at the N.Y. Public Library. A safe place to meet people, since she could get rid of them quickly. But something worked—a stroke of luck—because I suggested that two weekends from then I come down to New York and we go to the circus. I didn't know then, but of course that was a passion with her. She went every year at least once. So we went to the circus.

GS: Well, what tone did she take when she found out you were seriously considering giving four years of your life to medicine?

EB: Actually, I didn't tell her I wrote for a long time. Maybe I hadn't even told her then. I guess she must have known by the time I graduated. Even then—I suppose this was a little odd even then—we called each other Miss for about three years. I admired her very much, and still do, of course.

She had a review of Wallace Stevens that I don't think she ever reprinted. I went over there (to Brooklyn) and I went in through the back door (the elevator wasn't working). There were two of those baskets for tomatoes, bushel baskets, filled with papers, inside the back door. These were the first drafts of the rather short review. You can see how hard she worked.

She had a clip-board that she carried around the house to work on a poem while she was washing dishes, dusting, etc. . . .

Now all her papers, or almost all, are in the Berg Museum in Philadelphia. They have everything there, in fact they've reconstructed her New York living room and bedroom. I went to the opening and found it all rather painful. But the exhibit of manuscripts was marvelous. If ever you want to see examples of real work, study her manuscripts.

She wrote a poem about the famous racehorse, Tom Fool. The man who arranged the collection had done a beautiful job, in glass cases: dozens of little clippings from the newspapers and photographs of the horse. And then the versions of the poem. It goes on and on . . . The work she put in!

GS: I'd be fascinated to see how she did those inaudible rhymes—whether that came first, or kept changing. How that figured.

EB: She was rather contradictory, you know, illogical sometimes. She would say, "Oh—rhyme is dowdy." Then other times when she was translating La Fontaine she would ask me for a rhyme. If I could give her a rhyme, she would seem to be pleased. She liked a ballad of mine because it rhymed so well. She admired the rhyme "many antennae." You could never tell what she was going to like or dislike.

GS: But what an extraordinary stroke of good fortune to be a friend of Miss Moore's before she knew that you had ambitions . . .

EB: Oh, I didn't have many ambitions. As I said, I must have been half-asleep. There was an anthology that came out, with ten or twelve young poets—in 1935, I think. Each of us "young" poets had an older poet write an introduction. With great timidity I asked Marianne, and she did write a few paragraphs. And she disapproved very much of some of my language and said so, too. It is very funny. I think only one of those poems was in my first book.

The first reading of hers I ever went to, in Brooklyn, years ago, she read with William Carlos Williams. I think at that time she had given very few readings. It was in a church, I think, in a basement. It was a sort of sloping, small auditorium, very steep, and Miss Moore and Dr. Williams were sitting on Victorian Gothic chairs, with red plush backs, on either side of a platform with what looked like a small pulpit at the front. I went over on the subway and was a little late. I had planned to be there early but I was late. Marianne was reading. I was making my way down the red carpeted steps to the front—there were very few people there—and she looked up, noticed me, nodded politely and said "Good evening!" Then went right on reading. She and Dr. Williams were very nice with each other. I don't remember very much else about it, what they read, oh, except a young woman who is editing Williams's letters sent me a copy a month or so ago of something she had run across: a letter from Williams about this very same evening. And it says "Marianne Moore had a little girl named Elizabeth Bishop in tow. It seems she writes poetry." Something like that. Of course I never knew Dr. Williams very well.

GS: But you knew Lowell, Jarrell, so many of them . . .

EB: You know I think we all think this about everybody— every other poet. I didn't know a soul. That is, no one "literary" except Miss Moore at that time.

GS: When did you meet Lowell? I ask this because the way he brought your works into a writing class I visited once at B. U. some years ago, I had the feeling that he had known you and your work . . .

EB: In 1945 or 1946 I met Randall Jarrell, I can't remember how or where. He came to New York that winter to take Margaret Marshall's place on *The Nation* as book review editor. She left the Jarrells her apartment. I had just published my first book, and Robert Lowell had just published his first book. Randall had known him at Kenyon College. Randall invited me to dinner to meet him and we got along immediately. I'd read *Lord Weary's Castle,* but that wasn't it. For some reason we just hit it off very well. By chance we'd been to see the same art exhibits that afternoon and we talked about those. Almost everybody has this theory that everybody else has a fascinating social life . . .

GS: Did you meet [Reed] Whittemore? He was so active, as an editor, with *Furioso* . . .

EB: I never met him.

GS: Did you meet Berryman?

EB: No, I never met him. I've met more writers in the last three or four years than I had in all the rest of my life put together.

GS: And Brazilian writers?

EB: I didn't meet any of them. I know a few. The one I admire most of the older generation is Carlos Drummond de Andrade,

I've translated him. I didn't know him at all. He's supposed to be very shy. I'm supposed to be very shy. We've met once—on the sidewalk at night. We had just come out of the same restaurant, and he kissed my hand politely when we were introduced.

I do know a few of the others. Vinicius de Moraes, who wrote *Black Orpheus*. He was a very good poet, a serious one, somewhat Eliot-ish. He still is, but now he writes mostly popular songs, very good ones—"Girl from Ipanema," for example, an old one now. He plays the guitar and sings well, but without much voice, really. He's very popular with the young. He's been a very good friend to me. He gets married rather frequently. He says: "All my wives are such wonderful girls. It's always all my fault. Of course I'm broke. I leave them everything, and just take a toothbrush and go." One funny story: I was staying in the little town where I had bought an old, old house. It wasn't ready to move in to (that took five or six years) and I was staying at a small inn, owned by a Danish woman, an old friend. Vinicius was there, too—just the three of us. It was winter, cold and rainy, dreadful weather. We sat, for warmth, just the three of us, in a sort of back-kitchen, reserved for friends, all day long, and read detective stories. Once in a while we'd play a game of cards or Vinicius would play his guitar and sing. He has some marvelous, charming songs for children. Well, every afternoon a Rio newspaper arrived, one with a gossip column we read avidly. So, one afternoon the boy came in with the newspaper and there was a big gossip piece in it about the very same little town we were in, how it had become "fashionable with the intellectuals." And there we were, the only "intellectuals," if that, within hundreds of miles, handing around our Agatha Christies and Rex Stouts and so on . . .

GS: You seem to write more and more kinds of poems but without exhorting yourself to be suddenly different.

EB: I know I wish I had written a great deal more. Sometimes I think if I had been born a man I probably would have written more. Dared more, or been able to spend more time at it. I've wasted a great deal of time.

GS: Would it have been extra works in other genres?

EB: No.

GS: Long poems?

EB: No. One or two long poems I'd like to write, but I doubt that I ever shall. Well, not really long. Maybe ten pages. That'd be long.

Yes, I did know Cummings some. When I lived in the Village, later on, I met him through a friend. He and I had the same maid for two or three years. "Leave a little dirt, Blanche," he used to say to her. Blanche finally left them. They wouldn't put traps down for the mice. Mrs. Cummings told her a story about a little mouse that would come out of the wall and get up on the bed. They would lie in bed and watch her roll up little balls of wool from the blanket, to make her nest. Well, Blanche was appalled at this.

GS: Was he sparing the mice on humanitarian or vegetarian principles?

EB: Oh no. Cummings loved mice. He wrote poems about mice. He adored them. He used to . . .

Well, I haven't said anything profound.

GS: You tell a wonderful story.

EB: Oh, in their interviews, Miss Moore always said something to make one think very hard about writing, about technique—and Lowell always says something I find mysterious . . .

GS: Would you like to say something mysterious?

EB: !

Bibliography, 1933–81

I. Collected Works (Books)

A. *North & South*. Boston: Houghton Mifflin, 1946. Contents: "The Map," "The Imaginary Iceberg," "Casabianca," "The Colder the Air," "Wading at Wellfleet," "Chemin de Fer," "The Gentleman of Shalott," "Large Bad Picture," "From the Country to the City," "The Man-Moth," "Love Lies Sleeping," "A Miracle for Breakfast," "The Weed," "The Unbeliever," "The Monument," "Paris, 7 A.M.," "Quai d'Orleans," "Sleeping on the Ceiling," "Sleeping Standing Up," "Cirque d'Hiver," "Florida," "Jerónimo's House," "Roosters," "Seascape," "Little Exercise," "The Fish," "Late Air," "Cootchie," "Songs for a Colored Singer," "Anaphora."

B. *Poems: North & South—A Cold Spring*. Boston: Houghton Mifflin, 1955. Contents: *North & South* plus "A Cold Spring," "Over 2000 Illustrations and a Complete Concordance," "The Bight," "A Summer's Dream," "Cape Breton," "At the Fishhouses," "View of The Capitol from The Library of Congress," "Insomnia," "The Prodigal," "Faustina, or Rock Roses," "Varick Street," "Four Poems" (I / *Conversation*, II / *Rain Towards Morning*, III / *While Someone Telephones*, IV / *O Breath*), "Argument," "Letter to N.Y.," "The Mountain," "Invitation to Miss Marianne Moore," "Arrival at Santos," "The Shampoo."

C. *Poems*. London: Chatto and Windus, 1956. Contents: Twenty poems reprinted from *Poems: North & South—A Cold Spring*, 1955.

D. *The Diary of "Helena Morley"* (translated, edited, and with an introduction by Elizabeth Bishop). New York: Farrar, Straus and Cudahy, 1957. Reprinted with additional Foreword, New York: The Ecco Press, 1977.

E. *Brazil* (with the Editors of *Life*). Life World Library, New York: Time Incorporated, 1962.

F. *Questions of Travel*. New York: Farrar, Straus and Giroux,

Note: An asterisk indicates that the work is included in this volume.

1965. Contents: I. Brazil—"Arrival at Santos," "Brazil, January 1, 1502," "Questions of Travel," "Squatter's Children," "Manuelzinho," "Electrical Storm," "Song for the Rainy Season," "The Armadillo," "The Riverman," "Twelfth Morning; or What You Will," "The Burglar of Babylon." II. Elsewhere—"In the Village" (a story), "Manners," "Sestina," "First Death in Nova Scotia," "Filling Station," "Sunday, 4 A.M.," "Sandpiper," "From Trollope's Journal," "Visits to St. Elizabeths."

G. *Selected Poems.* London: Chatto and Windus, 1967. Contents: Forty-five poems from *Poems: North & South—A Cold Spring,* 1955, and *Questions of Travel,* 1965.

H. *The Ballad of the Burglar of Babylon* (with Introduction). New York: Farrar, Straus and Giroux, 1968.

I. *The Complete Poems.* New York: Farrar, Straus and Giroux, 1969. Contents: *North & South, A Cold Spring* (without "The Mountain" or "Arrival at Santos"), *Questions of Travel* (without "In the Village") plus Translations from the Portuguese—"Seven-Sided Poem," "Don't Kill Yourself," "Travelling in the Family," "The Table" (by Carlos Drummond de Andrade), "From *The Death and Life of a Severino*" (by João Cabral de Melo Neto); and New and Uncollected Work— "Rainy Season; Sub-Tropics" ("Giant Toad," "Strayed Crab," "Giant Snail"), "The Hanging of the Mouse," "Some Dreams They Forgot," "Song," "House Guest," "Trouvée," "Going to the Bakery," "Under the Window: Ouro Preto."

J. *An Anthology of Twentieth-Century Brazilian Poetry* (edited, with introduction, by Elizabeth Bishop and Emanuel Brasil). Middletown, Connecticut: Wesleyan University Press, 1972. Contents: Translations by Elizabeth Bishop include "My Last Poem," "Brazilian Tragedy" (Manuel Bandeira), "Cemetery of Childhood," "Elegy for Maria Alves" (Joaquim Cardozo), "Travelling in the Family," "Seven-Sided Poem," "Don't Kill Yourself," "The Table," "Infancy," "In the Middle of the Road," "Family Portrait" (Carlos Drummond de Andrade), "Sonnet of Intimacy" (Vinícius de Moraes), "From *The Death and Life of a Severino,*" I, II, XIV (João Cabral de Melo Neto).

K. *Geography III.* New York: Farrar, Straus and Giroux, 1976. Contents: "In the Waiting Room," "Crusoe in England," "Night City," "The Moose," "12 O'Clock News," "Poem," "One Art," "The End of March," "Objects & Apparitions" (by Octavio Paz), "Five Flights Up."

II. Uncollected Works
  A. Poems (including translations)
    1. "The Flood." *Con Spirito* (Vassar), February 1933.
    2. "A Word with You." *Con Spirito*, April 1933.
    3. "Hymn to the Virgin." *Con Spirito*, April 1933 (reprinted in *The Magazine*, April 1934).
    4. "Three Sonnets for the Eyes." *Con Spirito*, November 1933.
    5. "Three Valentines." *Trial Balances*. Ed. Ann Winslow. New York: Macmillan, 1935. ("Valentines I and II" reprinted from *Vassar Review*, February 1934.)
    6. "The Reprimand." *Trial Balances*. New York: Macmillan, 1935.
    7. "Rainbow," "Patience of an Angel," "Banks," "Hell is Graduated" (by Max Jacob). *Poetry*, May 1950.
    8. "The Wit." *New Republic*, February 13, 1956.
    9. "Exchanging Hats." *New World Writing*, April 1956.
    10. "A Norther—Key West." *New Yorker*, January 20, 1962.
    11. "Thank-you Note." *Harvard Advocate*, Spring 1969.
    12. Lines Written in *Fanny Farmer's Boston Cooking School Cookbook*. Christmas 1971 (published here for the first time).*
    13. "The Key of Water," "Along Galena Street," "The Grove" (by Octavio Paz). *Harvard Advocate*, Summer 1972.
    14. "January First" (by Octavio Paz), "Sambas" (anon.). *Ploughshares* 2, no. 4, 1975.
    15. "Santarém." *New Yorker*, February 20, 1978.
    16. "North Haven." *New Yorker*, December 11, 1978 (corrected *Harvard Advocate*, November 1979).
    17. "Pink Dog." *New Yorker*, February 26, 1979. (Elizabeth Bishop's last completed poem.—EDS.)
    18. "Sonnet." *New Yorker*, October 29, 1979.
  B. Prose (Fiction, articles, reviews, blurbs, translations, letters)
    1. "Then Came the Poor" (story). *Con Spirito*, February 1933.
    2. "Chimney Sweepers" (story). *Vassar Review*, Spring 1933.
    3. "Seven-Days Monologue" (story). *Con Spirito*, April 1933.
    4. "Time's Andromedas" (article). *Vassar Journal of Undergraduate Studies*, May 1933.*
    5. "Mr. Pope's Garden" (story). *Vassar Review*, Summer 1933.
    6. "Gerard Manley Hopkins: Notes on Timing in His Poetry." *Vassar Review*, February 1934.*
    7. "The Last Animal" (story). *Vassar Review*, April 1934.
    8. Review of *Journey to the End of Night* (Celine). *Vassar Review*, May 1934.

9. "Dimensions for a Novel." *Vassar Journal of Undergraduate Studies,* May 1934.

10. "The Baptism" (story). *Life & Letters To-day,* Spring 1937.

11. "The Sea and Its Shore" (story). *Life & Letters To-day,* Winter 1937 (also in *New Letters in America.* Ed. Horace Gregory. New York: Norton, 1937).

12. "In Prison" (story). *Partisan Review,* March 1938 (reprinted in *The Poet's Story.* Ed. Howard Moss. New York: Macmillan, 1973).

13. "Gregorio Valdes, 1879–1939." *Partisan Review,* Summer 1939.*

14. "The Farmer's Children" (story). *Harper's Bazaar,* February 1948 (reprinted in *The Best American Short Stories 1949.* Ed. Martha Foley. Boston: Houghton Mifflin, 1949).

15. "As We Like It" (article). *Quarterly Review of Literature,* Marianne Moore Issue 1948; reprinted 1976.*

16. "The Housekeeper" (story by "Sarah Foster"). *New Yorker,* September 11, 1948.

17. "It All Depends" (statement). *Mid-Century American Poets.* Ed. John Ciardi. New York: Twayne, 1950.*

18. Review of *Annie Allen* (by Gwendolyn Brooks). *U.S. Quarterly Book List,* March 1950.

19. Review of *XAIPE: Seventy-one Poems* (by E. E. Cummings). *U.S. Quarterly Book Review,* June 1950.*

20. "Love from Emily" (review of *Emily Dickinson's Letters to Doctor and Mrs. Josiah Gilbert Holland*). *New Republic,* August 27, 1951.

21. "What the Young Man Said to the Psalmist" (review of *Pantomime, A Journal of Rehearsals* by Wallace Fowlie). *Poetry,* January 1952.*

22. "Gwendolyn" (story). *New Yorker,* June 27, 1953.

23. "In the Village" (story). *New Yorker,* December 19, 1953; reprinted in *Stories from 'The New Yorker' 1950–1960,* New York: Simon and Schuster, 1960; and in *Questions of Travel,* 1965.

24. "The Manipulation of Mirrors" (review of *Selected Writings of Jules Laforgue,* ed. and trans. William Jay Smith). *New Republic,* November 19, 1956.*

25. Blurb. *A Cage of Spines* (by May Swenson). New York: Rinehart, 1958.

26. "I Was But Just Awake" (review of *Come Hither: A Collection of Rhymes and Poems for the Young of All Ages,* made by Walter de la Mare). *Poetry,* October 1958.

27. Blurb. *Life Studies* (by Robert Lowell). New York: Farrar, Straus and Cudahy, 1959.*

28. Blurb. *O to Be a Dragon* (by Marianne Moore). New York: Viking, 1959.

29. "A Sentimental Tribute" (article). *Bryn Mawr Alumnae Bulletin*, Spring 1962.

30. On "The Man-Moth." *Poet's Choice*. Ed. Paul Engle and Joseph Langland. New York: Dial Press, 1962.*

31. Blurb. *To Mix with Time* (by May Swenson). New York: Charles Scribner's, 1963.

32. "Three Stories by Clarice Lispector" (translations of "The Smallest Woman in the World," "A Hen," "Marmosets"). *Kenyon Review*, Summer 1964.

33. "Flannery O'Connor, 1925–1964," *New York Review of Books*, October 8, 1964.*

34. "On the Railroad Named Delight" (article; including "Sambas"). *New York Times Magazine*, March 7, 1965.

35. The "Darwin" Letter. Anne Stevenson. *Elizabeth Bishop*. New York: Twayne, 1966 (reprinted *Times Literary Supplement*, March 7, 1980).*

36. "An Inadequate Tribute." *Randall Jarrell 1914 1965*. Ed. Robert Lowell, Peter Taylor, Robert Penn Warren. New York: Farrar, Straus and Giroux, 1967.*

37. "Unamerican Editions" (letter). *Times Literary Supplement*, February 15, 1968.

38. Letter. *Kayak*, August 1969.

39. Preface to *Woodlawn North* (by Milton Kessler). Boston: Impressions Workshop, 1970.

40. Letter. *The Little Magazine*, Fall 1971/Winter 1972.

41. Blurb. *Golden State* (by Frank Bidart). New York: Braziller, 1973.*

42. Blurb. *Radiation* (by Sandra McPherson). New York: Ecco Press, 1973.

43. "A Brief Reminiscence and a Brief Tribute" (article). *Harvard Advocate*, Auden Issue 1975.*

44. Self-portrait. *Self-Portrait: Book People Picture Themselves*. Ed. Burt Britton. New York: Random House, 1976.

45. "Memories of Uncle Neddy" (story). *Southern Review*, October 1977.

46. "Laureate's Words of Acceptance." *World Literature Today*, Winter 1977.

47. Letter (March 26, 1977). *Peter Kaplan's Book*. Ed. Jaimy Gordon, Ray Ragosta. Providence: Pourboire Press, 1978.

48. "Letters from Elizabeth Bishop." Anne Stevenson. *Times Literary Supplement,* March 7, 1980.

49. Foreword. *Elizabeth Bishop: A Bibliography 1927–1979.* Candace W. MacMahon. Charlottesville: University Press of Virginia, 1980.

50. Selected letters to Candace MacMahon, Houghton Mifflin (on *North & South* and *A Cold Spring*), and Marianne Moore (on "The Weed," "Paris, 7 A.M.," "A Miracle for Breakfast" and sestinas,* "The Sea and Its Shore," "In Prison," "Florida," "The Fish," "Roosters," "The Mountain," "Manners"). Candace W. MacMahon. *Elizabeth Bishop: A Bibliography 1927–1979.* Charlottesville: University Press of Virginia, 1980.

C. Interviews

1. Ashley Brown. *Shenandoah,* Winter 1966.*

2. "Poets." *Time,* June 2, 1967.*

3. Eileen Farley. *University of Washington Daily* (Seattle), May 28, 1974.

4. Anna Quindlen. *New York Post,* April 3, 1976.

5. Jim Bross. *Norman Transcript* (Oklahoma), April 11, 1976.

6. Margo Jefferson. *Newsweek,* January 31, 1977.

7. Leslie Hanscom. *Newsday,* February 6, 1977.

8. David W. McCullough. *Book-of-the-Month Club News,* May 1977.*

9. George Starbuck. *Ploughshares* 3, nos. 3 & 4, 1977.*

10. Alexandra Johnson. *Christian Science Monitor,* March 23, 1978.

11. Sheila Hale. *Harpers and Queen,* July 1978.

12. Elizabeth Spires. *Vassar Quarterly,* Winter 1979 (reprinted in a different form in *Paris Review,* Summer 1981).

III. Bibliography

Candace W. MacMahon. *Elizabeth Bishop: A Bibliography 1927–1979.* Charlottesville: University Press of Virginia, 1980.

IV. Selected Secondary Material

A. Books, Monographs, Collections

1. Anne Stevenson. *Elizabeth Bishop.* New York: Twayne, 1966.

2. John E. Unterecker. "Elizabeth Bishop" (with selected bibliography by Lloyd Schwartz). *American Writers: A Collection of Literary Biographies,* Supplement I, Part 1. Editor-in-Chief Leonard Ungar. New York: Charles Scribner's Sons, 1979.

3. *World Literature Today.* "Homage to Elizabeth Bishop, Our 1976 Laureate." Ed. Ivar Ivask. Winter 1977.

a. Ivar Ivask. "World Literature Today, or Books Abroad II and Geography III."
b. Marie-Claire Blais. "Presentation of Elizabeth Bishop to the Jury."
c. John Ashbery. "Second Presentation of Elizabeth Bishop."
d. Elizabeth Bishop. "Laureate's Words of Acceptance."
e. Chronology
f. Octavio Paz. "Elizabeth Bishop, or the Power of Reticence."*
g. Célia Bertin. "A Novelist's Poet."
h. Penelope Mortimer. "Elizabeth Bishop's Prose."
i. Frank Bidart. "On Elizabeth Bishop."*
j. Helen Vendler. "Domestication, Domesticity, and the Otherworldly."*
k. Howard Moss. "The Canada-Brazil Connection."
l. Candace Slater. "Brazil in the Poetry of Elizabeth Bishop."
m. Anne R. Newman. "Elizabeth Bishop's 'Songs for a Colored Singer.'"
n. Lloyd Schwartz. "The Mechanical Horse and the Indian Princess: Two Poems from *North & South*."
o. Eleanor Ross Taylor. "Driving to the Interior: A Note on Elizabeth Bishop."
p. Jerome Mazzaro. "Elizabeth Bishop's Particulars."
q. Sybil P. Estess. "Toward the Interior: Epiphany in 'Cape Breton' as Representative Poem."

B. Articles and Reviews

A. Alvarez. "Imagism and Poetesses." *Kenyon Review,* Spring 1957.

John Ashbery. "*The Complete Poems*." *New York Times Book Review*, June 1, 1969.*

Harold Bloom. "The Necessity of Misreading." *Georgia Review*, Summer 1975.

———. "Books Considered." *New Republic,* February 5, 1977.

Louise Bogan. "On *North & South*." *New Yorker*, October 5, 1946.*

Philip Booth. "The Poet as Voyager." *Christian Science Monitor,* January 6, 1966.

David Bromwich. "Verse Chronical." *Hudson Review*, Summer 1977.

———. "The Retreat from Romanticism." *Times Literary Supplement*, July 8, 1977.

Ashley Brown. "Elizabeth Bishop." *Dictionary of Literary Biography*. Detroit: Gayle Research, 1980.

————. "Elizabeth Bishop in Brazil." *Southern Review*, October, 1977.*

V. L. O. Chittick. "Nomination for a Laureateship." *Dalhousie Review*, Summer 1955.

Alfred Corn. *Georgia Review*, Summer 1977.

Bonnie Costello. "The Impersonal and the Interrogative in the Poetry of Elizabeth Bishop," 1977.*

Peter Davison. "The Gilt Edge of Reputation." *Atlantic*, January 1966.

Martin Dodsworth. "The Human Note." *Listener*, November 30, 1967.

Irvin Ehrenpreis. "Solitude and Isolation." *Virginia Quarterly Review*, Spring 1966.

————. Letter to *Times Literary Supplement*, January 18, 1968.

————. "Loitering between Dream and Experience." *Times Literary Supplement*, January 22, 1971.

————. "Viewpoint." *Times Literary Supplement*, February 8, 1974.

Sybil P. Estess. "Elizabeth Bishop: The Delicate Art of Map Making." *Southern Review*, October 1977.

————. "Shelters for 'What Is Within': Meditation and Epiphany in the Poetry of Elizabeth Bishop." *Modern Poetry Studies*, Spring 1977.

Wallace Fowlie. "Poetry of Silence." *Commonweal*, February 15, 1957.

Lloyd Frankenberg. *Pleasure Dome*. Boston: Houghton Mifflin, 1949.

————. "Meaning in Modern Poetry." *Saturday Review*, March 23, 1946.

Jean Garrigue. "Elizabeth Bishop's School." *New Leader*, December 6, 1965.

Barbara Gibbs. "A Just Vision." *Poetry*, January 1947.

Lorrie Goldensohn. "Elizabeth Bishop's Originality." *American Poetry Review*, March/April 1978.

————. *American Book Review*, October 1978.

Jan B. Gordon. "Days and Distances: The Cartographic Imagination of Elizabeth Bishop." *Salmagundi*, Spring–Summer 1973.

Ian Hamilton. "Women's-Eye Views." *Observer*, December 31, 1967.

John Hollander. "Elizabeth Bishop's Mappings of Life." *Parnassus,* Fall 1977.*

Richard Howard. "Comment on 'In the Waiting Room.'" *Preferences.* New York: Viking, 1974.*

Randall Jarrell. "Fifty Years of American Poetry." *Third Book of Criticism.* New York: Farrar, Straus and Giroux, 1969.*

––––––. *Poetry and the Age.* New York: Farrar, Straus and Giroux, 1972.*

David Kalstone. "All Eye." *Partisan Review,* Spring 1970.

––––––. "Conjuring with Nature: Some Twentieth-Century Readings of Pastoral." *Twentieth-Century Literature in Retrospect.* Ed. Reuben Brower. Cambridge, Mass.: Harvard University Press, 1971.

––––––. "Elizabeth Bishop: Questions of Memory, Questions of Travel." *Five Temperaments.* New York: Oxford University Press, 1977.*

Penelope Laurans. "'Old Correspondences': Prosodic Transformations in Elizabeth Bishop," 1979.*

David Lehman. "'In Prison': A Paradox Regained," 1981.*

Herbert Leibowitz. "The Elegant Maps of Elizabeth Bishop." *New York Times Book Review,* February 6, 1977.

Robert Lowell. "For Elizabeth Bishop 1–4." *History.* New York: Farrar, Straus and Giroux, 1973.*

––––––. An Interview with Frederick Seidel. *Writers at Work: The Paris Review Interviews.* Second series. New York: Viking, 1963.*

––––––. Jacket blurb to *The Complete Poems.* New York: Farrar, Straus and Giroux, 1969.*

––––––. "On 'Skunk Hour.'" *The Contemporary Poet as Artist and Critic.* Ed. Anthony Ostroff. Boston: Little, Brown, 1964.*

––––––. "Thomas, Bishop, and Williams." *Sewanee Review,* Summer 1947.*

Jerome Mazzaro. "Elizabeth Bishop and the Poetry of Impediment." *Salmagundi,* Summer–Fall 1974.

Robert Mazzocco. "A Poet of Landscape." *New York Review of Books,* October 12, 1967.

Mary McCarthy. "Symposium: I Would Like to Have Written . . ." *New York Times Book Review,* December 6, 1981.*

J. D. McClatchy. "The Other Bishop." *Canto,* Winter 1977.

Nancy L. McNally. "Elizabeth Bishop: The Discipline of Description." *Twentieth-Century Literature,* January 1966.

William Meredith. "Invitation to Miss Elizabeth Bishop." Remarks read at Session 565, Modern Language Association Convention, December 28, 1977, New York City.*

James Merrill. "Elizabeth Bishop, 1911–1979." *New York Review of Books,* December 6, 1979.*

———. "An Interview with Donald Sheehan." *Contemporary Literature,* Winter 1968.*

———. "Her Craft." July 29, 1977.*

Arthur Mizener. "New Verse: *North & South.*" *Furioso,* Spring, 1947.*

Marianne Moore. "Archaically New." *Trial Balances.* Ed. Ann Winslow. New York: Macmillan, 1935.*

———. "A Modest Expert." *Nation,* September 28, 1946.*

———. "Senhora Helena." *A Marianne Moore Reader.* New York: Viking, 1961.*

Howard Moss. "All Praise." *Kenyon Review,* March 1966.

Lisel Mueller. "The Sun the Other Way Round." *Poetry,* August 1966.

Howard Nemerov. "The Poems of Elizabeth Bishop." *Poetry,* December 1955.

Majorie Perloff. "The Course of a Particular." *Modern Poetry Studies,* Winter 1977.

Robert Pinsky. "Elizabeth Bishop, 1911–1979." *New Republic,* November 10, 1979.*

———. "The Idiom of a Self: Elizabeth Bishop and Wordsworth." *American Poetry Review,* January–February 1980.*

———. "Poetry and the World." *Antaeus* 40/41, Winter–Spring 1981.

———. *The Situation of Poetry.* Princeton: Princeton University, 1976.

Peggy Rizza. "Another Side of This Life: Women As Poets." *American Poetry Since 1960: Some Critical Perspectives.* Ed. Robert B. Shaw. London: Carcanet, 1973.

———. "Elizabeth Bishop (1911–1979)." *The Real Paper,* October 20, 1979.

M. L. Rosenthal. *The Modern Poets.* New York: Oxford University Press, 1960.

David Schiff. "Elliott Carter: 'A Mirror on Which to Dwell.'" *New York Arts Journal,* Spring 1977.

Lloyd Schwartz. "Elizabeth Bishop, 1911–1979." *Boston Phoenix,* October 16, 1979.*

———. "Elliott Carter: Music in Words." *Boston Phoenix,* December 6, 1977.

_____. "One Art: The Poetry of Elizabeth Bishop, 1971–1976."
Ploughshares 3, nos. 3 and 4, Spring, 1977.*

L. F. Sensabaugh. *Hispanic American Historical Review*, August
1963.

Jane Shore. "Elizabeth Bishop: The Art of Changing Your
Mind." *Ploughshares* 5, no. 1, 1979.

William Jay Smith. "Geographical Questions: The Recent Poetry
of Elizabeth Bishop." *Hollins Critic*, February 1977.

Willard Spiegelman. "Elizabeth Bishop's 'Natural Heroism.'"
Centennial Review, Winter 1978.*

_____. "Landscape and Knowledge: The Poetry of Elizabeth
Bishop." *Modern Poetry Studies*, Winter 1975.

Stephen Stepanchev. *American Poetry Since 1945*. New York:
Harper and Row, 1967.

Mark Strand. "A Conversation with Norman Klein." *Ploughshares* 2, no. 3, 1975.*

_____. "Elizabeth Bishop Introduction." Delivered at the Guggenheim Museum, November 29, 1977.*

Helen Vendler. "An Anthology of Twentieth-Century Brazilian
Poetry." *New York Times Book Review*, January 7, 1973.

_____. "New Books in Review." *Yale Review*, March 1977.

Richard Wilbur. "Elizabeth Bishop: A Memorial Tribute."
Ploughshares 6, no. 2, 1980.*

Oscar Williams. "North but South." *New Republic*, October 21,
1946.*

Alan Williamson. "*A Cold Spring:* The Poet of Feeling," 1980.*

Michael Wood. "RSVP." *New York Review of Books*, June 9,
1977.

Lloyd Schwartz

POETS ON POETRY   Donald Hall, General Editor

Poets on Poetry collects critical books by contemporary poets, gathering together the articles, interviews, and book reviews by which they have articulated the poetics of a new generation.